STOP WAR AMERICA

Robert McLane

Robt McLane

Semper Fi !

Other books for sale by Corps Productions (please go to www.corpsproductions.com for more information):

Welcome to Vietnam Macho Man

The Petrified Heart

Thoughts Etched in Jade

Vietnam's Orange, White and Blue Rain Agents and Weapons of Mass Destruction

Red Plateau

Edited by Peggy Cheney
Published by Ernie Spencer
Cover design by Takashi Hiraga
Layout by Leo Wong
Copyright 2005 Robert McLane

ISBN 0-9618529-3-3

Corps Productions
www.corpsproductions.com

Library of Congress Cataloging-in-Publication Data

Table of Contents

I wish to thank the following people for their help in the telling of my story:

My beautiful daughter Tiffany, whose unconditional love and support has been such a source of happiness and joy in my life;

My brother Marines of Fox Battery, 2nd Battalion, 12th Marine Artillery Regiment;

My dedicated brothers in Vietnam Veterans Against the War, including Scott Camil, Mike Oliver, Joe Urgo, Ed D'Amato, Scott Moore, Al Hubbard, Bob Hanson, Joe Bangert, Jan Berry, John Kerry, Jack McCloskey, Ron Kovic, and far too many others to list here;

Donna Smith, who sent out a lot of queries for me;

Michael Downend, a fellow writer and former Marine pilot, who gave me a lot of encouragement and helped me with editing my story;

I especially want to express my gratitude to Peggy Cheney for her assistance in preparing and editing the final draft.

I also want to thank Ernie Spencer, a Marine Infantry Company Commander at Khe Sanh and fellow member of the Khe Sanh Veteran's Association, for his advice and decision to publish my story

This book is dedicated to the memory of

Hunter S. Thompson.
1937 – 2005

"I hate to advocate drugs, alcohol, violence, or insanity to anyone,
but they've always worked for me."

Robert McLane was born in Cameron, Texas, a small central Texas town ninety miles north of Austin. When he was twenty-two months old, he contracted polio but fully recovered. At three, his family moved to the East Texas town of Tyler where he spent his next fourteen years but often spent summers with his brother and sister in Cameron on his grandparents' farm.

He attended college in Tyler for two years and joined the Marine Corps Reserve in the summer of 1965. In the fall of 1967 he was returned to active duty. His tour of duty in Vietnam with an artillery battery along the DMZ included most of 1968, the bloodiest year of the war.

Upon discharge in January, 1969 he enrolled at Stephen F. Austin University in Nacogdoches, Texas but dropped out in 1970 to go to New York City to help form The Vietnam Veterans Against The War. He dedicated the next three years of his life to VVAW as the editor of their newspaper, The First Casualty and participated in most of their demonstrations.

In 1974 he was involuntarily committed to a Veteran's psychiatric hospital in Waco, Texas.

After being released, he headed back to New York City where he drove a taxi for five years and attended The American Academy of Dramatic Arts and Hunter College, majoring in theater and film.

He married in 1981 and moved back to Texas where his daughter Tiffany was born in 1982. In 1985, he divorced and moved to Shreveport, Louisiana and raised his daughter with the help of his mother as a single parent while struggling with his own PTSD.

When David Duke ran for senator in Louisiana, Robert founded an organization called DUKEBUSTERS and blanketed the state with anti-Duke bumper stickers. This led to his founding No Respect Publishing that continues to manufacture and sell anti-Republican bumper stickers and buttons.

He continues to dedicate his life to issues of peace and justice and manages to spend part of the winter at his hideaway in Mexico.

Stop War America: A Marine's Story

Cameron, Texas
April 1974

M y grandfather and I drove down the old black top road in silence. Texas built highways like this during the Depression and called them farm-to-market roads. It felt good to be home, a place where people lived normal lives, a million miles from the streets of New York City. Finally my grandfather spoke.

"It seems like that damn war is going to last forever, Robert. I wish they would just go in and get it over with."

I watched cattle grazing while men in straw cowboy hats and faded jeans mended fences. As the outskirts of Cameron came into view I looked at my grandfather,

"Well, I know more men and more bombs is not the answer. We ain't never gonna win that war, granddaddy. It's time to call in the dogs and piss on the fire."

My grandfather was a quiet man. We hardly ever had any long talks. He dropped me by the courthouse and headed to the feed store. Ever since I was a small child, I spent summers on my grandparents' farm. We drew our water from a well and drank it from a dipper. Life there was simple. Plant the crops and pray for rain. I saw Sheriff Black getting out of a big white Ford. Carl Black had been sheriff longer than I could remember. Someone told me that he once tried to court my grandmother. I guess she had other plans.

"Howdy, Sheriff." I smiled as the big man picked up a pile of papers from the front seat of his car.

He looked me up and down and smiled back. "Hello son, do I know you?"

"Yes sir. I guess I need a haircut. I'm one of Miss Peed's grandkids."

He studied my face for a moment. "Aren't you the McLane boy who went to Vietnam? What brings you back to Cameron?"

"I just stopped by to see my grandparents. Today I'm going over to the cemetery to visit my Daddy's grave."

Sheriff Black had been a pallbearer at my father's funeral. Daddy died while I was in boot camp. I flew home on emergency leave. I wore my brand new Marine Corps uniform to the service. Daddy would have been proud. Sheriff Black was a friend of my father long before I was born. My father was still a teenager when he started winning enough money playing dominoes and poker to make a living at it. One day he traded in his schoolbooks for a deck of cards. When he met my mother during the Depression, he was driving a new car that he had paid cash for with money he had made gambling. Later, my dad ran a domino hall in Dutch town, a rundown neighborhood just across the railroad tracks that ran through the middle of Cameron.

"Well it's good to see you again, son. That haircut sounds like a good idea."

Sheriff Black headed into the Courthouse and I started walking towards the cemetery. In a few minutes, the paved road turned to dusty gravel. I followed it though the gates of an old graveyard and past the faded headstones of some of the first families who came to Cameron by wagon train back when it was just another cow town. I crested a small hill and stopped by a huge oak tree,   large limbs spread out in every direction, providing precious shade over the McLane family plot. The graves were well tended.   My Uncle Shine saw to that. I knew most of my uncles by their nicknames, names like Speck and Buster. I loved them all.   The grass had been cut and watered and a small rosebush struggled against the hot Texas sun. I stared at my father's headstone. I missed him a lot. My grandmother was buried a few feet away.

She bore eleven children. My father was the seventh son. When I was a kid, he was my best friend. I spent my time after school and Saturdays watching my Dad play dominos with some of his regular customers. When I got bored, I stood on an empty wooden Coke box and rolled the colored balls across one of the pool tables with my hands. I don't remember my older brother ever setting foot in the place. He was studying to become an ordained minister in the Southern Baptist Church.   I was studying my bank shot. I was too small to hold a cue stick but I longed for the day when I would actually be big enough to play a real game.

In the back room there was a long running, no-limit poker game. Sometimes just as much money would be riding on a round of dominos.

The only movie theater in town was just down the street. On Saturdays, Daddy would slip me fifty cents. That was enough money for a hamburger and a chocolate malt in the drugstore and a ticket to watch Roy Rogers sort out some bad guys on the silver screen. Maybe that's where my troubles started. I always wanted to be one of the good guys, even if it meant getting into the occasional fistfight.

Unlike Roy, I didn't always win. It was against the law for anyone under the age of eighteen to set foot in my father's domino hall but I learned early on that such laws did not apply to everyone.

I sat down in the cool shade of the big tree and pondered my future. I was glad to be back in Cameron. The last month had been a rough one. I had been working as a 911 operator for the City of New York. I had taken the exam to become a cop. Then my life took an irreversible turn. My taste for risky behavior and illegal drugs finally caught up with me. It began with one more LSD trip. I rode the train up to Cape Cod to visit some fellow Vietnam Veterans for the weekend. We decided to take acid and play monopoly.

When I woke up the next morning, the drug was still racing through my brain. Everyone else was still asleep when I stepped out into the bright sunlight and wandered down the street. I ended up at the local Cape Cod Community College. Strange looking people wandering around on campus was a common occurrence at most colleges back then, and there probably wouldn't have been any trouble if it hadn't been for that damn bloodmobile.

I have O-negative blood. In spite of my fear and hatred for needles, I often sold blood when I was a poor underclassman going to junior college in Texas. Ten bucks was a lot of money back then. Thanks to my job as a 911 operator, I had plenty of money that weekend on the Cape, but this voice in my head wouldn't shut up. It kept telling me that someone desperately needed a pint of my blood. Finally I headed over to the blood mobile. The nurses looked me over and told me they wouldn't be taking any of my blood that day.

When I tried to argue, they called the cops. After they discovered I was a Vietnam Vet, they drove me over to the VA Psychiatric Hospital in Brockton.

"He's cute!" One of the nurses said to the cops as they brought me into the emergency room. I spent a week walking around in faded pajamas until the LSD wore off.

I signed myself out AMA (against medical advice) and caught a train back to New York City. My job as a 911 operator was history. So were my chances of ever becoming a cop. I began having flashbacks from the LSD. I wandered the streets of New York City looking for help that wasn't coming. I got into fights. This time the cops delivered me to a civilian hospital called Bellevue. I was tied down with bed sheets in a wheelchair while a policeman tried to get me to sign papers committing myself to the funny farm.

"Fuck you, I want outta here!" I glared up at the big Irish cop. I hardly noticed the small blackjack in his hand as he gently tapped my elbow. It felt like a flashbulb had gone off in my head as the pain knocked me out. When the room came back into focus, I looked at him and asked, "Where do I sign?"

Bellevue was a hellhole of mind-numbing drugs and the constant screaming of whacked out patients struggling with an endless parade of overworked doctors, nurses and orderlies. At last I again signed myself out and wandered down to the East Village. I watched a couple of guys arguing over a parking spot. Finally, I couldn't take it anymore.

"I can't believe you guys are fighting over some piece of rubber and steel. Don't you realize that in fifty years this car will be just another pile of junk rusting away in some automobile graveyard?"

To prove my point I reached over and snapped off the radio antenna. I traded punches with the owner until the cops showed up. A bystander told them what had happened. When they realized I was a veteran, they took me to the VA hospital on First Avenue. I knew the drill. This time I didn't resist. After spending a couple of days on anti-psychotic drugs and more Thorazine, I filled out the AMA form and signed myself out again.

Staring at the wall of taxis and buses rushing up First Avenue, I realized it was time to get out of New York City. I walked down to the Holland Tunnel and started hitchhiking west. In less than a week, an eighteen-wheeler tractor-trailer dropped me off outside of my grandparents' farm. It was a miracle that I made it.

Now I was lying in the cool shade beside my father's grave watching a chicken hawk slowly circling overhead. I drifted off to sleep.

The late model Oldsmobile rolled slowly down the gravel road and stopped by the big oak tree. A large man in a business suit and a crew cut haircut got out. He stood over me for a minute and then laughed.

"Baby brother, you are the only one I know who could lie down all alone in the middle of a damn cemetery and fall fast asleep. I been looking all over Cameron for you. I should have looked here first."

I sat up, rubbed my eyes and looked at my brother. "Someday we'll both sleep here. What can I do for you, Roy Joe?" All my life I had called my big brother by his first two names, a practice common in the South.

"Let's go get something to eat and talk about it. I'm about to starve to death."

We settled into a booth at the Texan café and ordered the lunch special. I stared at my iced tea. Back in Vietnam, I remembered looking at a photo of a glass of iced tea in an old issue of Sports Illustrated. I hadn't seen a piece of real ice in almost six months. I remembered thinking, that someday I'd drink iced tea again and I'd have all the iced tea I wanted. My brother looked at me.

"I want you to go back to Waco with me. I want you to check into the VA hospital there. They have a new drug out now called lithium. I think it may help you. I drove down here to take you back. Will you go with me?"

I looked at him and shook my head. "I have seen my share of hospitals for a while. Thanks anyway." I took another sip of tea.

"The problem is that you haven't stayed in one place long enough to get any help. Everyone is worried about you. They're afraid you are going to hurt somebody or hurt yourself."

"Look, Roy Joe, I know I had some problems in New York City, but other than getting in a couple of fist fights, I haven't tried to hurt anybody. The only thing I did that got me into trouble was trying to give some damn blood."

My brother ordered a cup of coffee. "Well, you sounded pretty unhappy when you called me from Bellevue."

"You'd sound unhappy, too, if you ever woke up in a hellhole like that. I was afraid they were going to keep me. I've had my fill of hospitals. I'm gonna rest on our grandparents' farm for a few days and when I feel ready, I think I'll head on out to California."

When we were kids, I would drive my big brother crazy arguing over anything and everything. He knew my mind was made up. He gave me a lift back to the farm. I watched his eyes drift over to the .30 caliber M1 carbine my grandfather kept leaning against the wall beside the front door. One of my uncles brought it back for him from Korea. As long as I could remember, the weapon had been resting there. Finally, my brother got up to leave.

"I sure wish you would change your mind. Peggy has them holding a bed for you and she is going to be real disappointed." His wife worked as a nurse at the sprawling hospital.

"Tell her I appreciate her concern and if I start feeling bad again, I will catch the bus up there right away. OK?"

We shook hands and he left. I walked back inside and took a nap. I seemed to be sleeping a lot lately. My grandmother woke me up to tell me the Sheriff wanted to talk to me.   He was standing out in the yard so I figured it wasn't a social call. I stepped out on the front porch.

"Howdy, Sheriff Black." I stared down at the big man.

"Son, I don't like to have to do this, but I don't have any choice. Your brother went before a judge in town and signed papers requesting that you be taken to the VA hospital in Waco. You got to come with me now. I'm not going to put you in handcuffs, but I have to do what the Judge ordered. You don't need to bring anything with you, but we ought to get going. It's a long drive to Waco. You can ride up front with me."

I said goodbye to my grandmother. She hugged me tight. I could see she was trying hard not to cry as we drove away.

In the car, Sheriff Black pushed his hat back and sighed. "Son, sometimes this job can get a little rough, like when I'm telling a pretty young woman that her husband has just been killed by a drunk driver or a father that his daughter has been arrested for dope. Sometimes things don't make sense, but a sheriff has to listen when the judge is talking, even if I don't understand a damn thing he is saying. I don't think there is anything wrong with you, but your brother thinks you're nuts and the judge agrees. Now, I have to deliver you to the Veterans' psychiatric hospital in Waco. Sometimes I think the whole world has gone rubber room crazy."

I was beginning to think that my life had turned into a never ending shit storm, a series of train wrecks where, despite my best intentions, all my dreams and plans had once again ended upside down in a pile of twisted and burning metal while passing strangers stared and shook their heads.

These were supposed to be the good times I had waited so long for, the dreams that I had held on to through all those endless nights and days along the DMZ. Texas was a distant memory when I was curled up in a fetal position in a muddy trench in Khe Sanh as North Vietnamese artillery shells screamed down from almost eighteen miles away. All I could think about back then was the day that I would climb on board the big freedom bird that would take me back to the world I left behind. I soon found out that it was a world that had changed forever.

"Don't worry about it, Sheriff. I've been in a lot worse situations than whatever is waiting in Waco. At least I'll be sleeping between sheets."

Sheriff Black drove around an old truck loaded down with bales of fresh cut hay as we entered the city limits of Lott, Texas. We waited for the one red light to turn green while beside us a long freight train headed north was slowly picking up speed. Sheriff Black looked at me.

"I appreciate what boys like you have gone through over there for this country.

A lot of folks don't, but I do. I appreciate it and I want you to know it."

I smiled. "Well Sheriff, I wish you appreciated it enough to let me hop on that old freight train out of here."

Sheriff Black laughed. "I would like to let you go, Robert, but I wouldn't be doing the job the voters in Milam County hired me to do. I can't just pick and choose which orders I will follow when the judge hands them down. He said to take you to the VA hospital in Waco and that's where you are going."

We pulled into a truck stop for gas.

"Son, I'm getting hungry. I guess we got time for a bite to eat. You can have anything on the menu. Milam County is going to pick up the tab."

We walked into the small café and found a booth. The waitress brought us two glasses of water as she looked me over.

"What did he do?"

Sheriff Black smiled. "Betty, he burned down a rock fence back in Cameron! Now get us some coffee over here and a couple of those chicken fried steaks before I arrest you too."

I smiled as I drank coffee and people looked around and wondered what was going on. It was pretty obvious from my shoulder-length long hair and beard that I wasn't the new deputy. One couple got up and paid their check and left.

"Looks like I am making some people nervous. Maybe you ought to have me in leg irons or handcuffs."

Sheriff Black shook his head as he cut into his steak. "Sheriffs in Texas have their own ways of doing things and if enough people don't like it, they can vote them out come Election Day."

He looked at me. "Son, I want to ask you a question. What was it like over there?"

I watched the waitress bringing my coconut pie.

"Remember the traveling carnival that you ran out of Cameron a few years back? The one with all those rigged games?"

Sheriff Black nodded his head. "Farm boys were losing all their hay money trying to knock over milk bottles filled with cement."

"Well, sheriff, that was sort of what the Vietnam War was like. Everybody was wearing out their arms trying to knock over some cement milk bottles. After throwing a couple of thousand baseballs, you feel like your arms are going fall off and the damn milk bottles are still standing. Instead of hay money, boys were losing arms and legs and lives. Only this time there wasn't any sheriff coming around to close the game down. Our job wasn't all that different from yours. We wore uniforms, carried rifles and tried to catch bad guys. Mostly we just tried to stay alive."

I finished my pie. The sheriff paid the tab and tipped the waitress. We drove through the main gate of the VA hospital and parked in front of the administration building. I guess he had made this trip before. He walked around the Crown Victoria and opened the door for me. I stepped out and followed him inside. We found a receptionist. The sheriff signed some papers while I sat in a chair and waited. I looked over my shoulder at a picture of Richard Nixon staring down at me. He was smiling. I smiled back up into Tricky Dick's eyes. I felt he was thinking, "I've got you now, my little war protester. You zigged when you should have zagged."

I saw my brother walk in. I looked at him. "Why are you doing this?"

"Because I love you." Tears welled up in his eyes and he turned away.

Sheriff Black walked over. "Son, I better get on back to Milam County. You take care of yourself, now, you hear?"

We shook hands. He left. A man in a white coat sat down beside me and took a ball point pen out of his shirt pocket. He began making notes on a clipboard. He glanced over at me.

"Sir, my name is Dr. Samuel Hoerster. If you don't mind, may I ask you a few questions?"

"Sure." I looked at him. He had a gentle, grandfatherly face and silver white hair. He started asking me questions, a lot of dumb questions. The first one was:

"Mr. McLane, who is the President?"

I looked up at Nixon. "That asshole in the picture."

I tried to humor him without being rude. Finally he finished and called to an orderly, "Jimmy, could you come here, please?"

A large man dressed in white pants and a white shirt walked over.

"This is Mr. McLane. Walk him over to Building 92 and see that he gets settled in. Thank you."

He handed the big man a file with my name written at the top. Jimmy smiled down at me and we left for Building 92. The sidewalk seemed to go on forever. The Waco Veterans' psychiatric hospital was a sprawling campus of three-story red brick dormitories encircling a large quadrangle of fresh cut grass and towering oak trees. The top floors were screened in. We passed men driving tractors that were cutting the parched grass. Some guys who looked like patients were milling around. They had earned what the VA called "grounds privileges." Their eyes were void of any expression.

They were walking in a manner later described as the "Thorazine shuffle." It was a ten minute walk to Building 92. We took the elevator up to the third floor. At the end of the hall, Jimmy took a large ring of keys from his belt and unlocked a gray metal door. Once we were inside, Jimmy locked the door again. We were standing in a large room filled with chairs, desks and people. Jimmy walked over to a nurse and handed her my file.

"This is Mr. McLane, he just came in."

The nurse smiled at me and asked me to sit down. She wasn't all that bad looking. I sat down in a chair beside her desk and waited.

"Welcome to Building 92, Mr. McLane. My name is Nurse Atkins. May I call you Robert?"

"Sure," I smiled.

I looked over at five guys in pajamas sitting in a row of over-stuffed chairs. They were puffing away on cigarettes and watching a "Green Acres" rerun on television. A guy in his twenties walked up. He was wearing a faded blue robe.

"Miss Atkins, I need a shot."

She smiled up at him. "Well Rusty, you are just going to have to wait. Right now I am busy."

Silently he turned around and walked over to the television and stared at the screen. After a few more questions, Miss Atkins asked me to roll up my sleeve. She smiled.

"First I am going to take your blood pressure. Then, I am going to draw some blood for our lab."

I rolled up my sleeve. She rubbed my arm with alcohol on a cotton swab. "Now, I'm going to stick you. This may sting a little bit."

Ever since I was a little kid, I have hated needles. But, after all the shots I had taken before going to Vietnam, I had made my peace with the process. She drew several vials of blood while I tried to concentrate on Eddie Albert. He was a veteran of World War II.

Doing stupid jokes on a television show must have seemed like a million miles from Tarawa for him. Nurse Atkins walked over to a locker and came back with a pair of pajamas.

"I would like you to put these on, please. You can put your clothes in this plastic bag." She pointed to a small room that had a single bed with spotless white sheets. I stepped inside. The pajamas were too big, but I managed to tie them on. At least the cloth slippers fit. I walked back out and handed her the bag. She handed me some pills in a paper cup.

"Dr. Hoerster has prescribed this medication for you. You have to take it. If you don't, we will give it to you by injection."

She handed me another paper cup filled with water. I tossed the pills down and drank the water. Thanks to the wonders of Thorazine, the seventy or so patients on the third floor of Building 92 could be easily managed by a handful of nurses and aides. Nurse Atkins told me I was free to watch television. I walked over to where Jimmy was folding some towels.

"So how are you doing, my man?" Jimmy smiled at me.

"A little nervous, I haven't had psycho playmates since I got out of the Marines."

Jimmy laughed. "Heck, don't you worry yourself none. You know I used to wrestle. Anybody who messes with you is going to have to answer to me. I can whip anyone in this building if I have to. Now, you just take it easy, you hear?"

I smiled. "Thanks, Jimmy."

A doorway beside the television led to a large screened-in front porch. I walked over and looked down at the trees and fresh cut grass below. I wished I could smell the grass and feel the sun on my face. What the hell am I doing in here? Will I ever get out? I had been in plenty of tough jams before. I did a year up to my eyeballs in a fucking war. At least now I was going to be sleeping between clean sheets.

"Play the hand you're dealt, boys. Play it with grace and style." I remember those were the words my daddy used to tell his customers back at his domino hall.

A short fat man in faded pajamas wandered by singing, "How much is that doggie in the window…the one with the wagging tail?"

I later learned he had been on the locked ward of Building 17 for almost twenty years. There were other patients who also looked like they had given up on ever getting out or being sane again. Suddenly, the thoughts that had been running through my mind slowed down to a crawl. Just forming words into a simple sentence seemed to take forever. I felt like I was walking uphill on an endless road of thick molasses.

"Hello." The guy who wanted a shot was looking at me.

"My name is Russell. I used to be a pilot in the Air Force. Then I tried to kill myself. Now I live here. What did you do?"

"Nothing that called for me being put in here. It seems I have a brother with an overactive imagination."

Russell smiled and began to unbutton his pajama top. "Wanna see where I shot myself?" He opened his shirt to reveal a large vertical scar running across his stomach.

"After I got out of the hospital, they brought me here. That was two years ago. This place ain't so bad. I can have a shot anytime I want one."

A middle-aged man, with thinning hair, wearing a bathrobe, walked over. He looked up at me, smiled with the rapture of a three-year-old, and announced: "Haircut day, buddy! Today is haircut day!"

Russell nodded at him. "That's Larry. He tried to kill himself, too. One day he closed the garage door and started his car. Unfortunately for Larry, the car ran out of gas, but he did succeed in destroying over sixty percent of his brain. He's also been in Building 92 for almost twenty years."

Larry walked over to tell the guys watching TV about haircut day. I liked the big porch. The screened-in windows were open and I could hear birds singing. Patients were free to come out here to stare at other red brick buildings and the long, high hurricane fence that surrounded everything. It felt good to get away from the damn TV and the blue cloud that floated over the entire room as the members of the Nicotine Club sat in their chairs and puffed away. I wondered how long I was going to be in Building 92. It was scary to realize that this place would be the final home for many of these poor bastards. They would never leave here alive. A buzzer announced someone at the front door.

One of the nurses reached for the big ring of keys in her pocket and opened the door. An aide dressed in white pushed in a large stainless steel cart. Trays of food were stacked inside. The evening meal had arrived. A line quickly formed as my fellow lunatics patiently waited for the nurses to pass out their dinners. The food was bland and starchy. I washed it down with a paper cup of Kool-Aid. On TV, "Green Acres" was replaced by a game show where contestants tried to guess the price of a new washing machine. The Nicotine Club yelled, "Higher!" as they puffed away.

I was getting a little bored when I noticed an old Monopoly set and a worn out deck of cards on a shelf. I decided to start a game of my own. I took the play money and the deck of cards and sat down at a card table. I stacked the different colored bills neatly in front of me and shuffled the deck. I invited Russell and some of his associates to join me in a friendly game of blackjack. I went over the basic rules as I gave each player five hundred dollars of funny money.

"Relax fellas, this is play money and this time we are just playing for fun." My daddy would have been proud of his second son. I dealt each player two cards, one up and one down. "Now don't be afraid to bet 'em up if you feel lucky."

Several patients bet their entire stake on the first hand. After they busted, I took back their money.

"Try to bet a little more carefully next time," I cautioned them. I smiled as I gave them another five hundred dollars. They promptly bet everything on the next hand and lost again. This time I gave them each a thousand dollars. Gambling with lunatics was like taking candy from a baby.

Nurse Atkins walked over and frowned. "Now Robert, I am not sure this is how the Monopoly money was intended to be used."

Russell looked up at her. "Don't worry Miss Atkins, this money is not real and neither are you!"

Miss Atkins wrote a short note on her clipboard. "Well, we'll have to see what Dr. Hoerster says." She walked away.

The two face cards Russell was holding weren't good enough, since the six of clubs I dealt myself gave me twenty-one. I gathered in the money from the losing hands and dealt another round. Here's the weird part. I knew when to take another card and when to stand. Every time. I continued to win each hand and lend out more money to the losers until Russell had had enough.

"Let somebody else deal," he growled.

"Sure boys, no problem." I passed the deck to Larry. I continued to manage the money and every few minutes I lent the losers another thousand dollars. I kept winning. My stake was now up past five thousand dollars.

Russell frowned at me. "How do you win every hand?"

I looked at Russell, then looked at the two face cards in my hand. I stared at the deck Larry was holding.

"Golly fellas, let me show you." I smiled at Larry. "Give me a hit, big guy."

Larry tossed me the Ace of Diamonds. I laughed as I showed them the two jacks in my hand. "That's why you can't beat me." Any other card in the deck but an Ace and I would have been just another loser. I didn't just hope the next card was an Ace. I knew it.

"That's it! I quit!" Russell shouted as he threw in his cards and started to walk away.

"Me too!" Larry growled as he got up and followed Russell.

"Relax boys, it was only play money." The game was over. I gathered up the different stacks of Monopoly money and put the box and the deck of cards back on the shelf.

Russell walked over and looked me in the eye. "I just want to know one thing. How did you know that last card would be an Ace?"

I smiled. "Being insane has its advantages."

At 8:45 Nurse Atkins turned off the TV and announced it was time for bed. Patients shuffled off to take their last meds of the day and brush their teeth. They climbed into beds that were arranged in a perfect line. At nine o clock, Nurse Atkins dimmed the lights and my first day in Building 92 was over. Thanks to the level of Thorazine in my blood, I quickly drifted off to sleep.

The lights were turned back on at 6am. It took a couple of minutes to realize that I had woken up in an asylum. I got up and washed my face. The Nicotine Club was lighting up their first cigarettes. They waited quietly for the TV to be turned on. I heard a key unlocking the big gray door that led downstairs.

An aide came in pushing a large cart that held our breakfast. Someone handed me a tray with a carton of milk and a box of corn flakes. There was also a plate with some lukewarm scrambled eggs and a piece of bacon. There was a small plastic cup of black coffee. I wondered why I was having so much trouble opening the box of corn flakes. Then, I remembered the Thorazine.

Accomplishing even the simplest task now required all of my patience and concentration. I gave up on the corn flakes and just ate the bacon and drank the coffee. I curled up in a stuffed chair and went back to sleep.

"Mr. McLane! Mr. McLane!" One of the day nurses woke me up. "You have lab work this morning." She made a note on her clipboard.

I shuffled over to a line of patients waiting by the gray door. One by one, an aide called out our names. Then he took a key from his belt and opened the door. We followed him into the hallway. In a few minutes, an old school bus pulled up and we climbed aboard. We rode along quietly to another red brick building and followed the aide off of the bus and inside.

I was handed a number and told to have a seat. I found out that "lab work" was the Veterans Administration code for blood tests. When someone called my number, I walked over to a small desk and rolled up my sleeve. I still thought of needles as instruments of pain and terror, but I waited quietly. The young nurse read the name on my wrist band and then drew several vials of blood. In a few more minutes we were on the bus and headed back to Building 92. All of the comfortable chairs were occupied so I curled up in a corner on the floor and went to sleep.

"Mr. McLane! Mr. McLane! You have to stay awake. The doctor will be here shortly making his rounds. He will want to talk to you."

"Goddammit! If you want me to stay awake, stop giving me pills that put me to sleep!" I glared up at the startled nurse.

She took her clipboard and made more notes. "Your medication is something you need to talk to your doctor about, but you have to stay awake."

She walked away. I walked over to the large screened in porch and stared down at other patients milling around on the grass below. I wondered how long I would be in this hell hole. The big gray door opened and several patients entered and were slowly led over to a table that held some leftover breakfast trays. They sat down and stared at the trays like they were some kind of puzzle.

Later I learned that while the rest of us were eating our breakfasts, these poor bastards were upstairs getting electro-shock treatments. First they were strapped down on a bed. Then a piece of rubber was inserted in their mouth and some kind of gel was smeared on their temples. Finally, a small metal paddle was placed on each side of their head and someone hit a switch, sending a jolt of electricity directly through their brain as their body convulsed and strained against the leather straps.

Back on the ward, the day nurse turned on the idiot box and the TV junkies began their morning fix. The gray door opened again and a large man in a white coat walked in.

Dr. Hoerster. VA regulations required an attending physician to spend a short daily session with each patient who was coherent enough to hold a conversation. Dr. Hoerster did this while sitting behind a small folding table. One by one, each patient was led over to a small chair for a short visit. Finally it was my turn.

"Good morning, Dr. Hoerster." I was amazed how long it took to form thoughts and then to transform those thoughts into speech.

"And how are you feeling this morning, Mr. McLane?"

"I am much, much better. I was wondering when I could leave here?"

Dr. Hoerster smiled and looked at his clipboard. "Well, you just got here. First we have to run some tests to determine just what caused you to end up here. When we have some answers, then we'll talk about when you will be ready to leave."

"Could you please reduce the dosage of my medication?"

"The current dosage is supposed to help you to stay calm. My notes here say that you snapped at one of my nurses this morning. She was just doing her job. If you continue yelling at my nurses, we may have to increase your medication."

Dr. Hoerster thumbed though the top pages of his clipboard. "It says here you took the Monopoly money and started a poker game. Gambling here is illegal, Mr. McLane."

"Dr. Hoerster, we were just playing for fun. There is nothing to do here but watch that stupid television."

"Well, it may just be for fun to you, but one of our long term patients is very upset. He thinks he owes you ten thousand dollars. There will be no more poker games. Do I make myself clear, Mr. McLane?"

"In that case he better pay up. Looks like I'm going to need the money to hire a lawyer to get me out of this dump. Say, they sent me to have blood drawn this morning. What happened to the blood they took yesterday? Did they lose it?"

"The combination of drugs we are giving you is very strong, Mr. McLane. If we didn't monitor it every day, it could even be fatal. I am afraid you will be having blood work done on a daily basis until I say otherwise."

"Daily?" I repeated the word as I stood up and gripped the edges of the small table and stared down at Dr. Hoerster. I wanted to flip it across the room, but even in my drugged condition I knew that was a no-no. I slowly released my grip and sat back down.

"I think that will be all today, Mr. McLane." He nodded at Jimmy and another aide who grabbed me and dragged me over to a bed. They held me down while one of the nurses shot another load of happy juice into my ass. Dr. Hoerster left. The Thorazine hit me like a monster wave at the beach. I was carried far out into a turquoise blue ocean where pretty mermaids rode side-saddle on prancing sea horses.

Marine Recruit Training Depot, San Diego September 1965

I got off the bus and joined seventy-nine other guys standing on a set of yellow footprints that were painted on the black asphalt. It had been a short ride from the airport in San Diego to the Marine Corps Recruit Training Depot.

We arrived about eleven o'clock at night and stood there in the dark for almost an hour. At last, a tall young man, wearing one of those well known Smokey-the-Bear drill instructor hats, walked up out of the shadows and looked us over.

His name was Lee Emery. He wore corporal stripes on his short-sleeved shirt. Years later, he would become famous playing a drill instructor in the movie *Full Metal Jacket*.

"So you ladies want to join my beloved Marine Corps?" His booming voice shattered the stillness of the night.

"I bet some of you girls think you are tough. Is there anyone of you who thinks she is bad enough to whip my scrawny ass?"

There were some large, powerfully-built young men standing on our yellow footprints, but no one took the challenge. Another DI walked up and joined Corporal Emery. Corporal Payne was a full-blooded Navajo Indian with the perfect name for a Marine Corps Drill Instructor. He stared at a short overweight white guy standing beside me.

"We got us a wide body here! What's your name, lard ass?"

The chubby one answered in a loud voice, "Richard Small."

His knees buckled as Corporal Payne slammed his fist into his stomach and screamed, "I bet the only thing small about you is your pecker! Well, from now on, lard ass, the first and last thing out of your mouth will be 'Sir'! Do you hear me, you fat piece of whale blubber?"

" Sir, yes, sir!" Private Small yelled as he struggled to stay at attention.

"I hope you enjoyed your last meal, Miss Thunder Thighs. My beloved Marine Corps has a special diet for wide bodies like you!"

Payne walked up and down the ranks, looking us over. Corporal Emery started screaming at some poor bastard who made the mistake of looking at him.

Emery's voice boomed. "What the fuck are you looking at, sweetheart? Are you in love with me? Do you like men?"

"Sir, no, sir!" the terrified recruit replied. The recruit dropped to his knees as Emery's fist slammed into his stomach.

"I can't hear you, faggot! Speak up when you address your drill instructor."

"Sir, no, sir!" The recruit yelled as he struggled back to his feet and returned to the position of attention.

Corporal Payne stared at the black recruit standing behind me. The young man's face bore the scars of a losing battle with acne.

"Goddamn!" Payne screamed as he grabbed the recruit by the arm and dragged him over to Corporal Emery. "Look at this motherfucker! Have you ever seen anything this fucking ugly in your life?"

Emery laughed. "We gotta get this scary fuck on a plane to Vietnam as soon as possible. One look at his face and the entire North Vietnamese Army won't stop running until they are back in Hanoi!"

Payne howled in glee. "We oughta drop leaflets with his picture on them all up and down the Ho Chi Minh trail! Now get back in rank, you ugly motherfucker!"

We spent the next several hours double-timing from one Quonset hut to another as we got haircuts, green fatigue uniforms, sheets and blankets, and new combat boots. About 2AM we finally made our bed and went to sleep. We were awakened less than three hours later to the sound of reveille being played on a scratchy phonograph.

"Platoon 3017! On the road!" Corporal Emery's voice boomed and we quickly laced up our boots and raced outside. We spent most of the day being issued more equipment, including helmets and M-14 rifles. We ran everywhere. Confused recruits were still learning their left foot from their right. The drill instructors never hesitated to plant their fist into the gut of anyone who screwed up.

Boot camp was normally a twelve-week introduction to random acts of violence and organized chaos. Because of the need for more Marines in Vietnam, the same training was now crammed into eight weeks. Emery and Payne constantly screamed in our ears while we stood at attention and tried not to blink. Often, all of us were punished anytime someone screwed up.

My knees buckled as Corporal Emery's fist slammed into my gut. I quickly got back on my feet and resumed the position of attention. My face turned blue as I fought for my breath. I had not yet learned the trick of rolling with any punch I saw coming. In theory, physical beatings are illegal in the Marine Corps. Drill Instructors solved this problem by assigning other recruits as birddogs to warn the DI of any approaching officer. This level of brutality was considered a vital part of the process to get these recruits ready for war, a real war that was just months away. The Drill Instructors took each returning body bag as a personal failure.

"Hey dickhead! What the fuck do you think you are doing?" Corporal Payne's voice roared while we stood in line waiting to take showers. "I'm talking to you, asshole!"

Corporal Payne walked up and looked down at a terrified recruit named Willard.

"Sir, nothing, sir!" Private Willard replied.

"Don't lie to me, slime ball! Do you think I am fucking blind?" Payne's eyes narrowed and he lowered his face until it was less than an inch from Private Willard's nose.

"You were scratching your balls, weren't you?"

"Sir! Yes, sir!" Private Willard shouted.

Payne grabbed Private Willard by his collar and jerked him out of line. "Come here, shithead! See that barrel? Climb up on it!"

Private Willard climbed up on the barrel. He stood there shaking in fear as he stared out at the other seventy-nine recruits and tried to keep his balance.

"Stand at attention, asshole! Do your balls still itch? Well, scratch them!"

Private Willard stood there looking confused and frightened.

"I said scratch your goddamn balls!" Corporal Payne roared.

"Sir! Yes, sir!" Private Willard shouted as his left hand slowly began to scratch his balls.

"Roll 'em around in your hand!" Corporal Payne screamed.

"Sir! Yes, sir!" Private Willard began rolling his balls around in his hand.

"Do your balls still itch, numbnuts?" Corporal Payne yelled.

"Sir! No, sir!"

"You don't want to scratch them anymore?" Corporal Payne asked in a loud voice.

"Sir! No, sir!" Private Willard replied as he tried to keep his balance on the shaky barrel.

"Do you think you can keep your hands off of your nut sack until I tuck you in bed tonight?"

"Sir! Yes, sir!"

"Then get the fuck back in formation! Private numb nuts, from now on I am going to be watching you." Corporal Payne looked over the rest of the formation. "Does anyone else want to scratch their balls?"

"Sir! No, sir!" the platoon yelled in one voice.

"Then move out on the double."

We ran to our evening shower. Our first full day of boot camp was over.

"Platoon 3017! On the road!" Corporal Emery's voice shattered the early morning quiet as we grabbed our covers and rushed out of the door. Cover is the Marine Corps word for soft cap. We were going on a run. The first mile went by quickly as we ran across the sprawling Marine Corps Recruit Training Depot. I glanced around at the long rows of kelly green Quonset huts that made up the living quarters for thousands of new Marines.

"Keep those eyes straight ahead!" Corporal Emery yelled as we ran up a dusty dirt road that seemed to go on forever.

Discomfort turned into real pain as we realized that Emery had barely begun this foot race into hell. No one wanted to be the first poor bastard to fall out. Somewhere in the second mile, Private Richard Small collapsed. He lay there puffing away like a beached whale. Corporal Emery kept the platoon moving on down the road as Corporal Payne raced over to where Private Small lay and began kicking him.

"Get on your feet, you goddamn pile of whale blubber!"

Private Small struggled to his knees.

"Get up, Mr. Wide Body!"

Slowly Private Small stood up. His face was beet red and his chest was heaving as Corporal Payne continued to scream in his face.

"Now move out!"

Private Small lurched forward and stumbled towards the rapidly disappearing platoon.

"Platoon halt!" Corporal Emery turned and faced us as we stood at attention and gasped for air.

"Assume push-up position!"

We quickly began doing push-ups as Corporal Emery raced around looking for slackers.

"Get your ass out of the air, motherfucker!" He kicked the offending recruit in the butt. "I didn't say stop!"

My arms ached as I wondered how many more push-ups I could do before I, too, collapsed on the ground.

"On your feet! Move out!" Corporal Emery raced to the front of the platoon and began singing cadence.

Like a chorus of trained parrots we repeated every word Corporal Emery said in the same sing song style:

"Jody said before he died

There were one or two things he would like to ride

A bicycle, tricycle, automobile...

A bowlegged woman and a Ferris wheel"

Finally, we made a U turn without slowing down and began the journey back. We passed Private Small still stumbling along under the rapt attention of Corporal Payne. We ran to the front of the mess hall and immediately began doing more push-ups.

Private Richard Small was having a bad dream. He wasn't supposed to be here. Back in Waterloo, Iowa, he wasn't really worried when he first read the draft notice. He weighed well over two hundred pounds. The short, nearsighted, Holiday Inn desk clerk had thought for sure he would fail the physical. To his utter dismay, he passed. Things got even worse when he learned he was being drafted into the United States Marine Corps.

PFC Neil Kenny was on mess duty. He watched Corporal Payne march two new recruits to the head of the chow line. One was a tall, lanky boy from Little Rock, Arkansas. The other was Private Richard Small.

Corporal Payne frowned at the skinny recruit and glanced at PFC Kenny.

"Look at this skinny motherfucker!"

"Sir! Yes, sir!" PFC Kenny replied as he stood at attention holding a large metal spoon at port arms.

"He's a skinny, scumbag piece of shit, isn't he?"

"Sir! Yes, sir!" PFC Kenny shouted as he continued to stand at attention.
"Give this skinny bag of bones some potatoes!" Corporal Payne growled.
"Sir! Yes, sir!" PFC Kenny placed a spoonful of potatoes on the metal tray and went back to standing at attention.
Corporal Payne screamed at the top of his lungs at PFC Kenny. "Are you fucking with me?"
"Sir! No, sir!"
"I said give this skinny motherfucker some goddamn potatoes!"
"Sir! Yes, sir!" This time PFC Kenny placed several large scoops of mashed potatoes on the metal tray.
Corporal Payne looked at PFC Kenny. "Do you like ice cream?"
"Sir! Yes, sir!"
"Do you think this skinny piece of shit likes ice cream?"
"Sir! Yes, sir!"
"Give this skinny motherfucker some ice cream!"
PFC Kenny placed a scoop of ice cream on the metal tray and resumed the position of attention.
Corporal Payne screamed, "I said give this skinny motherfucker some ice cream!"
PFC Kenny placed several more scoops of ice cream on the metal tray.
"Now go sit the fuck down, you skinny bag of bones and you eat every bite on that goddamn tray! Go!"
The skinny kid ran over and sat down at a table and started shoveling down spoonfuls of potatoes and ice cream. Private Small was soaked in sweat as he stood at attention and held out his tray. Corporal Payne stared down at the fat recruit and glared at PFC Kenny.
"Look at this fat piece of shit! He's a fat motherfucker, ain't he?"
"Sir! Yes, sir!"
"Give this fat scumbag a bean!"
"Sir! Yes, sir!" PFC Kenny placed a small scoop of beans on Private Small's tray.
Corporal Payne yelled at PFC Kenny. "Are you fucking with me again?"
"Sir! No, sir!"
"What did I tell you?"
"Sir, you said to give the Private some beans."
"I said 'A' bean! 'A' goddamn bean! Give that fat motherfucker 'A' bean!"

Private Small winced as he watched PFC Kenny scrape the small pile of beans off of his plate. He picked up one bean in the large spoon and looked at Corporal Payne.

"Put it on the goddamn tray!"

"Sir! Yes, sir!" He slammed the bean in the middle of the metal tray.

"Now go sit down and eat your goddamn bean, you fat cocksucker!"

Private Small sat down and stared at his bean. He stole a glance at the skinny recruit beside him. He watched him slowly eating another spoonful of the still large pile of potatoes and ice cream.

PFC Kenny looked at both of them. He could see it coming. Corporal Payne was yelling at the next private in line. Private Small's eyes darted back and forth between the bean on his tray and the pile of potatoes and ice cream on the tray beside him. Finally, Private Small couldn't take it anymore.

"Agggggggggggg!" He groaned as he quickly dug into the potatoes and ice cream with both hands. He started stuffing the gooey mess into his mouth while the skinny recruit stared at him with his own mouth frozen open in shock.

Corporal Payne came running. His fist slammed into Private Small's back. "Put my potatoes back! You fat piece of shit! Put them back!"

"Aggggggggggggggg!" Private Small ignored the pain in his back and continued to stuff more potatoes and ice cream into his wide open mouth.

Corporal Payne knocked Private Small off of the bench and onto the floor as Private Small continued to swallow and moan. As Payne kicked the fat recruit, Private Small began throwing up.

"Don't stop, you fat cocksucker! Spit my potatoes out! I want every bite back, you fat piece of shit!"

The next morning I was waiting to go inside the chow hall for breakfast when I saw Private Small walk by. He was being escorted by a military policeman.

He was wearing a pink shirt. He had on gold shorts. He had on one tennis shoe and one dress shoe. In spite of the ridiculous attire, Private Small was smiling. He was going home. He was being escorted to the front gate.

From there he would walk to the local bus station. Civilians who lived nearby stopped and stared. They had seen this procession before. Private Small didn't mind. His back was still sore from the beating the night before, but he couldn't stop smiling. Tomorrow morning he would wake up as Mr.

Small and someday forget all about Corporal Payne and his potatoes and ice cream.

Edson Range, Camp Pendleton 1965

S leet was falling as I lay on the frozen ground and tried to focus down the cold steel barrel of my M-14 rifle at a small bull's eye over two hundred yards away. I missed. I tried to hold the sights steadier and fired again. I hit the outer edge of the target. Recruits who shot below a certain score stood in line later that night to get a beating. I was in the line.

We had gone to Camp Pendleton for two weeks rifle training. We were still recruits and our time was spent learning to correctly clean and fire our M-14 rifles and going on constant runs through the frozen hills that surrounded Edison Range. It was Christmas. After lights out, some people from a local church strolled outside the barracks and sang carols. It was the saddest Christmas of my life.

"Tell me a word I don't know!" Corporal Payne was yelling in my face.

"Sir, Altomiter, sir," I replied in a loud voice.

"What the fuck is that?" Corporal Payne discovered, while looking over my records, that I had two years of college before joining the Marines. If I told him a word that he already knew, I got a fist in my gut. I solved that problem by making up words and then making up definitions.

"Sir, it is an instrument used to measure the purity of gold, sir."

Corporal Payne snorted and walked away. If he had ever discovered that I was playing him for the fool he was, I never would have made it out of boot camp alive.

The night before graduation day should have been an occasion of joy and pride. It wasn't. Eight weeks of boot camp were finally over. The day started on an up note. For the first time since we got there, we were allowed to visit the Post Exchange. First, we stood in line and counted the crisp new twenty-dollar bills and then signed our name in the paymaster's log, affirming that we had received our correct pay in greenbacks. Tomorrow we would line up on the main parade deck and march in review for the commanding general. After a couple of long speeches, we would be declared Marines. Today, we had just twenty minutes to browse the brightly colored shelves of the Post Exchange and buy small items of our own choosing.

Shelton was a large black kid from East St. Louis. At the PX, he purchased a bottle of Old Spice cologne. Later that night he dropped it on the barracks floor and the small bottle broke. He quickly cleaned up the mess but not in time to escape the nose of Corporal Fortney. Fortney was by far the most sadistic of our three drill instructors. His booming voice echoed through the room while we stood at attention.

"This place smells like a goddamn whorehouse! What the fuck did you girls do to my barracks?"

Shelton spoke up. "Sir, I broke a bottle of cologne, sir."

"Well, thank you very much for your honesty."

Fortney then picked up a towel and tied it around Shelton's head.

By now all of us had learned the painful lesson of how to take some of the steam out of a drill instructor's punch while standing at attention. At the last second, we would roll slightly with the force of the blow and try to catch some of his fist on the corner of our rib cage.

It still hurt, but at least we could still breathe while we waited for the pain to go away. Corporal Fortney was well aware of this recruit's trick. Thanks to the towel, he knew Private Shelton could see nothing, as he slammed his fist into the recruit's stomach. Shelton's knees buckled and he struggled to stay on his feet as Corporal Fortney hit him again. Shelton didn't make a sound. I stood at attention and stuffed the rage I had been holding inside for eight weeks. This was our last day in boot camp. Anything that another beating was going to teach us should have been learned by now.

Shelton was my buddy. I hated Corporal Fortney and I hated myself for quietly standing there at attention while my blindfolded friend was beaten. I made a silent promise to God that I would kill Corporal Fortney if I ever got the chance. I left boot camp with what is called a "bad attitude." This was not the Marine Corps I envisioned when I watched John Wayne in "The Sands of Iwo Jima."

Corporal Fortney was a sadistic bad apple who should never have been a Marine, much less a drill instructor. If the Marines needed a lot of angry young men in the winter of 1966, Corporal Fortney was doing his part to help them to meet their quota. I loaded the heavy sea bag on my shoulder and climbed on the bus for Camp Pendleton. I didn't look back.

Infantry Training Regiment, Camp Pendleton 1966

The Infantry Training Regiment (ITR) was a far different experience than boot camp in San Diego. We were now full fledged Marines – as much a Marine as any member of the Corps since its birth almost two hundred years ago. Our days of being beaten while standing at attention ended at San Diego. If any instructor at Camp Pendleton ever hit one of us, we could hit back. From now on, officers were the only people we were required to address as "sir." These young instructors still out ranked us, however, and we had to follow their orders. They could make us suffer as much as any drill instructor.

"What's you name, Marine?"

The Corporal with the Instructor's helmet yelled at the Marine standing beside me.

"Private Johnson!" He replied in a loud clear voice. The Corporal had been walking down the ranks asking each Marine his name. Next, he stood in front of me.

"What's your name, Marine?"

He looked me up and down. I knew he wouldn't like my answer.

"Robert." I replied in a calm voice.

"Robert?" He raised his eyebrows and asked in a mocking tone. "Robert?"

I answered again. He called a fellow instructor over.

"Hey Mac, come over here and meet Robert!"

A tall white guy walked over and stared at me. "Well, Robert, my name is Corporal McAlester. Do you like doing push-ups, Robert?"

I smiled, "I love doing push-ups!"

"Well, Robert, why don't you drop down and start doing push-ups and don't stop until I tell you to."

I immediately began doing push-ups and counting in a loud voice:

"One…two…three…four…five…six…seven…eight…niner…" I deliberately used the military version of the number nine.

"Start over Robert and this time say nine."

I began again. Once again when I got to nine, I said "Niner!"

Corporal McAlester yelled in my face. "Start over, Robert!"

I began counting once more. This time when I finished my ninth push-up I yelled "Niner!" and went back to one on my own. I did this several more times until I couldn't lift my arms.

"On your feet, Marine!"

My face was red and my chest was heaving as I got back up and stood at attention.

"Now, what is your name?"

"Robert," I replied as I gasped for air.

"What is your last name, mister?"

"McLane."

"Well, while you are here at ITR, your name will be Private McLane. Is that all right with you, Robert?"

I paused before I answered, like I was thinking about his question. "OK," I answered in a calm voice.

"And if it's OK with you, Private McLane, we are going to go on a little run this morning."

"Sure, I love to run," I smiled as I stared straight ahead. We began each morning with a six mile run, wearing helmets and carrying M-14 rifles. After the run, we went to breakfast. Our mission at ITR was to learn to fire every weapon in the Marine Corps arsenal. One day it would be flame-throwers, the next day we tossed our first grenade. We learned how to use our bayonets to probe the ground for land mines.

After evening chow we passed the time playing poker or writing letters. Mike Roberts threw his cards in and stood up. He was bored and tired of losing money. I saw a gleam in his eye as he sat down on his bunk and stared at an ace bandage someone had been using to wrap a sprained ankle.

There was a small rectangle of aluminum that held the bandage together. Mike took the piece of metal and placed it squarely in the center of his fatigue cap. He looked in a mirror.

I smiled as I watched Private Roberts promote himself to First Lieutenant. We left the squad bay and walked over to another platoon in the barracks next door.

"Attention!" I shouted as Mike walked in behind me. Everyone jumped to their feet and stood at attention while Mike strutted around and tried to act like an Officer.

"Keep those eyes straight ahead, Mister!" I yelled as I caught one private trying to study the funny looking piece of metal in the middle of Mike's cap.

"Get this place cleaned up, Marines! There will be an inspection at 0600!" I followed Mike as he strutted out the door and we ran back over to our own barracks. We lay on our own bunks laughing. Mike could have faced a court-martial and a long stretch in the brig if he had been caught impersonating an officer. He never tried that stunt again.

The black sky slowly turned to gray as a small red haze rose over the distant mountains. We had been running almost thirty minutes. At a designated point we turned without stopping and continued running in the direction we had came from. My arms ached as I held the M-14 rifle across my chest and followed the bouncing Marines in front of me. Private Aikman was wheezing louder with each step. He had a bad heart, bad enough to get him a medical discharge from the Army.

His dream of fighting in Vietnam seemed doomed until he stopped and talked to the Marine Recruiter sitting behind the card table at his local community college. After listening to his story, the recruiter looked up at him and smiled. "You look healthy enough to me. Perhaps the Army's loss will be the Marine Corps' gain. Let's send you over for a physical and see what our guys think."

Perhaps the doctor was in a hurry that day or maybe he just didn't care, but Mr. Aikman passed with flying colors. He raised his hand and became Private Aikman.

Every time we went on a run, we thought he was going to die, as he wheezed and fought for each breath, while the Marines beside him grabbed his arms and pulled him along. He didn't die and his dream of fighting in Vietnam eventually came true.

We had a young Mexican in our platoon who didn't speak English. Another Mexican trainee adopted him and became his protector and translator as he desperately tried to learn English. I could not believe how low the Marine Corps was scraping the bottom of the barrel to meet their demand for more recruits. If you had two arms, two legs, a head and a pulse, you were welcome to try out for the team. Guys who washed out were given a one-way ticket home.

I graduated from ITR and was sent to learn the specific job I had been selected to do in the Marine Corps. Instead of becoming a cook, truck driver or supply clerk, I went to artillery school. For hundreds of years, accurate artillery fire had been the ace in the hole that generals from Napoleon to Robert E. Lee had used to ensure victory in a pitched battle. The British found out the hard way in the battle of New Orleans, as they marched their smartly dressed soldiers in neat straight lines right into the jaws of Andrew Jackson's massed cannons. Those who survived didn't stop running until they reached the Gulf of México. General Giap used superior artillery fire to defeat the French at Dien Bien Phu.

I was a math major my first two years of college. That helped when I took the barrage of tests each Marine faces to determine what kind of job they will be trained to do. In 1966, most of the recruits taking these tests were being assigned to the infantry. These Marines were called "grunts."

I was assigned to Fire Direction Control School. I was being trained to make the mathematical corrections necessary to adjust artillery fire. My tools were a slide rule and a book of logarithms. Each day I would spend hours laboring over mathematical equations. At night, I struggled over more math problems as I did my homework.

Private John Mills had a genius IQ. Sergeant Hart caught him doodling with his pencil and staring out the window.

"Why aren't you working on your homework, Private?"

"I have finished my homework, Sergeant."

"Oh, really? Let me see?"

Private Mills handed Sergeant Hart a small stack of papers. Sergeant Hart flipped through them and discovered all the problems had been correctly solved. I was still working on problem number two.

"Well, here is some more homework, Private Mills."

Sergeant Hart smiled as he placed a new stack of papers on Private Mill's desk. In another twenty minutes Private Mills was doodling again. Sergeant Hart looked over the finished assignment and gave up.

At the graduation ceremony, Private Mills was unimpressed with his Fire Direction Control Diploma. He folded it into a paper airplane and sailed it across the parking lot.

Private Wilson stood off to the side and watched our graduation. He had just gotten the bad news that he had flunked out of Fire Direction Control School and was being reassigned to a gun crew. He would shoot cannons for the rest of his time in the Marines. Private Wilson watched Private Mills laughing as he sailed his paper airplane across the parking lot. He knocked our genius out cold with a right cross to the jaw and walked away.

I finished up my six months active duty and reported to my reserve unit in Dallas. It was May 1966. From here on, I would be a Marine just one weekend a month—or so I thought.

Cameron, Texas
June 1967

I didn't want to go to this goddamn war. I didn't think the crooks running the Saigon government were worth dying for. In 1963 I remembered watching Madam Nu give an interview on television while her husband was cracking down on all the Buddhists in Vietnam. Her brother was a good Catholic boy and he had thrown several hundred monks in jail. To protest this political repression, several other monks had burned themselves to death in front of television cameras. These shocking images were broadcast all over the world. Madam Nu called these tragic deaths "Bar-B-Ques," and offered to supply more matches. She was the "First Lady" of Vietnam.

A few weeks later, President Diem was assassinated in a CIA-approved coup, and Madam Nu became a widow on the run. Ten days later President Kennedy was assassinated in Dallas. In 1965, I joined the Marine Corps Reserves. This was the only option available to avoid being drafted besides going to Canada. I didn't like snow.

In June of 1967 I was busted in Dallas for possession of a small amount of marijuana. The District Attorney promised not to indict me if I agreed to go back on active duty for two years. Since I had missed a drill while I was in jail, I was being recalled to active duty anyway. I took the deal. The good news was that I didn't have to report to Camp Pendleton until September. In July I packed a small bag and started hitchhiking west.

At the time there was a song on the radio by Bob Dylan called "Mr. Tambourine Man." There was a message in between the lines about the joys of pot smoking. I had already tried pot and decided that Dylan was right and I wanted some more.

I was headed for Haight-Ashbury. I took Interstate 10 to Los Angeles and turned north. I was waiting by an on-ramp on Highway 101 when I saw my second hippie.

The first hippie I had ever seen was named Rodney. When he first stumbled onto the campus of my junior college in Tyler, Texas, all the girls went running to their dorms for their cameras. Rodney was the real deal, right down to the hair just over his ears, the ragged blue jeans, and his pierced ear. We became instant friends. That weekend, I hopped a freight bound for Dallas with Rodney and his runaway girlfriend.

We stood in the open doorway of the boxcar and sang "Goodbye Ruby Tuesday" for the startled citizens of Chandler, Texas, as the freight train rolled though the middle of town. Sunday afternoon, I said goodbye to Rodney in Dallas and hopped another freight train back to Tyler.

Hippie number two was Jimmy Rizza. He was on his way to a commune just north of San Francisco. Jimmy was a bona fide flower child, right down to his feathers and bells. I was standing on a northbound entrance ramp to 101, just south of Santa Barbara when Jimmy came walking up.

"Hey, brother!" he greeted me as he took out a shiny harmonica and began to blow it as cars flew past. Where are you bound?" he asked between blasts on the harp.

"Headed for the Haight," I replied.

I had a feeling I was going to be stuck here for a while. Hitching alone, I felt I could pass for a college student going home for the weekend. The folks, who might have stopped and given me a ride, blew right on past this colorful harmonica player and his sad looking friend.

Jimmy was one of those rare people who only lived in the moment. He never thought about yesterday or tomorrow. I sat down on my sleeping bag and watched the cars and trucks flying by. I wished Jimmy would offer me a joint. He didn't. I sat there watching the sunset for a couple of hours listening to Jimmy playing the blues.

Suddenly, a VW bug pulled over to the side. Jimmy and I grabbed our stuff. I couldn't believe my eyes. The bug already had four guys inside, and they were picking us up! I climbed in the back. We were a mass of elbows and feet as the bug lurched forward and started rolling. Now I was in the company of five hippies.

Janis Joplin was moaning on the radio about a good man gone bad and The Beatles were singing "Paperback Writer" as we headed up the Coast Highway. Around midnight they dropped us off at the city limits of Santa Cruz.

"I know some people we can spend the night with," Jimmy smiled.

I discovered nights in California can get cold. Jimmy continued to play his harmonica as we walked along in the darkness.

The house Jimmy said we could stay in was locked. Jimmy explained that the guy who lived there had already gone to bed. "He has a job at a record store. He has to get up early."

He raised a window in the back of the house and climbed in. He walked to the front door and let me in. "There's an extra bed in the back."

Jimmy unrolled his sleeping bag in the living room. I tiptoed into the back bedroom. There were two beds. Someone was sleeping on one of them. I lay down on the other one and fell asleep. Early the next morning, an alarm clock started ringing. My roommate woke up. He walked over and looked at me. I felt like Goldilocks as I pretended to still be asleep. I must have looked like I was cold. He walked back over to his bed and picked up a blanket. He draped it over me and went into the bathroom. A few minutes later, I heard the front door slam as he left for the record store. I lay there, amazed that someone could wake up with a total stranger sleeping in his room and do what this guy did. There was something to this "free love" that hippies talked about and I wanted to learn more.

Later that morning, we headed back for Highway 101. I never got to say thank you to my host. We hitched all day up the Coast Highway. We got stranded along a deserted stretch of road just south of Big Sur. After it got dark, I wanted to crawl in my sleeping bag and start fresh the next morning. Jimmy wanted to keep going.

I was considering parting company with my new road buddy when a late model Cadillac pulled over to the side of the highway. Inside were two Mexicans. I thought they were dressed like a couple of gangsters, fancy shirts and hats pulled low. They didn't speak any English and Jimmy and I didn't know any Spanish. We climbed into the back of the big car and sped away in the night. This was a lot more comfortable than six hippies in a VW bug. I stretched my legs out and watched the lights of distant ships on the Pacific Ocean. I wondered where they were bound. I wondered where I was bound.

Quietly the driver lit a cigarette. It smelled funny. He passed it to his friend. His friend took a hit and passed it to Jimmy. In the silence I watched Jimmy take a toke and then he handed it to me. I inhaled deeply and passed it back to the driver. Twice more the joint went around as we drove on north though the dark California night.

We stopped at an all-night diner. I climbed out of the car and stood trans-fixed, staring at the most beautiful neon sign I had ever seen. The red letters simply said, "GRILL."

Jimmy led me inside. The Mexicans thought I was funny. I bit into the most delicious hamburger I had ever tasted. We paid for our meal and went back outside. I stared again at the neon sign, until Jimmy called me to join him in the back of the car. As we headed north, the driver turned the radio on to some Spanish station. Everyone was lost in their own thoughts as we rolled on up the Coast Highway. I woke up when we stopped for gas on the outskirts of San Francisco. We unloaded our bags and thanked the Mexicans for the ride. Jimmy wanted to head on across the bay to his commune. We parted company.

"Good luck, my friend, in Vietnam. Be careful." Jimmy smiled as he glanced back at me one last time.

I walked a few blocks and started hitchhiking again. My next ride dropped me off at the edge of Haight-Ashbury. The street was deserted as I walked along in the early morning fog.

"Buffalo Bill is dead!" I stopped and listened to a skinny guy wearing glass-es reading poetry from a ragged paperback.

"God, he was a handsome man!" I spoke the line from memory. The guy in the glasses looked up and smiled.

"Oh? You're into Cummings?"

I was first introduced to e.e. cummings in high school. I was hooked immediately by his simple poems and his unusual style of writing. "Buffalo Bill Is Dead" was one of my favorites.

"My name is Clyde. Would you care for a cup of tea?"

"That would be a perfect way to start my first day in Haight-Ashbury."

I followed him up five flights of stairs to a large run down apartment. Over tea, I learned that Clyde had once studied for the priesthood. He had just quit his last job as a short-order cook. It seems that one afternoon he put six ham-burger patties on the grill and three of them immediately hopped off. He turned in his apron and never went back. Clyde had a fat hooker girlfriend named Betty. Betty worked nights in the Tenderloin, a seedy part of town crawling with whores and junkies.

Betty gave Clyde walking around money while Clyde pondered what to do with his life. They shared the large apartment with David, a college kid from Dallas. The rent was paid by an ex-con from Puerto Rico named Angel. Angel didn't sleep there, but he sometimes used the place to store the drugs he sold every week.

Angel learned to knit when he was in prison. He made sweaters that he would sell to some of the dress shops on Haight Street. Angel was no hippie. He looked a little weird sitting on the couch with his knitting needles and a .38 caliber snub-nosed revolver tucked away in a shoulder holster. Every night around midnight, David and I would take a ride down the entire length of Haight Street looking for anyone that needed a place to crash. We headed back to the apartment with a car full of hippies.

Since there was no TV, Clyde provided the entertainment. He was a great storyteller. We crashed around dawn and slept until the afternoon. There was an open drug market that flourished on Haight Street twenty-four hours a day. You might buy a gram of hashish for ten bucks and later trade it for two hits of mescaline. Later you could trade the mescaline for a hit of LSD. You just kept trading until you got whatever drug you wanted to take. At the end of Haight Street was Golden Gate Park. The park was a haven for stoned hippies to throw Frisbees and play guitars.

I rolled out of bed at the crack of noon and headed for the bathroom. Contrary to the thinking of Middle America, this hippie liked to start the day with a nice hot shower. Rising early meant there would be plenty of hot water, water that would not last with a dozen houseguests. I hated being stoned when I needed a bath. Every grain of dirt felt like a sharp rock against my skin. I had just enough money for a cup of coffee, and it cleared out the cobwebs from last night's party.

I walked over to the office of the Oracle, an underground newspaper that would front a hippie willing to work, ten newspapers to sell on the street. Because of my good work history, I was trusted with an extra ten newspapers. Each paper sold for a quarter. I made ten cents. I signed for my papers and headed down Haight Street.

"Get your hippie paper!" I yelled at the busload of tourists stuck in traffic. I walked along a row of hands holding quarters as they reached down from the open bus windows and quickly sold all of my papers. I walked back over to the boys at the Oracle and paid them off. This time I took fifty more papers and headed out again.

My favorite spot to peddle newspapers was where Haight Street ended at the entrance of Golden Gate Park. I had tour buses coming from three different directions. Two guys in an old pick-up truck pulled up beside me.

"How about letting us look at your newspaper while we drive around the block? If we like it, we'll buy it."

I looked into their eyes and smiled. "Sure, brother! Welcome to the Haight. Take your time, I'll be right here." I handed them a newspaper and they drove away.

Pony Boy came by. This fifteen-year-old runaway from Oregon had found a home in the Haight. "Hey man, wanna buy a hunk of hash?"

"Let me see it."

He put a small brown cube in my hand. It looked like a bullion cube. I held it up to my nose. The rich smell of Marijuana resin filled my nostrils.

"How much, Bro?"

"For you my man, five bucks!"

I paid him in quarters. The guys in the pick-up truck returned.

"How did you know we would come back?"

"I didn't. But I was willing to take a chance. This is a place where most folks trust people, even strangers. Find somewhere to park your truck. Get out and walk around. You might decide to stay."

In less than an hour, I had paid the Oracle folks off again. I was through selling papers for the day. I bought some fish & chips at a sidewalk stand and walked into the park. In a rolling meadow, hippies were blowing soap bubbles, monster soap bubbles that were made by dipping a long piece of cloth attached to a stick into a large pan of soapy water.

I sat under a huge eucalyptus tree and ate my fish & chips. I finished my soda and made a pipe out of the can. I used a pin from a peace button to punch holes in the can. I broke off a small piece of hashish and tried out my new pipe. I sat under the tree smoking and trying not to think about how many days I had left before I had to report to Camp Pendleton. I tried to think of some way to get out of going to this stupid war.

I thought about reporting in with a purse, maybe something with a shoulder strap. Would they buy it? Could I pull it off? I didn't think so. Most of the Marines I knew were cynical and sadistic types that would just love to see some stupid asshole walking in carrying a purse. That would make their day. After putting the poor bastard through a couple of days of hell, he would still be in the Marine Corps, minus one purse. Maybe I should just accept my fate and go to war. Vietnam seemed a million miles away from this peaceful meadow in Golden Gate Park.

I headed back down Haight Street. Two guys who looked like truck drivers were driving down the street with a sign that said, "Free rides for hippie chicks to the East Coast." A Hell's Angel walked over to the driver, opened his door, and planted his boot alongside the guy's head. Violence was rare in the Haight. The cops arrested the Hell's Angel. A couple of hippies walked around shaking a can at people trying to raise bail.

I wandered into a coffee shop that looked like a Middle Eastern tearoom. There were cushions all over the floor and the sweet smell of incense drifted though the air. You had to buy something, but you could hang out as long as you wanted to. I ordered tea and found a comfortable cushion to recline on. This was a lifestyle a guy could get used to.

In a world gone crazy with greed and power, the Haight was a place where those things didn't matter, a place of beauty and love, where for the briefest of shining moments, time stood still.

A group of performers and dancers formed an acting troupe called the Bread & Puppet Theater. They put on performances in an old movie house. As the light dimmed, I found a seat in the back of the balcony and quietly lit up a joint. After passing it to the guy beside me, I heard a noise above my head. I looked up and saw a hand extending from a small hole in the projection booth. The hand took the joint and disappeared. A few seconds later, the hand reappeared and I took back the joint.

I continued to share the joint with the guy beside me and the hand while watching the show. This was the Haight-Ashbury that I quickly came to love.

I met a cute blonde from Manchester, England who came here with her sister. Like the Van Morrison song, she became "my brown-eyed girl." We shared fish & chips in the park and made love in Clyde's apartment.

One night Clyde brought home some methamphetamine, then known as speed. I sat on the floor of the bathroom while Clyde poked at the top of my forearm with a needle. A houseguest I didn't know came in to take a pee and looked at Clyde.

"What are you doing? Give me that!"

He took the needle and rolled my arm over. Quickly he found a vein and pushed the plunger until it was empty. The rush was incredible. I knew if I hung around the Haight, I would do this shit again and again until I turned into one of those human scarecrow speed freaks that roamed the nights looking for one more fix. These speed demons would soon turn Haight-Ashbury into just another ghetto.

I knew it was time to leave. I had less than two weeks to report to Camp Pendleton.

David had to get back to Dallas to get ready for the fall semester and the English sisters were headed home to Manchester. We filled David's Mustang with gas and headed east. I told my hippie friends goodbye and hitched south towards my grandparent's farm.

The big eighteen-wheeler pulled over to the side of the road and I got out. I crossed some railroad tracks and followed a winding dirt road uphill to a small two-story white frame farmhouse. I told my grandparents I had been, "Out in California." I rode into town with my grandfather and got a haircut.

That night I went to a high school football game with a couple of my cousins. I had one hit of LSD that I had brought with me from Haight-Ashbury. I washed it down with a coke. I tried to explain what I was doing to my cousin.

"Charles, I just took something called LSD and tonight, if things get a little strange, you're gonna have to be my friend. I need to know I can count on you."

My cousin looked at me like I was some kind of burned out wino asking for some spare change. Christ, I used to play cowboys and Indians with this guy.

One look in his eyes and I knew that no matter what happened that night, I was on my own. I tried to relax and watch the football game. Someone threw a pass. The ball continued spiraling upward into the night sky until it disappeared. I continued staring up into the sky while everyone else was watching the game. I realized that the acid had kicked in. I put on some dark shades and tried to act normal.

Later my cousin dropped me off at my grandparent's house. He didn't mention the LSD. I went to bed.

I awoke the next morning to the smell of fresh coffee and hot cakes cooking in my grandmother's kitchen. I slowly pulled on my faded jeans and tightened the shoelaces of an old pair of tennis shoes. I wanted the moment to last forever.

"Breakfast is ready, Mr. City Boy," my grandmother teased me as I came down the stairs. Some of my earliest memories are of the meals I ate at this same table while a man on the radio talked about someplace called Korea.

After breakfast, I took a walk. I followed an old path that led to a small creek at the edge of a field of fresh-cut hay. In front of me, a huge oak tree leaned over like an old woman pulling on a stubborn weed. I was happy to see the tree was still healthy and strong. High among the sprawling limbs lay the ruins of an old tree house.

The rotting boards that were nailed in the trunk were warped and splintered but they held firm as I climbed up into the remains of what once was a mighty fortress.

From the lofty shelter of this natural hideout, my young cousins and I had held off many determined bands of fearless lawmen. We never surrendered. We never ran. We kept fighting until the posse was all dead, or it was time for supper.

The sight of a young man sitting in an old tree house may have looked strange to the long distance truck drivers passing by, but I didn't care. This time the fight was real. I had received orders from the United States Marine Corps to report to Camp Pendleton in September, to begin the final training I would get before leaving for Vietnam.

I wanted to go on sitting in the old tree house forever, at least until the damn war was over. I decided that I wasn't going to come down until I had a plan that I was absolutely, one hundred per cent, sure would bring me back home alive.

I went over every lesson my cousins and I had learned from our many summers as desperadoes: Keep your head down. Listen up. Keep your eyes on the look out for the subtle signs of another attack. No matter what, we had to be brave. No one wanted to be remembered as a coward. I would rather not be remembered at all. The ones who got remembered were the ones who didn't come back.

There were a lot of different ways to say someone had been killed. "He didn't make it," was the most common way Marines in Vietnam told each other about another KIA, (killed in action). Back in the Civil War, Mama would tell her neighbors about the dreaded letter from the War Department by saying that her son had "fallen." They tried to make it look like getting killed in a war was no worse than taking a header down a flight of stairs. What they called it made no difference to the undertaker. I had no interest in needing his services anytime soon.

Most of my thoughts that morning were not making much sense. Neither had a lot of lessons I had learned in the Marines. They didn't have to make sense, they just had to work. I believed that God really did like me in spite of all my bad habits and wanted to keep me around for a long time. I was a member in good standing of one of the finest fighting outfits in the world, next to my cousins.

Finally, I decided it was safe to come down. I picked up an acorn from underneath the old tree and slipped it into my pocket. I walked back across the field to the white farmhouse my grandfather had built at the end of World War II. I was filled with the confidence of my newfound faith. I felt good about the plan I had chosen. I sat down to another old-fashioned country meal.

My grandmother avoided looking at me as we started to eat. She looked like she was trying not to cry. I told a joke to break the tension. No one laughed.

"Don't worry folks. I'm coming back from this thing. I guarantee it."

My grandmother put down a pitcher of tea and looked at me. "Of course you are."

The next day my grandfather drove me to a small airport and I caught a plane to Dallas. The stewardess was kind enough to provide me with several miniature bottles of bonded whiskey. I poured them in a cup with ice and tossed them down as the plane headed north. I looked around. The lady sitting beside me was a schoolteacher on her way to visit her grandchildren. I eyed the tiny bottle of Jack Daniels sitting beside her tray.

"Pardon me, Madam. You aren't planning to drink that, are you?"

"Of course not!"

"I don't mean to be rude, Madam. You see, I am a little nervous. I am a Marine, on my way to Vietnam. I'll settle down once I've killed some Viet Cong. Are you sure you aren't saving it for later?"

"You may have it, if you'll just be quiet."

She picked up the tiny bottle and set it on my tray. I asked for some more ice and opened the small bottle. Another shot of this stuff and I could ignore anybody.

I reported into the Marine Corps Reserve Center in Dallas, drunk and belligerent. "Just keep your mouth shut!" The Marine Sergeant in charge of processing my paperwork wasn't in the mood for any shit from a drunk private. Depending on how the next couple of hours went, I would face the morning in a Dallas jail or a Marine Corps base in California. It was a no win situation.

"Whatever you say, boss. Just get me to the plane on time. I'm going to war!" I wanted to get this over with. Sign here. Sign there. You can't go to war until the paperwork is done. They took fingerprints and photographs. Finally I was ready. I slept on the plane and woke up in California. My head was splitting with a bad hangover.

Camp Pendleton was an endless maze of Marines standing in different lines - lines for shots, lines for haircuts, lines for new uniforms, and lines to designate next-of-kin on insurance papers. There was a final six weeks of training. The instructors were combat veterans who had just returned to the States after finishing their own tour of duty. Hopefully, knowledge was being passed on that would save lives, once these new warriors were actually in harm's way.

There were daily courses on everything from recognizing booby traps to Vietnamese culture and the importance of taking malaria tablets. I filled out one more form and handed it to an office clerk who was supposed to assign me to a training regiment. In the blank for religion, I wrote "hippie." It didn't take long for someone to notice.

"Hey, we got us a genuine hippie here!" One of the laughing clerks handed my form to a sergeant in charge of processing the paperwork. He got up from his desk and looked around.

"OK, Marines, who's the hippie?"

I slowly raised my hand. He called me up to the front of the room.

"Are you for real?"

"What do you mean by real?"

The sergeant laughed. "He's for real."

He motioned for me to follow him behind the counter. Cautiously, I followed. He told me to have a seat across from his desk. I discovered that this was not your average Marine sergeant. First of all, he was only twenty-one. He had just finished a tour in Vietnam. Since he only had a couple of months left on active duty, he was put in charge of the office clerks processing the paperwork of Marines on their way to Vietnam. He hated the Marines and couldn't wait to become a civilian again.

He had plans for a real live hippie. He forged the signature of his commanding officer on my orders and tossed them in the bottom drawer of his desk.

"You're not going to a training regiment right away. You're going to hang with us for awhile, bro. There's so much confusion around here, nobody's even going to miss you. My name's Murphy."

A North Vietnamese bullet had left a long ugly scar down the calf of his leg. His face still had the look of innocence, but that was deceptive. He couldn't wait to get out of the Marines. He had seen more death in the last year than most men three times his age. He mistrusted anyone in authority. He started his mornings with a joint.

He stared at the long line of Marines bound for Vietnam and smiled. If these poor bastards only knew. The arrival of a genuine hippie was a refreshing break to another boring day of supervising these Remington raiders.

The phone rang and Murphy picked it up. Someone from Ohio was trying to find their son. Murphy listened patiently as the woman gave him all the details she thought would help find her boy. Finally he cut her off.

"I'm afraid I can't help you lady. Your son left for Vietnam last week, some kind of secret mission. I have to go now." Murphy hung up the phone and got up from his desk.

"Let's go get some chow. You can tell me about Haight-Ashbury." We left the barracks and headed for the mess hall.

Thanks to Murphy I had fallen between the cracks. I kept moving, eating in different mess halls every day and sleeping in different barracks at night. I could have gone back to Texas. No one would have missed me. I didn't know how long this would last.

During the day I went to the base library and read magazines or went shopping at the Post Exchange. At night I partied with Murphy. With all the confusion of hundreds of new arrivals every week, it was pretty easy to become invisible. It came to an end late one night.

The best way to smoke pot at Camp Pendleton at night was to go for long walks in the vast open darkness while we passed around a joint. We walked back to the barracks where Murphy lived. I had to piss. So did Murphy. We went into the bathroom. The Marines call it the head. I still don't know why. I was standing at the urinal when we heard the First Sergeant singing in the shower. There was a seven foot wall separating the showers from the rest of the bathroom. Murphy grabbed a huge industrial mop that was leaning against the wall. He was going to throw it over the wall. I grabbed onto the mop and tried to take it away from him.

"Are you crazy? That's the First Sergeant!"

We struggled over the mop.

"He's a lifer, ain't he?" Murphy snarled. He twisted the mop out of my hands and heaved it over the wall. I heard the First Sergeant yell as the mop hit him in the face. I ran after this laughing mad man, out into the cold, dark night with an angry naked First Sergeant in hot pursuit. Somehow we got away.

The next morning I saw the First Sergeant walk by. He didn't recognize me. The big mop had caught him square in the face. He had a black eye and his nose was swollen. This was too much for me. I knew the First Sergeant would turn Camp Pendleton upside down looking for whoever threw the mop. I found Murphy and told him I was headed back to Haight-Ashbury for a few days 'til things cooled off. I never saw him again.

I put on civilian clothes and took a bus to Los Angeles. I started hitchhiking north. I made it to San Francisco the next day. I didn't recognize anyone as I walked down Haight Street. Clyde was gone. My brown eyed girl was back in England. I saw Angel walking out of a record store. He hardly knew me with my Marine Corps haircut.

"What are you doing back? I was relieved to see him smile. We walked back to his apartment. These days he lived alone. Angel said I could crash there for a while.

"What should I do?" I asked Angel as he rolled a joint and passed it to me. I shook my head and stared at the ceiling. "Sooner or later they are going to realize that I am missing and the FBI is going to start looking for me. It's hopeless, Angel."

I watched the blue smoke slowly curl towards the ceiling. I walked over to the window and looked down. A hard rain was beginning to fall. Tourists and hippies were scurrying under the alcoves and doorways of the various shops and bookstores along Haight Street. Angel went to the kitchen and brewed up a pot of herb tea. He brought me a cup as I continued to stand at the window and watch the rain coming down.

"I wish I could just go on hanging out here in the Haight, but sooner or later I will get picked up. Like it or not, I gotta go back."

"You wouldn't want to stay here anyway. This place has gone to hell since you left. Everybody is ripping each other off over dope. Last week three hippies were found in their apartment shot to death. I'm thinking about moving on myself."

The tea was bitter but I drank it anyway.

"Why did it all have to end this way? This place was so full of peace and love. I could have gone on living here forever."

Angel sat down on the couch and picked up his knitting needles. He was finishing a sweater. He shook his head. "Peace got drafted and love caught the clap."

I looked at Angel. "I don't want to kill anybody. Not in this war, not in any war. I want to think about living and deciding what I want to do with my life. Two months from now I could be headed home in a body bag, all because of a bunch of lying politicians!"

I decided to go to a movie, anything to keep from thinking about the insanity of going back to Camp Pendleton. I put on my coat and walked out into the rain.

The next morning I told Angel goodbye and started hitchhiking back to Camp Pendleton. I was standing at the edge of the freeway when a highway patrolman decided to check me out. The only identification I had was my dog tags.

He turned me over to the Shore Patrol. They kept me at a Navy base called Treasure Island for a couple of days and then transported me in handcuffs in the back of a paddy wagon back to Camp Pendleton. My time in limbo was over.

"Where have you been, Marine?" The captain sat at his desk and looked at my orders. I stood at attention and stared straight ahead. "It says here that you reported into Camp Pendleton over a month ago."

"Well, sir, it's all been kind of confusing. Lieutenant Atkinson told me that a new company was forming up and that I was to hang loose in the area until I heard my name called. I have been waiting for someone to do that for over a month."

Murphy had covered his tracks. The lieutenant whose signature he forged left for Vietnam the same week I reported in. They knew I had been goofing off but they couldn't prove it. They could prove I had been off base without authorization and that cost me a hundred dollar fine and the only stripe I had. Hanging out with Murphy for a month was worth every nickel.

I was assigned to a training regiment and reported to the First Sergeant.

Every day was filled with runs, marches, and classes about Vietnam. There were mock-ups of Viet Cong villages, complete with tripwires that set off devices that splattered us with red ink. We crawled through tunnels made by connecting fifty gallon barrels end to end for almost a hundred yards. I climbed out of a well back into the bright sunlight. We played war with Vietnam veterans dressed up like Viet Cong.

They delighted in making us look like fools and told us we were all going to die. We stood in line to get gamma globulin shots, monster shots in the ass with needles that looked like they were made for racehorses. I tried to look away.

The sadistic corpsman reached around and held the huge needle in front of my face. "What's the matter, bro? You don't like needles?"

Christ, I wondered. Where the hell does the Marine Corps find these people? I limped over to the next line.

After supper I got into a poker game. I stared at some graffiti on a wall locker. It simply said, "Gone to war. August 23rd." I wondered if the poor bastard who wrote it was still alive. I looked at the guys I was playing cards with.

"Do you realize that in six months, one of us is going to be dead?"

A PFC from Chicago glanced at me, "So what? As long as it ain't me, I don't give a good goddamn."

I looked at him and smiled. "Well, I am just so proud to be serving with you happy warriors. You're all so sensitive and caring. You're such jolly good sports to be willing to die for a buncha drug dealers and pimps. I'll give them your regards when I am buying some of their fine products or procuring the services of some of their sisters."

An eighteen year old Kansas farm boy challenged my sarcasm with a little Republican swill about fighting for freedom and democracy. "We're just trying to help them build a free country."

"They have been doing just fine for the last couple of thousand years without help from us or any other misguided missionaries." I threw in my hand. I couldn't believe the gullibility of some people. These were the same folks that lost all of their money at the state fair trying to knock over those cement bottles.

"The average Vietnamese wouldn't know democracy if it bit 'em in the ass! They do know a thing or two about war. In the last thousand years, they kicked out Genghis Khan, the Chinese, the Japanese, and the French. Now it's our turn."

"Lyndon Johnson snaps his fingers and a million young boys step up and drop their pants, bend over and smile for the cameras!" I bailed out of the card game and took a long walk in the cool night air.

My situation was completely hopeless and out of control. Every plan I had made up not to be here had gone horribly wrong. I felt like an overweight cow in a Kansas City stockyard. I wasn't the only one feeling despair. Fights broke out every day for no other reason than to relieve the tension.

At last it was time to go. We followed our sea bags onto a bus headed for Travis Air Force Base. I felt like a condemned man traveling his last mile in an overcrowded wagon. I watched the cars passing us on the freeway for any sign of pretty women. It would be over a year before I saw any more of them. At the airport, guys rushed to pay phones to say goodbye to wives and sweethearts. I had neither.

In 1944 my uncle crossed the ocean in a slow moving ship called a troop transport. Twenty-three years later I was sitting in a comfortable window seat courtesy of Delta Airlines. We spent three days in Okinawa getting last minute shots and our final orders for just where we were bound in Vietnam.

I left one sea bag in Okinawa to be picked up on my way home. I wrote a small note to myself and left it in the top of the bag. That night a buddy and I crawled through a hole in the fence and flagged down a taxi into town. The next night I stayed on base and went to a movie. Coming out of the theater I had an LSD flashback. I had heard about this strange phenomenon, but it had never happened to me before. I came out of the theater into a different world. At times like these, other folks in a similar situation were observed taking off their clothes and climbing flagpoles. That kind of behavior would not do on a Marine Corps base in Japan. My only option was to maintain my cool in the middle of 20,000 Marines until this shit wore off. The solution was simple. I would just pretend I had just dropped some really good LSD. This was definitely not the best environment for psychedelic adventures, but the renegade chemicals dancing in my brain didn't care.

I took a long walk and found sanctuary in the dark shadows of a palm tree. I did not panic. I sat quietly and waited for this shit to die down. Veteran acidheads will tell you that what makes LSD so much fun is the hallucinations. Only rookies think that stuff is real. The pros just sit back and enjoy the show. Finally the uninvited drugs started wearing off. I walked back to my barracks and went to sleep. The next morning everything was back to what passed for normal is those troubled times.

Kadina Air Force Base, Okinawa October 1967

M arines spend a lot of time standing in lines. It comes with the job. I had a lot of interest in this line. One Marine would be assigned to the First Marine Division.

The next Marine would be sent to join the Third Marine Division. The First Division was stationed in Da Nang. The Third Division was somewhere on the border just south of North Vietnam, in a place called the DMZ. I counted heads to make sure I was going into the First Division. Then I counted again, to make sure. I was one head away from going into the First Division when my scheme went to hell. The guy in front of me should have gone into the Third Division, but at the last minute, some office clerk yelled out, "I need one more for the First Division."

He took the guy in front of me. Then he looked at me and nodded towards the line of Marines going into the Third Division. The next morning I flew out of Okinawa bound for Vietnam. We broke through the clouds over the huge air base at Da Nang. Much too soon for me, we landed. I stared out of the window at a long row of stacks of aluminum coffins.

Each shiny metal box represented a family back in America whose worst nightmare had come true. Da Nang was a mass of confusion—guys just arriving, guys leaving for home. Military Police stood on almost every corner directing traffic.

Da Nang looked like a military version of old Dodge City. Everyone was wearing or carrying a rifle. There were some American women working at a Red Cross center. The Marines called them "Round-eyes" or "Doughnut Dollies." They were the last white women these guys would see until they either went on R&R or went home.

Every day a lone plane took off headed north for the DMZ. Every day I missed it. This foolishness had gone on for almost a week. I didn't want to get on that plane. I knew there was a real war going on where that plane was headed and I wanted to put off taking that flight as long as possible. The previous two days, all flights north were canceled because the airport at Dong Ha was closed due to damage from incoming artillery.

I couldn't keep missing that flight. I wanted to spend the next year just wandering around Da Nang but I knew that wasn't going to happen. M.P.'s were constantly checking orders. If the date on your orders was too old, you went straight to jail.

That night I met a Marine who was on his way home. I could tell by his scruffy boots that he had done his time in the bush. I asked him a question.

"Are we winning this war? Can you see any progress during the year that you have been here?"

"Forget winning the war. Just keep your head down and do your best to stay alive. Do your thirteen months and go back home. We ain't never gonna win this damn war."

"Say, by the way. What is the Vietnamese word for Marijuana?" I asked like I was doing research on the Vietnamese language.

"Tuc Fein. It's the best shit you'll ever smoke. Just be careful and don't get caught."

Later that night I traded my Zippo lighter for seventeen joints. My connection couldn't have been more than ten years old. I took a walk in the shadows and got stoned. The next morning I went to the airport early and signed my name on the manifest for the morning flight to Dong Ha. It was a small flight. There were about eight Marines and a couple of Green Berets headed north.

The Marines sat on their sea bags and waited for someone to pick them up. I stared at a chicken chasing a bug.

"See," I thought to myself, "The DMZ is not such a bad place. This chicken is doing OK. He is surviving." A small voice inside me asked, "What about the bug?"

Finally a duce-and-a-half truck pulled up and we threw our bags in the back and climbed on. We stared out at the rice paddies and water buffalo as we followed a winding muddy road towards the Headquarters for the Twelfth Marine Regiment.

This was headquarters for the largest concentration of artillery batteries in the history of the Marine Corps. Their job was to provide fire support for tactical operations all over the DMZ. The truck dropped us off outside the Regimental Headquarters tent. We stood around waiting for someone to tell us what to do.

Finally, a fat, pale sergeant stepped outside the tent and spoke to us. It was obvious that life in the rear suited him very well.

"Welcome to the Nam. We'll tell you where you are going as soon as we figure it out. Can anybody here type?"

My ears perked up. Two years ago I needed a half a credit to graduate from high school. I took a six-week typing course in summer school. I looked around. No one had their hand raised. Slowly I raised mine.

"I can type about twenty words a minute if nobody rushes me."

He walked me inside the tent to an old Smith-Corona typewriter sitting on a field desk and handed me a blank piece of paper.

"Write me a letter."

I sat down and wrote a letter to my grandmother to let her know that things were looking up. I handed it to the sergeant.

"What's your name, Marine?"

"McLane."

"Well McLane, it looks like you're the new battalion legal clerk."

I was issued an M-14 rifle and assigned to a tent. I told the sergeant I needed some jungle boots. I didn't want to look like a new guy. He sent me over to the supply tent. They didn't have any boots in my size so I walked over to the medical battalion tent set up by the Landing Zone (LZ). This place served as an emergency room for incoming casualties. Outside the tent was a large pile of slightly used one owner jungle boots. I sat down and started digging through, looking for a pair that would fit. I called them my lucky boots. What were the odds on two guys getting wounded in the same pair of boots? I left my new Stateside boots in the pile. I walked back over to the headquarters tent and reported in. I spent the day typing legal papers for the second battalion commander. It was a dirty job, but someone had to do it. Every other night, I pulled guard duty.

I spent the night in a bunker made of sandbags and took my turn staring out into the darkness. The rats and mosquitoes kept me awake as I wondered where the war was.

Dong Ha, Vietnam
November 1967

I t was Sunday. The big supply tent was quiet, except for Gladys Knight and the Pips singing "I Heard it Through the Grapevine" on the battery-powered radio while about a dozen of the craziest free spirits ever to go to war were rocking and rolling the afternoon away.

It was American Bandstand dancing in combat boots, with an occasional artillery shell thrown in to keep the party jumping. The lack of women did not inhibit the wild gyrations of these brothers-in-arms. Different dance styles were being demonstrated by happy warriors from various places around America.

Zimmerman was from Wisconsin, a good-looking kid who liked to fight.

He pointed a finger at a slender black PFC and shouted, "Chicago!"

He looked over at another black Marine named Dumas and yelled, "New York!"

Dumas was doing his version of a dance called the funky chicken with the trick knee. Behind him was a tall white Texan named Walsh, who was doing something a little more basic. Zimmerman shouted at Walsh.

"Get down, Dallas!"

Gunnery Sergeant Houten was walking by and heard the racket. He stuck his head in the door of the tent. He looked around and shook his head. Gunnery Sergeants ran the Marine Corps and this one ran Headquarters Battery.

He worked his Marines hard, but he also allowed them time to fight and gamble. He wasn't so sure about dancing. This was a new breed of Marines he had never seen in Korea. He was sure they were breaking some regulation, he just didn't know which one. He made a mental note to ask Captain Stack if he could order the men not to dance.

"Come on, Gunny!" Zimmerman waved for him to join them. He grimaced and shook his head in disbelief. He turned and walked away. Gladys Knight was replaced with the honey throated voice of Hanoi Hanna telling everyone we were losing the war and time was running out to surrender.

"Happy Thanksgiving, Marines!" she purred as she started playing a record called Bad Moon Rising, by Credence Clearwater Revival. Hanoi Hanna talked a lot of commie trash, but she played some great rock and roll.

Dumas looked outside and made sure the gunny had left. He sat down by a row of sandbags and lifted one up. Underneath was a joint that looked like a machine rolled Camel. He fired it up as Janis Joplin wailed, "Take another little piece of my heart, now baby!"

Dumas passed the joint to Zimmerman and lifted up another sandbag. He picked up a fifth of rot gut Vietnamese whiskey that had been poured into an empty Jack Daniels bottle that someone at the officer's club had forgotten to smash. He put two Styrofoam coffee cups together and poured a shot of the bootleg booze. Dumas used the second cup for good measure. Sometimes the illegal booze ate a hole in the bottom of a single cup.

"Seven days! Seven days and a wake-up!" Dumas laughed and toasted his last week in Vietnam.

Zimmerman passed the joint to a blonde-haired Corporal everyone called "Smurf."

Smurf was a beach boy from Anaheim, California. He should have been hanging ten at Huntington Beach instead of ducking shrapnel in the DMZ.

Smurf passed the joint to a curly-haired Irish Canuck named Doyle.

The guy wasn't even an American. Some estimated that about one in ten Marines serving in Vietnam was from Canada. Doyle was a drifter who had wandered into a war. He passed the joint back to Dumas as I stepped outside to get some air.

I watched a skinny white dude walking by. I recognized him immediately. "You're that guy in the picture!"

He stopped and looked at me. I smiled at him. Six months ago, Life magazine had done a front page story on an outpost about ten miles up the road called Con Thien. While they were up there, a forward observer was wounded by enemy artillery fire and taken out by helicopter on an emergency medevac.

Several photos of Sergeant Hutchinson ended up in the December issue of Life. I read the issue back in the States. He was from Kansas. He had been in Vietnam almost three years. Each time a tour was almost over, he extended for another one. He wasn't planning on going back to the States. He had a brown belt in karate.

He wanted to finish his hitch in Vietnam and be discharged in Okinawa to continue studying martial arts. Hutch was a straight arrow. His idea of a thrill was a cup of coffee at bedtime. After he picked up his third Purple Heart at Con Thien, he was sent to Dong Ha to finish out his current tour of duty. The Marine Corps rewarded anyone who had been wounded three times by letting them finish their time in the rear.

Getting a Purple Heart in the Marines wasn't easy. It wasn't just a case of getting hit, you had to be hurt. If they didn't have to medevac your ass to the rear—sorry pal, no cigar.

Suddenly, an incoming artillery shell screamed in and exploded about a sixty yards away, followed by two more. We scrambled into the nearest trench. Hutchinson pressed against the side of the trench and looked over at me.

"Did they mention anything about the incoming when they told you about this place?"

Since Dong Ha was considered the rear, this only happened once or twice a week. Sometimes I heard our own artillery answering. The guys in the tent never stopped dancing. The shelling ended as quickly as it started.

My biggest enemy at Dong Ha was a guy about my age who happened to be my boss. In another time we might have been friends. We were both a couple of fellas who had been to college and ended up in Marine Corps uniforms. His happened to come with captain's bars. Whenever Captain Thomas Stack felt he was not getting the level of respect he felt he deserved, he tried to remedy his insecurities by thinking up some ridiculous job for the poor fool who offended him.

I offended him a lot. I looked at him and saw a kid who was still getting used to shaving every day, a kid who got picked on often in school, a kid who felt other people were laughing at him. His high-pitched voice only made matters worse.

Making Tommy Stack a Marine Officer was one of God's little jokes.

For guys like me, the joke wasn't funny. An asshole with a little power can make war hell. Our relationship got off on the wrong foot. Maybe I didn't salute him fast enough. Maybe it started that first night in the shower tent. I was drunk and stoned and I decided to take a shower. I was covered in soap when Captain Stack walked in. Suddenly, I could not stop laughing. Captain Stack's eyes narrowed.

"Are you laughing at me?"

"No, sir!"

I answered between chuckles.

"Well then, what the fuck are you laughing at?"

I caught my breath.

"Well, sir. In the shower, no one can tell the generals from the privates!"

I grabbed my soap and walked away. I knew I would pay for my humor someday.

Right now, I was stoned and I didn't give a shit. I started laughing again as I stumbled alone in the darkness.

Dong Ha, Vietnam
December 1967

It was Christmas in Dong Ha. We tried not to think about it. There was a convoy taking hot chow up to a small isolated Marine Base called Con Thien. It was as far north as you could go and still be in South Vietnam. I volunteered to ride shotgun on the lead truck. If there was a land mine or an ambush waiting down the road, the driver and I would be the first to know.

I had heard about what happened to trucks that hit land mines. Often, the guys inside the cab had their legs blown off at the knees. I decided to take my chances with snipers and rode on the roof of the truck. I got a can of hard rock candy from the mess tent. I sat cross-legged on the roof of the truck with my M-16 in my lap and the candy beside me as we rolled out of the gate and headed north past the rice paddies and small villages of this beautiful part of Vietnam. As we passed small children tending to their family water buffalo, I threw them pieces of candy and wished them "Merry Christmas."

Once we were past the village of Cam Lo, we entered something called a free fire zone. Leaflets had been dropped from helicopters warning everyone that anyone caught in this area would be considered VC or NVA soldiers and they would be shot on sight. The countryside seemed deserted as we rolled past another isolated Marine artillery outpost called C-2. As the morning fog burned away, I could see the distant mountains of North Vietnam.

The Ho Chi Minh trail snaked through the mountains, bringing thousands of bicycles and small trucks carrying tons of rice and bullets to resupply the people we were fighting. Countless 500-pound bombs falling from flight missions of B-52's had failed to stem the flow of supplies headed south. From as far as seventeen miles away, long range North Vietnamese artillery batteries hidden in caves along the border of the DMZ pounded Con Thien night and day. I had been up here a few times before, riding shotgun on convoys delivering ammunition to the isolated base.

This time we were bringing hot turkey and cold eggnog. We rolled through the barbed wire gate around noon and began unloading our Christmas cargo.

Con Thien was a cluster of sandbagged bunkers surrounded by minefields and razor wire. The six 105 howitzers of Fox battery were set up and firing support for any Marine grunts patrolling in the area.

The cooks set up a chow line and started serving Christmas dinner. They were in a hurry to get this over with and get the hell out of there before something bad happened. The gunny walked over to me and held out a carton of eggnog.

"This is for you, McLane."

I looked at him and shook my head. "No, that is for the guys up here."

He smiled at me and shook his head. "No, this eggnog is for you. Watching you riding on the roof of that truck this morning made me proud to call you a Marine, in spite of your weird ways."

The gunny didn't have to twist my arm.

The guys in Fox battery were like Marines in any line outfit, they could use a shave and a hot shower. It was a hot day. Most were shirtless in the hot sun. All wore helmets and flak jackets.

So far the artillery on both sides had honored the Christmas truce.

The food disappeared fast and it was time for us to head south. I climbed back on the roof of the lead truck and waved goodbye to the guys in Fox battery as we rolled out of the gate. We made it back to Dong Ha without any trouble.

Christmas Eve turned into one big old-fashioned Marine brawl.

Everyone was already in a bad mood. It all started about midnight. Each Marine picked out the asshole he hated the most. The fights went on for about twenty minutes. After we had bloodied each other's heads, we all felt better.

We were glad Christmas was over.

* * *

They called me "Buddha." I was a good Catholic boy when I left the States. I carried a new St. Christopher's medal an old girlfriend had given me. My faith fell by the wayside one night on a listening post outside the wire at Dong Ha.

As artillery shells screamed down around me, I realized that I didn't really believe in the big guy in the sky that I had learned about in Sunday school. I became an atheist. That changed when I met a sergeant whose Japanese wife had converted him to Buddhism. He explained that the Buddhist concept of life and death was like a revolving wheel of good Karma and bad Karma. The old Karma wheel goes on rolling forever. The only way off of this endless ride was to slip into the void, a place beyond good and evil, a perfect place called Nirvana. The bad news was that no one, including Buddha, could take you there. You had to find your own path. In the meantime, my path would be spent following around a mechanical revolving duck in a shooting gallery called the DMZ. This duck was wearing captain's bars so I followed, but he was still a duck.

My teacher about the basics of Buddhism was a supply sergeant nick-named Ski. As a child, he was a member of Hitler's youth corps. His only memory of those days was of American soldiers giving him chocolate bars. He met his wife while stationed in Japan. There are as many different variations of Buddhists as there are Baptists. The sect Ski belonged to was over a thou-sand years old. The main temple was on Mount Fuji. They had a mantra that they repeated every day. Ski told me that if I repeated the mantra over and over, I could have anything I wanted. It sounded good to me.

I put this mantra to the test the very next morning. I was on a working party filling sandbags. As I worked, I said the mantra over and over. After a couple of minutes I said to myself, "I want off of this working party and I want off right now!"

I looked up and saw the gunny running towards us.

"Grab your rifles and get down to the front gate, go!"

I threw down my shovel and ran to my tent. I got my weapon and ran to the front gate. I thought about the mantra as I ran towards the gate. What had I gotten myself into? There was a two and a half ton truck waiting at the gate with the engine idling. A minute later we were speeding down Route 9. I thought to myself, who am I: a Christian or a Buddhist? If I met my maker today, which hat would I be wearing? Buddha had gotten me off of the work-ing party. Buddha had me riding down the road in this truck. No reflection on Jesus, but I wasn't gonna quit the fat man now. If, today, the great cosmic wheel of birth and death turned for me, I was going out as a Buddhist. We were headed to the scene of an ambush. A lone truck driven by a Seabee, had taken a direct hit from a rocket-propelled grenade. Seabees were glorified carpenters who carried hammers in one hand and M-16s in the other while they ran around building plywood shelters for the Marines.

The RPG had passed through the driver's door. He was lying on the ground with a hole in his leg as big as a grapefruit. We fanned out and started looking for who fired the RPG. We walked along the road looking for any sign of which way they went.

"Freeze!"

The voice had caught me with both feet on the ground and I froze. Someone had spotted a claymore mine that had been set up beside the road. It was pointed at us.

We waited while a Marine disarmed the mine. I hoped the guy on his knees knew what he was doing as I thought about the C-4 explosive and the rounds of buckshot inside the mine. The NVA had sneaked up to our lines and stolen one of our claymores. Now they were trying to give it back.

The bastards were always cheating at war. This delay was giving whoever did this some time to get away. As soon as the claymore was disarmed we started looking for bad guys again. We entered a small village alongside the road and approached a small group of old men, women and children. They had to have seen what happened.

"Which way VC?"

We knew they understood our question. They knew which way Charlie had gone, but they weren't talking. They just stared down at the ground in silence.

I switched my M-16 to full automatic.

"You don't want to talk? No? You assholes don't ever have to talk again!"

I was ready to waste them all. The people who ambushed the Seabee were getting away. We couldn't find them, but we had this sorry bunch. Nobody moved.

"Cool it, McLane!" the gunny yelled at me. "Start searching these huts and be careful."

I gave them one last glare over my shoulder as we began to search the crude huts. We found nothing, no trace of Charlie, no signs of a tunnel, not even suspicious footprints. Every home had clay pots filled with rice.

We knew the local VC would come in here at night and eat. During the day they would pull off ambushes like this one and disappear. We called off the search and headed back to the site of the ambushed truck. Traffic was backed up in both directions. Nobody passed until we checked their identification papers.

"Hey! Look at this one."

Someone pointed at a young woman sitting beside a window in the overcrowded old bus. She was probably half French and truly beautiful. We walked over to get a better look. She knew we were talking about her, but she stared straight ahead and said nothing. After checking everyone's papers we waved the bus to move on.

"Stop! Stop!"

Marines were yelling at two guys on a motorcycle that were trying to ease through the stalled traffic. I held my M-16 in a horizontal position and stepped in front of them.

"Dong Lai!"

They stopped about a foot away from me. I checked their papers and let them go.

Charlie got away that day. The poor Seabee should have had someone riding shotgun with him that morning, not that it would have made any difference. After a medevac helicopter picked up the wounded driver, we climbed into the back of our truck and headed for Dong Ha.

I was becoming someone I did not like, someone who almost shot some innocent people in cold blood. I didn't want to try this mantra stuff again until I talked some more with Sergeant Ski.

At lunch time I sat down beside him in the mess hall. I told him what happened.

"You should not use the mantra in such a casual way. That can lead to misfortune. This is a religion – not some kind of Cosmic Cookie Jar."

"I just wanted to get off of the working party. The next thing I knew, I was looking down the wrong end of a claymore mine. Then I almost killed some innocent people. It all started with that damn mantra."

Sergeant Ski frowned.

"Keep doing the mantra. Don't ask for anymore stupid shit like getting off of a working party. You've got to learn about the laws of cause and effect. People who don't understand those laws are trapped on a revolving wheel of birth and death. This religion is a way off of that wheel. Go to the head temple at Mt. Fuji. I've been practicing Buddhism for ten years and I still have a lot to learn. You have a long way to go."

A nearby B-52 strike shook the ground as I went back to filling sandbags.

I kept seeing the faces of the women and children I almost killed. I had to get a tighter grip on my emotions. It was hard to control my feelings as I watched that Seabee lying in his own blood, silently staring up at the clear blue sky.

* * *

Captain Stack's voice boomed from the back of the tent, "McLane! Get a broom and sweep the roof off."

"Sir?"

"The roof, McLane! Get a broom and start sweeping!"

I got a ladder and broom and climbed to the top of the huge tent that served as the headquarters of the 12th Marine Regiment. The old canvas was covered with a thick layer of red dust. The side I was standing on faced due north. Some of Uncle Ho's finest artillery batteries were set up and doing business less than ten miles away. Those boys had to be good—they practiced every day. I walked along the top of the tent to the spot directly over Captain Stack's desk. I took the broom and swept the dust away to form a circle about three feet wide. Next I made a ring around the circle about a foot wide. Then I made a larger ring around the first one. In about ten minutes I had drawn a perfect bull's eye clearly visible to any North Vietnamese forward observer who happened to be in the area. Guys walking by were getting a laugh out of my little joke. Captain Stack did not laugh when he walked out to check on my progress.

"So you think you're a wise guy, Mister? Maybe thirty days on mess duty will change your attitude."

The next day I began thirty days of KP. I reported to the mess tent at 5am. I was assigned to the pot shack. This was a small tent where all the dirty pots and pans ended up after each meal. Since there was no running water, cleaning this huge pile of greasy cookware was a real challenge. I carried water in five gallon cans from a large portable tank the Marine Corps calls a "water buffalo."

They could have parked the water tank closer to the pot shack, but that would have been too logical. I attacked the huge pile of dirty pots and pans with gusto. It was after dark when the last steel pot was squeaky clean.

I went straight to my tent to try to get some sleep before my 4:30 am wake-up call to start this shit all over again. In the mornings I worked in the officer's mess tent as a glorified waiter. I would relay the way the officers wanted their eggs prepared to the cook and serve them promptly from the kitchen.

Since there weren't enough fresh eggs for everybody, the enlisted Marines ate the powdered version. There was a rumor that these eggs had saltpeter in them to keep anyone that ate them from having an erection. Saltpeter or not, they tasted like carpet pile, and every day most of them were uneaten and thrown out. One morning a huge fight broke out next door in the enlisted mess tent. I watched the officers enjoying a leisurely breakfast while the battle raged on. The melee was finally over when one Marine knocked the other guy out. The officers never got out of their seats as they continued enjoying their breakfast. It was as if a couple of dogs were fighting in the yard while these gentlemen ate their morning meal.

"Pot shack!" The cook's voice cried out in the middle of the afternoon.

I counted one.

"Pot shack!" He yelled again. That made two. I never answered until the third call. They never caught on.

"Pot shack! Goddammit! Where the fuck are you?"

I walked to the door of the pot shack and yelled, "Whatta ya want?"

The cook yelled back, "I want a Goddamn clean pot! That's what I want! Make it two!" He disappeared back into the mess tent. I picked up two large pots and stepped out into the hot sun.

The head cook was a black guy from Detroit named Moe. Funny thing was, unlike most white guys, Moe liked me. He admired my habit of fucking with people. Sometimes after work I would stop by his tent for a game of chess and a gin and tonic. Moe was the only enlisted guy I knew in the DMZ who had access to real gin and ice.

Moe once passed through my home town in Texas on a Greyhound bus. He had a short layover while the bus changed drivers. He noticed a couple of guys looking him over, the kind of hustlers and strong-arm men who often hang around bus stations. Moe looked like fair game. He liked to fight, but this time Moe didn't like the odds. He waked across the street to a pawn shop and looked at some pistols. He purchased a small .25 automatic and some bullets. Back in the bus station, he stepped into a rear stall of the men's room. Moe loaded the pistol and slipped it under his shirt. He got a magazine and went back to waiting for his bus. The kind of low lifes who hang around bus stations are natural born predators. They develop a sixth sense that keeps them alive and out of jail.

They know when to attack and when to lay back. Moe's trip to the pawn shop did not go unnoticed. They left him alone. He sold the pistol when he joined the Marines.

A week didn't pass without Moe getting into a fight with somebody. At Dong Ha, he was undefeated. Moe was short, but he had the build of a middleweight boxer. His fights didn't last long. It was usually over once he got his hand around the poor bastard's neck. Moe was lucky that he never crushed someone's windpipe. I walked into the mess tent, carrying the two clean pots. Moe was opening a large can of potatoes. I sat the pots down and smiled at Moe.

"Tonight, I am going to kick your ass…on a chessboard, that is."

Moe smiled.

"Is that right, homeboy?"

"Yeah! And to make it extra sweet, I'm gonna let you play the white pieces. For the coup de grace, I'm gonna send one of my pawns out to put your King out of his misery."

Moe smiled again, something he seldom did unless he was bullshitting with me. He picked up one of the two clean pots. I smiled too.

"Enjoy these pots with my compliments. Tomorrow, I must move on to more interesting challenges in our never-ending struggle to hold back the rising red tide of Godless Communism."

Moe laughed.

"Tonight, make sure you have some old-fashioned capitalist money to back up that big mouth."

I laughed and walked back to the pot shack. My tour of mess duty was down to a couple of hours. I finished washing the last of the pots and pans and hung up my apron. I took a shower and changed clothes. Moe walked in with his chessboard. He handed me a joint. While Moe set up the board, I opened a small package that an old high school buddy had mailed me from the States.

Inside was a carefully wrapped fifth of Southern Comfort whiskey. I didn't see Captain Stack until he stepped into the tent. I hid the joint. Captain Stack smiled.

"I knew it wouldn't take you long to fuck up."

He picked up my bottle of whiskey.

"Report to my office tomorrow morning at 0800 for office hours. I'll keep this for evidence."

He took the bottle and disappeared into the night. Moe and I walked the other way as I lit the joint.

"I knew I would get into it with this bastard again. I just didn't think it would be so soon."

Moe smiled as I handed him the joint. "What's he gonna do? Send your sorry ass to Vietnam?"

Moe was still smiling when the night suddenly filled with the staccato bursts of AK-47s going off as green tracers streaked through the air. Moe and I split up. I raced back to my hooch for my M-16. Moe ran towards his tent.

I ran inside and stared at my cot. My rifle was missing. I grabbed my flak jacket and ran back out into the darkness. The firing was coming from the front gate. Marines were running in every direction. I ran over to the armory.

The front door was locked. I kicked it open and stepped inside.

I lit a match. Brand new M-16 rifles were stacked everywhere. I picked one up and helped myself to several loaded magazines that were lying on a countertop.

Tracers were still arcing through the sky as I ran back out of the broken door.

"Halt! Who goes there?"

The gunny yelled as he leveled a .45 automatic pistol at me.

"McLane!"

We both headed for the front gate as the firing continued. I jumped in a trench and pointed my M-16 out into the darkness. Pop-up flares were slowly drifting down giving the night an eerie light. The AK-47s stopped firing just as quickly as they had started. More flares lit up the sky but nothing was moving.

"McLane! Where is your helmet?"

Captain Stack was crouched down beside the trench.

"I left it back at my tent, sir."

"I don't want anybody up here without a helmet. It looks like it's over. I am ordering you off of the line."

I climbed out of the trench and headed back to my tent. Smurf was on a reactionary team that night. He couldn't remember where he put his rifle so he took mine.

The next morning I cleaned the extra M-16 and returned it to the armory. They had already repaired the door.

"Well, if it isn't the Incredible Hulk?"

Sergeant Dodson eyed me as I waked in. I smiled and flexed my muscles. "Next time, leave the key under the mat."

I handed back the weapon. Sergeant Dodson examined the rifle and put it back in the rack. I walked over to the battery headquarters tent for my scheduled office hours. Captain Stack was sitting at his desk. I came to attention.

"Private McLane reporting as ordered, sir."

"At ease, McLane. I have decided to let you slide on the bottle of whiskey. You acted like a real Marine last night, except you forgot your helmet. There also won't be any charges for breaking into the armory. This deal is good only if I have your permission to destroy the evidence."

I breathed a sigh of relief.

"Be my guest, sir."

Captain Stack looked up at me. "Have you ever driven a stick shift?"

"Yes, sir. I learned to drive on a stick shift."

"Good. I am assigning you to the motor pool. They need another duce-and-a-half driver. Report to Lieutenant Wheeler."

I headed for the motor pool. They needed a driver to make a run to the garbage dump every day. I was given the worst looking truck in the motor pool. It was old and ugly. The door had a large shrapnel hole in it. Three of the tires were flat. I went to work changing the tires.

A mechanic named Doyle walked over and said hello.

"Welcome to the motor pool, bro. You'll like it here. We cover each other's ass and we like to party. You'll fit right in, McLane."

I smiled. "Anything's better than mess duty."

I jumped up and down on the big lug wrench trying to break loose the rusty wheel lugs.

"I'll keep this old bucket of bolts running for you, McLane. Just don't wreck it."

Lieutenant Wheeler yelled at Doyle.

"Get back to work, Corporal!"

He walked over and stood behind me with his hands on his hips. I had already gotten the word on this guy. He was a real asshole. Everyone in the motor pool hated his guts.

"I hear you are a real wise-ass, McLane. This is my motor pool. You fuck up around here and you're gonna wish you were back on mess duty. Mister, I want this truck ready to roll when I get back from chow. If it ain't ready, I'm gonna kick your butt."

I stood up and turned around. This guy was much too soft and skinny to be threatening anybody. I threw down the lug wrench.

"If you want to kick my ass, sir, you don't have to wait until you get back from chow. You can take off those pretty bars and start right now."

I stared the little turd down. He turned and walked away. I went back to fighting with the rusty lugs. Finally I got the tire loose and rolled it over to Doyle.

I waited while he fixed the flat.

"Don't worry about Lieutenant Wheeler. He was just trying to test you."

I laughed.

"One of these days he's going to pull that crap on the wrong Marine."

I rolled my tire back over to my truck. I knew that it would not be ready when that asshole got back from chow. I didn't care. I decided it was time to eat.

I walked back over to where Doyle was working and cleaned up for lunch. Doyle was working under a jeep. He looked up at me. "How's my truck?"

"Your truck is a rusty old piece of crap, but it's coming along. Right now I'm going to the mess hall. Care to join me?"

Doyle smiled.

"Sounds good to me. I want to be there if Lieutenant Wheeler decides to kick your ass."

"First he better rent some balls."

After lunch, I took the last flat tire off and rolled it over to Doyle. It was too damaged to repair. Doyle gave me a new tire.

Next I slowly drove the truck over to where Doyle was working. The brakes were bad. This truck would not be ready for the road until sometime tomorrow. Fuck Lieutenant Wheeler.

After supper I moved my gear over to the motor pool living quarters.

Every other night I pulled guard duty. Tonight I was off, so I shared a joint with some of my new friends and relaxed. We listened to some tapes of Jimi

Hendrix.

Doyle wanted to know about Haight-Ashbury.

"Forget about Haight-Ashbury. It was a great party, but it's over. You missed it. Now the place is nothing but a ghetto full of speed freaks and junkies. "

The next morning I did a final check of my truck. Doyle had repaired the brakes and took it for a test drive. It was a gasoline-powered, two-and-a-half-ton ticket off of the base.

Each day I made a trash run to the dump just outside the village of Dong Ha. It beat scrubbing dirty pots and pans all day. Private Lopez walked up carrying his M-16. He grinned at me.

"Hey McLane, the gunny told me to ride shotgun with you today. Now this looks like a job I can handle."

I grinned back.

"It is if you don't mind lifting barrels of trash. Someone's got to drive this baby and I already got that job, unless you planned on me doing everything while you catch up on your Z's"

Lopez frowned. I kept smiling.

"Sorry Lopez, you got to pull your own weight around here in spite of what Jesus told the Mexicans."

Lopez looked confused. "OK, wise-ass, what did Jesus tell the Mexicans?"

I narrowed my eyes and lowered my voice. "He said, 'Y'all don't do anything 'til I get back.' It'll be our little secret that you learned that from a Texan. Leave your M-16 in the front of the truck. You won't need it while you're wrestling with these trash cans."

Lopez leaned his rifle against the side of the truck. He took a couple of steps towards me. "Why you got to be such a smart ass, McLane?"

I smiled at him. "Don't take it so personal. It's just my nature. I like to fuck off as much as the next Marine, so we'll take our time and see if we can make a whole day out of this trash detail."

Lopez smiled back, "Maybe you're all right after all, bro."

I showed him the joint I had cupped in the palm of my hand. "Sure, amigo, forget the Alamo. We can buy some more of this shit on our way to the dump."

In front of almost every tent at Dong Ha was a large metal barrel. Our job was to take whatever was in the barrels to the dump. Hopefully we could stretch this out into the afternoon and get back from the dump just in time to wash up for supper.

Lopez was OK once we got the ground rules worked out. After lunch we rolled out of the front gate and headed for the dump. About a hundred yards away I pulled over beside a young girl dressed in a black shirt and pants and wearing a straw hat.

"Yo, Mama San! What's up?"

She ran over to my side of the truck.

"Where you been McLane? Now you drive truck?"

"Yeah, baby, it's all mine. Wanna ride?"

She frowned.

"No, no McLane. I much too busy to ride with you."

Lyndon Johnson would have been proud of how fast this twelve-year-old kid had caught on to the fundamentals of capitalism. She cut to the chase.

"What you want, McLane?"

"Just two bags of smoke, sweet thing."

I handed her two ten dollar notes of the military script that Marines used for money. She gave me two sealed bags that each contained ten joints. They looked like the Camels that my old man used to smoke.

"I gotta run, darlin."

I blew her a kiss as she ran back to the side of the road. She added my money to the fat roll she kept under her shirt. We drove on toward the village of Dong Ha.

Traffic was light. I drove around a few mopeds and dilapidated buses filled with civilians, pigs, and chickens.

"Once we get into the village, you want to keep an eye out for snipers. If we get ambushed or hit a land mine, we're fucked."

I lit a joint and passed it to Lopez.

"I thought Dong Ha was supposed to be a friendly village, right?"

"Sure it is—as long as the sun is up. Remember, North Vietnam is about an hour's stroll from here."

We finished the joint and rolled into the dump. A mob of Vietnamese children glared at us from a distance. After we left, they would pounce on anything that wasn't burning. We dumped the trash and poured a five gallon can of diesel around the edges. Lopez lit a cigarette and tossed the match at a puddle of fuel.

The kids inched in closer as we walked back to the truck. Lopez fired a couple of rounds at their feet to keep them back. This might not win any hearts and minds, but if we didn't do it they would be swarming all over the truck. As we drove away they rushed in, determined to grab anything worth saving.

A boy about ten years old picked up a can of foot powder and smelled it. He threw it at us and gave us the finger. We flipped him back and kept rolling. We drove through the front gate right on schedule. I dropped Lopez off and headed for the motor pool.

Doyle walked over as I got out of the truck.

"Hey, McLane. You got guard duty tonight. You're on post twelve with me and Smurf."

"Oh damn! Tonight is my bowling night. I'll just have to cancel."

Doyle laughed.

"I got some balls you can play with."

I smiled.

"You won't like my secret grip. It made me a legend back in Texas."

After chow, I picked up my helmet and rifle and a blanket and headed out to post twelve. This was a listening post. It was a small bunker made up of sandbags and tin, about fifty yards outside the triple stand of concertina wire that surrounded the large base. Inside were a couple of crude bunk beds. We watched the sun slowly set over the minefield and trip wires that stood between us and the North Vietnamese Army. At least we didn't have to sweat the officer of the guard coming around. Nobody came near post twelve after dark. If any tripwires went off during the night, it would either be a wild pig or a clumsy Viet Cong. Smurf lit a joint. I set up the .50-caliber machine gun while Doyle scanned the darkening countryside with a pair of binoculars. He stepped back and looked through the field glasses backwards.

"Wow! This is just like being back home, watching Vietnam on the six o'clock news."

He leaned against the bunker and watched Smurf with the reversed binoculars.

Smurf held an empty C-ration can up to his mouth and looked at Doyle.

"Fighting intensified today outside the small village of Dong Ha, as a small band of determined, dug-in Marines refused to surrender in the face of relentless air raids from low flying Russian MIG fighter jets and continued ground attacks from a division of Russian tanks. The sounds of bugles fill the night as thousands of hard-core North Vietnamese ground troops get the signal to begin a human wave charge. These gallant Marines have drawn a line in the mud. Well, there was a line here a minute ago, but the mud sucked it away. Against impossible odds, these determined Devil Dogs will not back down! Particular praise must be singled out for Private Robert McLane. Before sunrise, with no regard for his own safety, this brave Marine single-handedly wiped out three North Vietnamese Regiments and strangled twenty-seven water buffalo! Since all of the dead animals were the property of local farmers, the financial loss will be compensated by deductions from Private McLane's monthly paycheck in an installment plan that the young Marine agreed to in an out of court settlement. Unfortunately, this payment plan will require Private McLane's tour of duty to be extended another five years. This is Percy Merriweather signing off, somewhere in the DMZ, in South Vietnam."

I finished setting up the machine gun while Doyle took the joint from Smurf. I looked down at Doyle.

"Did anyone double-check these tripwires?"

"I personally checked them while you were canceling your bowling date."

I laughed.

"In that case, I better check them myself. You might have tied one of the wires to your dick by mistake."

Smurf went inside the bunker and tried to get some sleep. He had second watch.

Doyle took out a little radio and tried to find some music he could listen to through an ear piece. One night he got some Vietnamese disk jockey talking away and held the radio up to the field telephone. That shook up the other guys on guard duty.

Since the field telephones are set up like a party line, they couldn't prove who did it, but they knew, they always knew. As night fell, it started to rain. Smurf was almost asleep when a rat scurried across the floor. "What the fuck was that?" Smurf asked.

"House pet." Doyle answered.

Doyle tossed the remains of a bag of M & M'S on the bunker floor.

"What was that?" Smurf asked.

"I dropped my vitamins," Doyle giggled. He was standing in the door of the bunker as the rain poured down. The rats went into a feeding frenzy fighting over the spilled candy. Smurf stood on the top of his bunk and yelled.

"You asshole! Paybacks are a motherfucker!"

Doyle laughed. "Wait till the big rat daddy of 'em comes out! The first time I saw him, I thought he was a sandbag with legs. He's gonna be pissed that he missed out on the party!"

Doyle kept laughing as the rain poured down. I finally fell asleep.

"Wake up McLane!" Smurf was kicking my bunk. It was time for my watch. I sat up and put on my boots. I stumbled outside and took a piss. The rain had stopped and the moon was breaking through the clouds. I was shaking my dick when the first rocket roared by, sounding like a 747 going past about fifty feet off of the ground. Of all possible incoming rounds, rockets are by far the worst. Their high pitched scream sounds like the damn thing is headed right up your ass.

I didn't think I had time to make it to the bunker door. I dove through a small opening on the side of the bunker, right into Doyle's lap. For a moment my butt got stuck. I had this image in my mind of red-hot jagged steel slashing through my ass as I wiggled and pulled myself inside. More rockets roared past as we hugged the bunker floor. These missiles were as big as telephone poles. Chunks of red hot steel as big as your leg flew, spinning through the air, cutting down anything that got in the way. In a few minutes it was over. Smurf and Doyle went back to sleep.

I stared out into the darkness looking for signs of an attack I hoped would never come. Post ten thinks they hear something. They request permission to fire a pop-up flare. I watch it slowly swinging back and forth from a small parachute as it drifts down through the darkness. I could see nothing. Post ten was probably just bored.

We did have a few aces in the hole we could play. Claymore mines were set up about fifty feet in front of us. They were hooked up to wires that ran back to the bunker. In a jam, you could even set them off by rubbing the ends of the wire in your hair. The static electricity could set off the blasting caps, sending hundreds of rounds of buckshot out into a killing zone.

I lit a heat tab and boiled a mess cup of water from my canteen. I added a small packet of C-ration coffee and sugar. I sipped the hot coffee and looked at my watch. It was still two hours before dawn. Well into my third month of Vietnam, I had settled into a routine of driving the trash truck during the day and pulling guard duty at night. Things could be a lot worse. Somewhere out there a real war was going on and men were dying. The ground rumbled and shook as a B-52 strike lit up the horizon. I wrote a letter to my grandmother as the first streaks of dawn lit up the sky. At six o'clock I woke up Doyle and Smurf. We loaded up the .50-caliber machine gun and humped it back to the armory. I skipped breakfast and walked back to my tent. I lay down on my rack and stared at the ceiling. It was almost time to head to the motor pool.

"Damn!" There must be some way I could lie here a little longer. Then it came to me. I'll shave! There was nothing in the Marine Corps guidebook that said I had to shave standing up. I grabbed my shaving gear and lay back down. With the mirror in one hand, I lathered up my face. I put down the shaving cream and picked up my razor. I had just started dragging the blade across my chin when Captain Stack walked in. I jumped out of bed and stood at attention.

"What the fuck are you doing in the rack, McLane?"

"Shaving, sir!"

"Why are you shaving in bed, mister?"

"The light was better, sir."

Captain Stack was screaming. "You don't shave in bed, mister. I don't know how the fuck you got into my Marine Corps, but I am going to make you my personal project. Maybe burning shitters for a couple of weeks will give you a better attitude. Report to the corpsman. Now!"

I put on my flak jacket and walked over to the corpsman's tent. They were in charge of burning all the 12th Marine Regiment shitters in Dong Ha every day. Of course, they didn't actually burn the shit themselves, they had poor bastards like me to do that job. They explained my new routine to me. There were twelve shit-houses set up at various locations in Dong Ha. Some were two-seaters, while others accommodated up to six customers at a time. Beneath each seat was a fifty-five gallon barrel that had been cut in half. In each barrel, numerous turds of various colors, shapes and sizes marinated in several gallons of diesel fuel. Every day each barrel would be pulled out and burned. It was, without a doubt, the shittiest job on the base. Until I heard otherwise from Captain Stack, it was my job.

Sometime into the second week, I started thinking about killing Captain Stack. The traditional weapon of choice for murdering officers was a fragmentary grenade. The Marine Corps doesn't like to talk about that tradition. It was a little messy, but highly efficient and mostly anonymous. The thought of one of your own rolling such a lethal object into your tent late at night was enough to discourage most officers from ever becoming a total asshole.

Burning shitters for the rest of my tour in Vietnam would not have changed my mind about how I felt about the Marine Corps, Captain Stack, or this fucking war. I had never been so miserable in my life. I thought about killing myself.

I tried to think of some way that the Brass wouldn't cover it up. A high rate of suicides would not look well in their personnel records. If I shot myself, they would just tell my folks that I had an accident while cleaning my rifle. I thought of going out in a blaze of glory like Buddhists in Saigon, but I knew my folks would be told I was smoking around a gas can. I decided to hang myself. I knew the bastards couldn't hide the rope burns on my neck.

Late that night, I quietly slipped into an empty supply tent and looked around. I took a rope and a folding chair to the center support pole. I stood on the chair and secured the rope high up on the pole. I tied the other end into a hangman's noose. I had learned to tie the knot while I was in the Boy Scouts.

I slipped the noose around my neck and tightened it. I stood alone in the shadows and waited. I thought about what I was going to do. I realized the finality of making such a choice. I still believed in God and I knew this would piss him off. I didn't care. I stared out the darkness and wondered if I was ready to really do this.

After about ten minutes, I took off the noose, untied the knot, and put the chair back where I got it. I decided as miserable as I was, I still wasn't ready to throw my life away. I walked over to the corpsman's tent. He was smoking a cigarette and reading a paperback by candle light. I invited myself in and sat down.

"You got to help me, Doc. I need to take some pills to help me calm down or I'm gonna frag the captain and laugh my ass off all the way to Leavenworth."

He stared at me poker faced.

"Goddammit Doc! If you don't help me, you can testify that I came to you for help and you turned me down. Now give me some goddamn pills!"

He got up and walked over to a wall locker and took out a small amber bottle. He handed it to me. He growled. "Relax! This is Librium. Take one of these every six hours. Try to get some sleep. You'll be fine."

I opened the lid and stared at the small black and green capsules. "They better work or you're gonna have a dead captain to clean up and mail home!"

I walked back out into the night and headed for my tent. The next afternoon I was back.

"You got to give me something stronger! This shit ain't working."

He went back to the wall locker and came returned with another bottle. "These are Valium. Take one of these every four hours and try to relax."

A couple of days later, I was sent to the hospital at Quang Tri. The red tag on my wrist said, "Psychiatric."

My DI back in boot camp used to refer to shrinks as the "Ha Ha Doctors." The corpsman walked me out to the LZ and made sure I got on a helicopter bound for Quang Tri. I reported in to the hospital. I was given pajamas and blood tests. That night I slept between clean sheets in a real bed. The next morning I reported in to the "Ha Ha Doctor." In a soft voice he invited me to sit down.

"And what seems to be your problem, Marine?"

I smiled. "Other than being on the losing side of a war and burning shitters all day under the command of a certain captain that I want to kill, I'm doing fine, sir!"

I wasn't trying to bullshit this guy, but I didn't see the need to paint him any pretty pictures either. After a few minutes of more questions, he told me I could go home if I wanted to. I looked in his eyes. Was this some kind of trick question? Trick question or not, the answer was no.

"I'm afraid I couldn't do that, sir."

He raised his eyebrows and looked at me. "And why is that?"

"You see, sir, I come from a small town in Texas. Everyone there knows I am in Vietnam. I couldn't have people talking behind my back about how I was only in Vietnam for four months and then I came back home without a scratch on me. What I think about this stupid war doesn't matter to anybody. I got to stay for the entire thirteen months, no matter how much I hate this place."

He made some notes on a pad and told me I could go. The next day I was discharged from the hospital and caught a helicopter back to Dong Ha. My shit burning days were over. I went back to driving my truck.

I was helping Lopez pick up trash when something fluttered to the ground. I bent over and picked it up. I couldn't believe my eyes. It was a black and white photo of the gunny in bed with a hooker. OK, I could call her an unknown young Oriental lady.

But one thing was sure, it was the gunny. He had his hands folded behind his head. He was grinning like the Cheshire Cat. He must have had it taken while he was on R & R in Thailand. I put it in my pocket. Later I showed it to Smurf and Doyle.

I tried to think about what to do with it. I wanted to cause this asshole as much misery as possible. I showed it to Corporal Cooper, the Headquarters Battery Clerk.

He didn't like the gunny either. Nobody liked the gunny. I told him of my dilemma. He stared at the photo and his face lit up.

"I know! Give it to me and I'll mail it to his wife!"

"That's perfect!" I wrote, "Semper Fi, Gunny! Greetings from McLane," on the back of the photo. I gave it to Cooper and walked back over to the motor pool. This bastard would continue to give me grief at every opportunity but the payback of all paybacks would be in a mail sack headed for the States tomorrow. I bet his old lady took him for the car and the house and a big chunk of his pension.

I walked into my tent. I stared at the empty space where my cot used to be. "What the fuck is going on?"

Smurf and Doyle were laughing. Doyle stopped long enough to tell me. "The gunny moved your stuff out in back. He said to tell you that you could move back in when you were ready to stop living like an animal. I guess he didn't like the way you keep house, you animal!"

Smurf stopped laughing and yelled. "Yeah! He said you're just a beast!"

They continued to laugh and kick their feet. I stared at the empty space where my cot had been. I wondered how I could really piss off the gunny. Tonight. Right now. It was time to turn this bullshit up a notch. I picked up a Life magazine off of Doyle's cot and started thumbing through the pages. I came across a full page photo of LBJ and another one of Ho Chi Minh and carefully tore them out.

I smiled to myself. I borrowed a magic marker from Smurf. Under LBJ's ugly mug, I wrote, "Wanted for murder and crimes against humanity." Beneath the picture of a smiling Ho Chi Minh, I wrote in big letters, "George Washington of the People." I stuck them side by side on the wall of the tent where my stuff used to be. I smiled. I would like to see the gunny's face when he sees these.

I walked outside where the gunny had put my cot. I sat down and looked around. I said to Doyle and Smurf, "You know it's kinda nice out here, fresh air and a great view. I think I'll just live out here."

Smurf laughed. "Until it starts to rain."

I straightened my gear out at the end of my cot. I took a walk over to Moe's tent and got stoned while I waited for the shit to hit the fan. Moe looked at me as I lit another joint. "Man, you took it too far this time. The Captain is gonna burn your ass this time, for sure! But I got to hand it to you, I never met a white boy who liked to fuck with people the way you do, McLane."

I passed the joint to Moe. "What the fuck can he do to me? Cut off my hair and send me to Vietnam? Send me back to the pot shack? Put me back on shit burning detail? I tell you Moe, I just plain don't give a shit!" The marijuana put a nice edge on everything. Fuck 'em. I walked back over to my open air cot and called it a night. I was eating breakfast in the mess hall the next morning when the gunny came running in. His face was red and he was out of breath.

He headed straight for me and yelled, "The Captain wants you over at his office on the double, mister!"

"Gee gunny, what do you think he wants?" I smiled as I stood up and took a last sip of coffee. "You think it's another promotion?"

I walked over to the battery tent and told the clerk I wanted to see the Captain.

He rolled his eyes and motioned me back towards the rear of the tent.

I walked up to Captain Stack's desk and stood at attention. "Private McLane reporting as ordered, sir!"

The Life magazine photos of LBJ and Ho Chi Minh lay on top of his desk.

He yelled as I continued staring at a spot on the wall behind his head, "What the fuck do you think you are doing, mister?"

I tried to look confused. "Are you referring to my new pictures, sir? The gunny was unhappy with my living quarters, so I thought I would brighten up the place a little. I haven't had any luck finding frames, sir."

Captain Stack's face got red and he screamed, "You think this is all one big joke, do you?"

"Sir, it's never any fun being on the losing side of a war. Especially when your side won't even admit it is over."

Captain Stack got up from behind his desk and walked around it 'til he was standing beside me. In a low voice he said, "That man you made a wanted poster for just happens to be your Commander-In-Chief!"

"Yes, sir, and it's unfortunate his unlawful conduct in Vietnam has made him an outlaw in the eyes of the international community of civilized nations."

The Captain's voice rose again, "You think he's an outlaw?"

"Sir, the Geneva Convention is quite clear about acts that are defined as war crimes."

Captain Stack sat back down and stared up at me like he was looking at a bug. "Well it's damn clear what we are going to do with you, mister. You are facing a general court martial, Private McLane."

He paused to let that sink in. Poker faced, I continued staring at my spot on the wall.

"You are in a lot of trouble, mister. You are even entitled to a civilian lawyer if you want one."

I replied, "That's fine with me, sir. I think I might need one."

He frowned, "You have to pay for his plane ticket over here."

"Yes, sir, I have about $900 dollars saved up in the bank. That'll pay for his ticket. I'll work out his fee when he gets here."

"It sounds like you already have someone in mind."

"Sir, if you would just contact the San Francisco Chapter of the American Civil Liberties Union, whoever they send will be fine with me."

Captain Stack leaned back in his chair and stared at the ceiling. After a couple of minutes, he looked at me, "Private McLane, I am confining you to your quarters. Report back here at 0800 hours tomorrow. You can make one phone call to your fucking lawyer."

I turned around and headed back to my tent. Things were looking up. I had an ACLU lawyer in the works and I wasn't burning shitters today. I dragged my cot back inside. I stared at the empty spot where my pictures of Ho and LBJ had been. They had been taken as evidence.

Cooper told me CID, (Criminal Investigation Division) was flying in from Da Nang. Someone was assigned to escort me to the mess tent for evening chow. The guys looked at me like I was some kind of condemned prisoner eating his last meal. I smiled, "Relax boys, I got my ducks lined up."

I couldn't wait for some suit to show up at Dong Ha with a briefcase full of motions and objections. This was going to be fun. They were charging me with putting offensive writings on the wall of my tent. Guys could walk around with "fuck the world" written on the side of their helmet and nobody said a word. I pin up a magazine picture of the most crooked politician that ever came out of Texas and these bastards want to draw names for a firing squad.

The gunny stuck his head inside my tent. He walked in and stood at the end of my cot. "Look McLane, the Captain doesn't want you to have to go to the brig over a stupid mistake. He is willing to offer you a deal. If you are willing to accept a non-judicial punishment, you can get this over with just a fine and nothing on your permanent record. If I were you, I would take his deal and put this mess behind you."

I looked up at him and smiled, "Thanks, gunny. That is real nice of the captain, but I believe I'll take my chances in court. Those ACLU boys are pretty good. I think I'll just roll the dice with them."

The gunny frowned, "Suit yourself. It's your funeral."

He turned around and left. The next morning I was escorted from the mess hall over to the battery headquarters tent to make my phone call. The captain was nowhere in sight. The battery clerk looked at me and smiled, "Go pack your gear, you've being transferred."

The charges had been dropped. The bastards had folded. They couldn't handle the idea of some damn civilian lawyer walking around Dong Ha with a briefcase asking a lot of questions. What if the civilian press got a hold of this? How could they expect the ACLU lawyer to keep his big mouth shut? The bastard would probably want to hold a press conference. There wasn't time to tell the guys goodbye. I threw my gear in a sea bag and grabbed my helmet and M-16 and walked out to the front gate. A truck was waiting for me and we quickly drove north up Route 9.

The place we were going didn't even have a name. It was simply a spot on the map the Marines called C-2. The truck pulled over to the side of the dirt road. I grabbed my gear and hopped out. This was where Fox Battery was currently living. I had not seen these guys since Christmas Day at Con Thien. C-2 was a half a mile south of their old home. I was supposed to report to the commanding officer, but first I had to find him. I asked a shirtless Marine where I could find the CO. He pointed down a dusty trail. I followed it and found him waist deep in a hole with a pick in his hands.

I had never seen an officer doing manual labor before. I walked up and stood at attention and saluted,

"Private McLane, reporting as ordered, sir!"

He looked just like any other Marine on a working party, except for the Captain's bars on his soft cap. He was the commanding officer in charge of the six guns and fifty-five Marines in Fox Battery. He was the first officer I ever respected.

"At ease."

He gave another shirtless Marine the pick and climbed out of the hole. We shook hands.

"Let's take a walk, McLane. I'll show you around."

We walked past men on gun crews unpacking artillery shells and stacking sand bags.

"I heard you had some problems back at Dong Ha. I have plenty of problems already up here at C-2. I don't need anymore. As far as I am concerned, you are starting out with a clean slate. Everyone up here has a job to do and I expect you to do yours."

"No problem, sir."

Captain Daniels looked at me, "I understand your original MOS was Fire Direction Control."

I nodded my head, "Yes, sir. It has been a while since I have shot a mission, but I'll catch on pretty quick."

He showed me the bunker where the guys in FDC lived, "You can store your gear in here. Sergeant Friedman is in charge of FDC. Tomorrow, he'll check you out."

I saluted my new CO and he turned and walked away. I went in the door of the big bunker. The entrance way made a ninety-degree turn into the living quarters. I found an empty rack and threw down my gear. The Vietnamese Army built these bunkers last year. They did a good job. They were made of heavy beams and lots of sandbags. The walls were a fine barrier from flying shrapnel, but there wasn't a single bunker anywhere in the DMZ that could take a direct hit from one of Ho Chi Minh's long range heavy artillery batteries, scattered up and down his side of the DMZ. That hard lesson was learned last summer up at Con Thien. A direct hit on the command bunker killed every man inside. Most died from the concussion.

Still, it felt safe leaning against the cool damp walls of my new home. FDC did the math that was necessary to shoot a mission with accuracy. Most of the petty shit that made life so miserable back in Dong Ha did not go on up here. The CO set the tone and Fox had a good one. The bad news was that several times a day, and often in the middle of the night, North Vietnamese long range heavy artillery batteries would rain down hellfire from the entrances of various caves scattered across the DMZ.

Most of the time the only damage was a new hole in the ground. Sometimes, unlucky Marines got in the way. Your best chance of surviving was to hit the deck at the first sound of incoming. The closer you were to the ground, the better. Weather can also be a factor in your chances of seeing another day. Mud is your best friend during an artillery attack. It sucks down a lot of red-hot razor sharp Russian steel that would be flying though the air if the ground weren't so delightfully wet. Twice as many Marines would be wounded during dry weather, when the ground got as hard as brick.

I walked over to the FDC bunker. A tall skinny guy was checking communication wires that led to each of Fox Battery's six guns.

The jailhouse tattoo on his forearm simply said "Rail." Rail liked to fuck with people. Just like me, it seemed to be a calling. He eyed me up and down. "Welcome to C-2! What's the story on you? You must have fucked up big time to get sent up here."

I smiled, "You might say me and a certain captain back at Dong Ha had a slight misunderstanding."

Rail studied my face. "I remember you. You're the John Wayne who rode in on top of the lead truck of that convoy up at Con Thien on Christmas Day. You were lucky that day, bro. Don't try pushing your luck at C-2. Up here, you zig when you shoulda zagged and they'll carry you out in a body bag!"

Four months at Dong Ha didn't mean shit to these guys. Until I showed them otherwise, I was just another new guy, a walking fuck-up, an accident waiting to happen. The next morning Sgt. Friedman led me through an imaginary fire mission. He made up the coordinates and watched me crunch the numbers.

I did this with the help of a book of logarithms and a slide rule. Sgt. Friedman gave me a new set of coordinates and I did it again. Captain Daniels stopped by.

"How's he doing, Sergeant?"

"Well, Captain, he's a little slow, but accurate"

Accuracy was good. Speed would come in time. In a real fire mission, two FDC teams crunched the numbers at the same time. If their answers differed by more than the smallest of margins, they did it all over. Only when the numbers matched up would they send the data to the gun crews. I wasn't ready to shoot a real fire mission yet. I spent the afternoon on a working party filling sandbags. Later, the gunny decided to put up a volleyball net.

We had to dig holes in the rock-hard ground with a pick. It was a hot day. After we started on the second hole, I tossed my flak jacket and helmet on the ground, followed by my T-shirt. Saluting and dress codes were a lot more casual here than back at Dong Ha. I liked that. Suddenly a huge explosion covered everyone with dirt and smoke. I dove down beside some sandbags. I had heard about guys who were hit and, in the excitement, didn't realize it right away. I decided to do a roll call of all my vital parts. Quickly I ran my hand up and down my arms and legs.

Everything looked OK, until I was checking my left arm. I was amazed to see the palm of my hand was covered in blood. I was bleeding from a small hole halfway between my elbow and shoulder. I never felt a thing. As I lay beside the sandbags, I realized that it was not much more than a scratch, the same kind of wound the Lone Ranger used to get every Saturday morning. I started laughing. Some of Uncle Ho's arty boys had just tried to kill me! That was my blood flowing down my arm. Strangely I wasn't very upset—I even felt happy.

Unlike our shells, there was no symmetry to the shape or size of the chunk of hot Russian steel that flew past my arm. I'll never know how big or small it was. Luck at C-2 was measured in inches. I looked behind me and discovered a young Marine lying on his back on the open ground. He was unconscious and bleeding from his nose and ears. I helped carry him over to the LZ. We laid him beside two other Marines who had been hit by the same shell. While we waited for a medevac, the corpsman administered morphine and tried to stop the bleeding. In about ten minutes, a helicopter landed and took off with the wounded Marines.

I went back to swinging my pick. Now I had my flak jacket back on and my helmet. Guys heard that I had been wounded and came around to see for themselves. They stared at the fresh scab on my arm. I tried to be cool about it, but I was on cloud nine. I felt like Tom Sawyer showing off a brand new black eye.

Rail walked over. He looked at my arm and smiled. "Well bro, you ain't a new guy no more."

I was disappointed to see my arm heal without even leaving a scar. The next morning I reported to the command post that was set up on the roof of the battery headquarters bunker.

We maintained radio contact with various forward observers from different infantry companies and recon teams operating within range of our guns. My job this morning was to relay data from the fire direction control center to the officer in charge of shooting fire missions. I made entries in a log book of each shell fired. About ten miles north of us, Ho Chi Minh had his boys doing the same thing, just another day at the office.

They always liked to let us have a few rounds during lunch. Their forward observers must have noticed that it was quite a long walk to the mess tent. Some days they shot early, some days they shot late. It was one big guessing game about when to go to lunch. Guys would argue about when was the best time to go. Sometimes, I would be halfway to the mess tent when I realized that I had guessed wrong, as I hugged the ground while shells screamed down around me.

Days at Fox Battery were spent shooting fire missions or unloading pallets of fresh artillery shells. At night we pulled guard duty.

Gun Four was my favorite gun crew. Sometimes, late at night they passed around a joint and tried to relax. These guys had been shooting missions long enough to do it in their sleep.

"Fire Mission!" The forward observer's voice cracked over the radio. A patrol was pinned down by machine gun fire. Two gun crews sprang into action as I relayed the coordinates to Lieutenant Wong. The executive officer in Fox Battery was a Chinese-American.

He talked to the gun crews on the field telephone,

"Charge   six...Shell...Hotel...Echo...Fuse quick...Azimuth...Four...niner...six...deflection...two...five...seven...four! Is Gun Three ready?

Gun Four?"

"Gun Three is ready."

"Gun Four is ready."

Lieutenant Wong looked at me.

"Guns are ready."

I passed the word to the forward observer. He gave me the order to fire. I looked at Lieutenant Wong and passed the word to fire.

Lieutenant Wong spoke into the field telephone. "Fire!"

The forward observer's voice cracked over the radio. "Left one hundred! Add fifty!"

I picked up a field telephone and passed the corrections to the FDC bunker.

I entered the new coordinates in the log book and passed them on to Lieutenant Wong. He passed them on to the gun crews. We shot again.

"Rounds on target! Fire for effect!"

The gun crews fired several more times under Lieutenant Wong's command. The Marine patrol was no longer pinned down.

"End of mission. Great job, Fox! See you next time!"

The NVA soldiers set up on both sides of the road and waited. A quarter of a mile away, a truck towing Gun Two and an empty supply truck rolled out of the gate at C-2 and began their trip to the rear. Gun Two was being taken back to Dong Ha for maintenance. In less than a minute, the ambush was over.

The truck that was towing Gun Two sat in the middle of the road with the windshield and radiator full of bullet holes. The Marines who were riding in it jumped in the back of the supply truck and kept rolling south.

Captain Daniels yelled, "I want two Marines with rifles from each gun and FDC down at the gate on the double!"

I hurried to my bunker and grabbed my M-16. We ran to the gate and joined Captain Daniels in the back of another truck. We raced down the road and formed a perimeter around the abandoned artillery piece. The NVA soldiers who sprang the ambush were nowhere in sight.

I'll bet they were already halfway back across the DMZ. I tried in vain to start the truck. We unhooked the gun and towed it back inside the gate. Then we went back and towed the truck. Because of the ambush, Captain Daniels decided we would start sending out our own daily patrols. A truck drove the thirteen man squad about a half a mile down the road and dropped them off. Sergeant McBride was the squad leader. These guys were not grunts and they were a little nervous as they headed into the bush. Yesterday, when Rail stumbled while his finger was on the trigger, his M-16 went off. No one was hurt, but everyone within a mile knew exactly where they were. The next day Sergeant McBride gave the squad a warning before they headed to the drop off point: He brought up yesterday's incident.

"That had better not happen again, Marines."

McBride carried a 16-gauge shotgun, a weapon prohibited by the Geneva Convention accords. When he jumped off of the truck, the shotgun went off straight up in the air. Marines were rolling on the ground laughing at our red-faced squad leader. Finally the laughter stopped and they headed out into the bush to look for bad guys. Just before sunset, they walked up the road and back inside the wire.

The North Vietnamese Army discovered a long time ago that attacking fixed artillery positions could have disastrous results. Marine artillery crews would just level their cannons at the attacking NVA and blast away. There were special "Beehive rounds" for just such occasions. Fortunately, they were rarely needed.

* * *

Rail held up an old copy of Seventeen magazine and considered his choices. Slowly he studied the full-page layout of about eight beautiful young girls and smiled. Each Marine took his turn to claim one of the models as his own personal girlfriend. He gave her a name, talked about her background, and told how they first met. When he was finished, he passed the magazine to the next Marine.

Rail picked out a redhead. "Her name is Heather. She's attending the University of Chicago on a scholarship. Her interests are theater, classical music, and making her number one Marine happy! We met in church. She writes me twice a day."

Fox battery had been shooting fire missions all morning. The crew on Gun Four passed the magazine around during a break.

Smoke chose a pretty brunette. "She's a biology major at Berkeley. She has a part-time job in a doctor's office where she keeps a big picture of me on her desk."

Mick laughed. "I bet she gets her examinations for free!"

After each Marine had picked out his fantasy girlfriend, things quickly turned ugly.

Rail smiled at Smoke. "I used to date your girlfriend before she got pregnant and left town. She didn't have a clue who the daddy was. I still miss her."

Smoke looked at Rail. "I played high school football with your old lady, of course, that was before the surgery. Back then, his name was Arnold. He lettered in football and track."

Before things got any uglier, a tractor-trailer with a full load of pallets of fresh artillery shells drove through the main gate. Sergeant McBride walked over, "OK ladies, we got a truck to unload!"

The Marines formed a human chain that led from the back of the truck to the entrance of the ammo bunker. Each Marine took one of the heavy shells and tossed it to the next Marine. While they were unloading the truck, some Army tanks rolled in and set up camp across the road. They moved into some empty bunkers and heated up C rations for dinner.

Above their command bunker, beside the radio aerials, a small triangular orange and yellow flag fluttered in the afternoon breeze. The Army called these things battle pennants. The Marine Corps never had much use for any kind of pennants or patches. In the Army, they inspired unit pride. In the Marines, they just started fights. Many a barroom brawl started because some Marine walked in wearing a different colored patch. In service towns like San Diego or Oceanside, this became a nightmare for the Shore Patrol, as fistfights over different patches broke out every night in bars all over town. The fighting continued in the holding cells until the Marines with different patches were separated. Finally, the Marine Corps admitted they had made a mistake and took back all the patches.

Sergeant McBride eyed the fluttering pennant, "I sure would like to have that doggie flag."

I looked at him and asked, "Is it worth twenty bucks?"

Sergeant McBride smiled, "I'd be happy to pay twenty-five!"

I shook my head, "Who knows? They might lose it. You know how careless those doggies can be."

We went back to unloading the artillery shells. This was one working party where it was impossible to fuck off. Sweat poured off of the shirtless Marines as they kept tossing the endless stream of shells. This time they would work straight through until the job was finished. Rail glanced back at me as I tossed him another shell.

"You know, this is how they built the Pyramids, with thousands of dumb peasants just like you."

I tossed him another shell.

"Rail, you know you contradict the whole theory of evolution. In thousands of years, your ancestors haven't evolved a fucking day! The whole purpose of your species is to roll a ball of shit up one hill and down another!"

Rail laughed. "That's funny, McLane. According to your service record, you are still the hands-on champion shitburner of the entire 3rd Marine Division."

"That's true, Mr. Rail, but I gave up a safe and comfortable bed back at Dong Ha, just for the opportunity to study at the feet of a true shitmaster like you."

I tossed Rail another artillery shell. He loved to practice the fine art of giving insults. Some Marines would get mad and want to fight. That was OK with Rail.

He liked to fight. He was always ready to top the last insult. It was a way to pass the time during a hot afternoon. A truck pulled up beside the front gate and two Marines hopped out. I recognized them right away. It was Moe and Smurf. Before Smurf became a truck driver, he was a cannon cocker. He replaced one of the Marines who was wounded last week. Moe replaced a cook who rotated home.

I walked over and said hello. I could tell that they weren't too happy to be at C-2.

I grinned, "Don't sweat it, boys. This place ain't so bad, once you get used to being shot at."

They picked up their sea bags and started looking for the CO. I gave Moe directions to the mess tent and went back to unloading shells.

Rail looked at me. "Hey Buddha, Smoke got a letter from his girlfriend." I asked, "You mean Miss Ann Buke?"

He tossed me another shell. "Yeah, that's her! The bitch writes one helluva letter."

Miss Ann Buke was a code word for a bag of joints. Smoke was a black guy on Gun Four. He must have scored some weed from somewhere. Sergeant McBride didn't have a clue about what we were talking about.

Night fell quickly in February. I headed over to Gun Four after dark.

"Yo, Buddha!" Rail greeted me as I walked inside the bunker. He had gotten a small bag of weed from a truck driver. A joint was already going around. Someone passed it to me. I took it and inhaled deeply. Rail had covered the interior light with a red bandanna, transforming the bunker into a small nightclub. Smoke turned up a tape of Jimi Hendrix as Koontz jumped on top of a small table. He had a shirt tied around his waist.

Rail raised his hands and looked around, "Ladies and Gentlemen! Welcome to the ZIG ZAG CLUB! Get ready for a night of excitement, as we bring you, fresh from her European tour, the mysterious, the exotic, the lovely, Olga!"

Koontz waved to the crowd as he turned around and shook his ass. He pretended to be a go-go dancer.

Rail continued his introduction. "Olga hails from a small town in Yugoslavia where she was discovered driving a beer truck. Say hello to the boys, Olga!"

Koontz smiled and waved and kept shaking his butt.

Smoke yelled, "Take it off, baby!"

Rail raised his hands, "Gentlemen, please! Olga is a professional dancer and this is a respectable club. She is engaged to a sausage salesman in Belgrade."

Smoke yelled, "I got your sausage, Sweetie!"

Koontz rolled his eyes and pretended to be offended. Mick looked at Smoke, "Hey, you just stepped on my girlfriend's foot, you asshole!"

Smoke laughed, "Her feet shouldn't be so damn big. "

Smoke pretended to look under the table. "Is this her glass eye rolling across the floor?"

Mick held out his hand, "Yes it is, now hand it over!"

When the song ended, Koontz bowed and hopped down from the table. Rail encouraged the audience to show their appreciation with applause. Things suddenly got quiet when the gunny walked in.

He looked around and asked, "What's that stinking smell?"

Smoke replied, "I farted."

"Why are these lights red?"

Rail answered, "It enables us to keep our night vision in case we get a fire mission."

The gunny started to leave, he paused at the steps leading out of the bunker. "You men keep it down. In case you forgot, there's a war going on."

He walked away. Mick peeped out the entrance of the bunker to make sure he was gone.

Rail looked at Smoke, "How about farting again, bro?"

Smoke fired up another joint. We decided to send Mouse to the supply tent to steal a case of C-rations. It seemed appropriate for someone named Mouse to be stealing food. He slipped in the back of the tent and hoisted a case of C's on his shoulder and started walking away. Cyrus saw Mouse leaving the tent in the darkness and mistook him for a Viet Cong sapper. Lucky for Mouse, Cyrus was not carrying a weapon. He started chasing after our food thief yelling, "VC! VC!"

Mouse started running and the race was on. Mouse tried to take advantage of the darkness to escape, but the case of C's slowed him down and Cyrus was relentless as he ran after his Viet Cong. Rail heard the commotion and quickly stepped outside the bunker.

He grabbed Cyrus by his collar and lifted him off of the ground, "Shut the fuck up, you misguided midget, before I introduce you to a real Viet Cong!"

He dropped Cyrus to the ground.

"Now get the fuck outta here, you dickhead!"

Rail looked at Mouse, "You should have turned around and cold-cocked that little bastard! "We're lucky he didn't wake up the Captain."

Everyone crowded around as Smoke broke open the case of C-rations. There were only a couple of meals considered desirable. One included a can of pound cake. Another held a can of peaches. Third prize was a can of fruit cocktail. The other nine meals weren't worth fighting over. There wasn't time to read labels as everyone grabbed a box at once. You just hoped you got lucky. I said goodnight to my friends at the ZIG ZAG CLUB and slipped outside into the cool night air.

Rail was right. The red light worked, my eyes were instantly adjusted to the darkness. I walked over to the mess tent to visit Moe. He was sitting on a box of potatoes listening to Smoky Robinson and the Miracles on a small tape player. We took a walk to the edge of the compound. I lit a joint and passed it to Moe. We watched a B-52 strike light up the horizon just across the DMZ.

"You must have fucked up big time to get sent up here."

Moe smiled, "I guess I beat up one white boy too many."

I looked at Moe, "I'm the last guy in the world to be giving advice about how to get along in the United States Marine Corps, but one of these days you're going to break some poor bastard's neck with that famous choke of yours and you are going to be in a world of shit."

Moe grabbed my arm, "I joined the Marines to fight and so far, it's been a pretty good ride!"

I smiled at him, "You're still the only guy I know in the DMZ that can get real ice and real gin."

Moe shook his head and let go of my arm, "Even I can't get that shit up here."

"You got two months left in Vietnam, Moe. Do it and go home, back to Detroit. There's all the ice and gin in the world waiting just sixty days away."

Moe lit a cigarette. "Maybe I want something more than ice cubes and booze. I might want more than thirty years on a fucking assembly line. Maybe I want a little respect and dignity."

I looked at him, "Well, you won't get respect or dignity while you're doing twenty years in some prison yard for manslaughter."

Moe frowned, "What do you know about what I want? Every morning you wake up white and I wake up black. I'm just a slave who has been trusted with a gun. Brothers like me are trusted with guns because right now there's a hell of a lot of killing to be done. The powers that be got it all worked out so that their own kids don't have to go to war, they've arranged deferments or got them hidden away in some graduate school. Meanwhile Uncle Sam needs more warm bodies. All this killing don't come free. Some of us got to die and die hard, screaming and crying for our Mama. It don't matter to the Grim Reaper as long as his body bags keep getting filled regularly. Twenty years from now, nobody but their own Mama is gonna remember their name, much less give a damn."

Gun Six began firing some harassment and interdiction rounds. These were literally shots in the dark, artillery rounds that were intended to catch Charlie as he was walking down some trail at two o'clock in the morning. We walked back to Moe's tent.

"I can't really say I am glad to see you. I wouldn't be happy to see anyone up here, except maybe Captain Stack."

Moe smiled, "Well, you are about to get your wish. The word I got back at Dong Ha was that your dear Captain Stack is headed this way. He must have pissed off the Colonel."

Moe turned down my offer to play a game of chess. A light rain started to fall as I walked back to the FDC bunker. Suddenly, I remembered the Army pennant.

I walked over to an ammo bunker located directly across the road from our doggie neighbors. I climbed up on the roof and sat down facing their camp.

The rain came down harder. I stared out at the darkness looking for any sign of activity. There was nothing, not even the faint glow of a late night cigarette, nothing between me and them but a muddy road and eighty yards of open ground.

I waited five more minutes. There was still no sign of life. The rain fell harder. I stood up and walked slowly across the road and towards their camp. I squatted down and waited another couple of minutes. I moved another fifty feet closer and sat back down on my heels. There was still no sign of life. I walked up to their command bunker. I quietly climbed up on the sandbagged roof and sat down. I listened for the sound of voices, footsteps, anything. Two minutes passed. Slowly I picked up the flagpole and climbed off of the bunker. I was careful not to hurry or trip over anything. I walked out of their camp and crossed the dirt road back over to Fox battery. It was a piece of cake. I hid the flagpole in the ammo bunker. I put the pennant under a sandbag and went to bed.

I was walking back from breakfast when Sergeant McBride saw me.

"There's a couple of Army lieutenants talking to Captain Daniels right now and they are pissed! They say their pennant disappeared last night and they want it back now."

I looked at Sergeant McBride and smiled, "Maybe the NVA took it. There's a war going on, you know."

Sergeant McBride wasn't laughing. "Don't bullshit me McLane! If you don't give that flag back, it could cause serious trouble between the Marines and the Army."

"I thought you were going to give me twenty-five bucks for it?"

Sergeant McBride spit on the ground.

"I didn't know the bastards would get so bent out of shape over a damn flag. You've got to give it back. Captain Daniels doesn't know you took it. I told him I would ask around and try to find out who took it."

I smiled, "Did they offer a reward?"

McBride frowned, "How would you like to spend the rest of your time in Fox battery on permanent guard duty?"

I threw up my hands. "Alright, they can have the damn rag! But I'm keeping the fucking pole. Take a look on the shitter floor in twenty minutes. Maybe it'll be there."

What a bummer. After stealing their pennant fair and square, I had to give it back.

I walked over to the sandbag it was under and stuffed it in my pocket. I'll bet their faces were red when they asked Captain Daniels to help them find their precious pennant. It must have been pretty embarrassing to have a total stranger walk into the middle of their camp, in the middle of the night, in the middle of a war, and take their most prized possession and nobody saw a damn thing! I left the flag on the floor of the shitter. Give the crybabies back their precious pennant. Next time they set up camp beside some Marines, I'll bet they pay closer attention when the sun goes down. I kept the flagpole. It had a shiny brass tip that made it look like some kind of fancy spear. Sergeant McBride "found" their pennant and gave it back to the Army lieutenants.

* * *

Captain Stack had smiled when he signed the orders sending me to C-2. He could spend the last six months of his tour at Dong Ha in peace, no more bull's-eyes on the roof of his tent, no more office hours for silly shit that ended in acquittals. It still hurt that the Colonel reversed the only conviction he ever got against me. He wasn't smiling when the Colonel told him to pack his bags for C-2. This time it was his gear bouncing around in the back of a duce-and-a-half as they rolled along the deserted road headed north.

Captain Daniels was rotating home. Tommy Stack was taking his place. He loaded his sea bag on his shoulder and looked around. It was my turn to smile. I knew he would have a much better attitude in a place where a real war was going on. This was no place for the kind of fun and games he was used to playing back at Dong Ha. When he got closer, I stood at attention and saluted. He returned my salute with his free hand.

"Hello McLane."

"Welcome to C-2, sir."

He stopped for a moment and spoke to me in a low voice, "I'm replacing Captain Daniels. Now I know we had our differences back in Dong Ha, but we're on the same team up here and I want to know that I can count on you. I know you can be a good Marine when you want to."

I smiled, "You don't have to worry about me, sir."

The month that I had been away from this asshole had mellowed me somewhat. I no longer had the burning desire to roll a grenade under his butt. I still practiced my mantra every day but I no longer made any stupid requests.

In fact, I wasn't asking for anything. Asking for stuff was not the way off of the Karmic wheel. Every day brought more incoming shells from Uncle Ho. It seemed Russia had given him a lot of the long range artillery left over from World War II. The same guns that Stalin used to shell the Nazis were now aimed at us. You never got used to that shit screaming down. I felt like an ant running around on a dartboard. Each miss was a glorious affirmation that God really did want me to live. Fuck the law of averages. The bastards were shooting at us from as far away as seventeen miles. Fox battery did not have the artillery to return fire that far.

The doggies did have some 175-millimeter cannons at Camp Carroll. I later found out that the NVA had over a hundred and thirty long range artillery cannons scattered across the DMZ and into Laos. I had found the war.

"Did you salt these potatoes?" Moe asked as he tasted the water with a large spoon.

"Yeah!" Duluoz replied, as he checked the flame on a kerosene burner.

"Well, salt 'em again!"

Moe growled and walked away. The big Cajun frowned and reached for the salt.

He couldn't figure Moe out, but one thing was for sure, if the little Nigger was looking for a fight, he would give him the fight of his life. Broad shoul-dered and over 250 pounds, Duluoz was a soft-spoken, gentle giant. The rea-son Moe was in a bad mood had nothing to do with Duluoz, it was just one of those days when Moe was mad at the world and the big cook was boiling potatoes at ground zero.

Moe stepped back into the cook tent and walked over to the big pot. He dipped a spoon into the hot water and blew on it. He took a small sip.

"Fuck! How much salt did you use?"

He spat the water out and threw the spoon at the big man. Duluoz ducked the spoon and lunged at Moe. They tumbled out of the tent and rolled on the ground.

Moe jumped up and grabbed a shovel and started beating Duluoz's head as he struggled to his feet. The big Cajun got on his feet. He snatched the shovel out of Moe's hand and swung it at his head.

"Let's see how you like getting hit with a shovel, you black bastard!"

Moe ducked his head and slipped around behind Duluoz. He locked his hands around his large waist and hung on. Duluoz swung the shovel behind him and tried to hit some part of Moe. Moe pressed his head into the back of Duluoz's shoulders and held on. He locked his hands with all of his strength. Duluoz tried to twist free. Suddenly, Moe let go and ran back into the mess tent with Duluoz chasing after him.

Ten seconds later, Duluoz burst back out of the tent being chased by Moe. The black cook held a ten-inch butcher knife in one hand. Duluoz disappeared into one end of his living quarters with Moe right behind him. He burst out of the other end with an M-16 in one hand and an ammo magazine in the other. He tried to load the rifle as he ran from Moe. Most of the time, whenever Marines fought, other Marines would gather around to watch the free show. This time they watched from a distance. Suddenly, Duluoz spun around and knocked Moe down with the butt of the rifle. The Marine Corps Manual of Arms describes this motion as a horizontal butt stroke.

As Moe tried to get to his feet, Duluoz hit him again, knocking him out cold. Duluoz reached down and took the knife out of Moe's hand and staggered back to his tent. He glanced back to make sure Moe was still down. Duluoz's eyes were starting to swell shut. The next day Moe was on a truck back to Dong Ha.

Doc Haig said he had a broken jaw. We ate C-rations until Duluoz's eyes opened enough for him to go back to cooking. I never saw Moe again.

* * *

"Buddha!" Smurf called out, "The Captain wants us filling sandbags down by the river!"

I got my helmet and rifle and walked down to the gate. Smurf was there along with Micarelli and a new guy from Georgia named Coppa. We climbed into the back of a duce-and-a-half and headed south to the Cam Lo River. A small group of fishermen were repairing nets beside their boat. With all the Agent Orange that had been dumped on the DMZ, any fish caught in these waters ought to glow in the dark. Rail climbed out of the truck and walked over to the fishermen. Three of them agreed to fill sandbags in exchange for five gallons of cooking oil that Rail had stolen from the mess tent. I bought a bag of smoke from two small boys playing on the riverbank. Kids liked to sell you the stuff and then watch you smoke it. Watching live Marines acting silly was a form of entertainment. I sat down on my helmet and lit up a joint.

My eyes drifted along the riverbank as the fishermen began filling up the sandbags and loading them in the back of the truck. Smurf got bored and started throwing dirt clods at our work crew. It was just in fun and finally, one of the Vietnamese threw a dirt clod back at Smurf. Rail came to Smurf's aid and the war of the dirt clods began to escalate. Everyone on both sides was just kidding around and laughing when a member of our work crew did a very foolish thing. One of the Marines had carelessly left his M-16 lying on the roof of the truck.

Suddenly he stood up and laughed while he held the rifle above his head. He was holding the weapon straight up in the air and his fingers were nowhere near the trigger. He had no idea of the danger he was in. Coppa grabbed his rifle and pointed it at the Vietnamese in the truck. He slammed a round into the chamber.

"Hold it!" I screamed at Coppa. My M-16 was pointed at him. He looked at me and froze. I yelled at the Vietnamese to get out of the truck. He realized by the tone of my voice that something was wrong. He put the weapon down and climbed out of the truck. I lowered my weapon and took another hit on the joint. Coppa put down his M-16 and walked over to me. A look of disbelief was on his face as I smiled up at him and offered him the joint. He took it and things started to calm down a bit. I looked up at him and smiled, "I was just trying to keep you out of trouble, bro. The Captain would have burned your ass."

He handed me the joint, "I just want to know one thing. Would you really have shot me?"

I thought about it for a moment as I looked back in his eyes.

"I guess we'll never know the answer to that one, will we?"

Rail gave the cooking oil to the fishermen and we headed back to C-2.

I decided to have a little fun with Captain Stack. The afternoon supply truck from Dong Ha brought the latest mail. It was the CO's job to pass out the mail and he noticed the Time magazine with my name on it.

"Say, McLane, could I see that Time magazine when you are finished with it?"

"No problem, Captain."

Naturally there was a problem.

"I promised it to Rail, but I am sure you can have it when he is done."

Rail was ready when the Captain asked about the magazine.

"I'm sorry Captain, I already promised it to Koontz."

After Koontz told him he had already promised it to Smoke, Captain Stack realized the only thing he was getting was the shaft. I walked into the FDC bunker to begin my watch. Captain Stack was looking at some maps. I tossed the magazine down on the card table.

"Here's that Time magazine, Captain. Smoke likes to have something to read when he's sitting on the shitter. He's finished and it's all yours."

When my shift at the Fire Direction Control center ended, I walked over to Gun Four. A light rain was falling. Rail was reading a comic book in the fading light.

After looking around to make sure the coast was clear, he lit a joint and passed it to me. He looked at me and spoke quietly, "You know, Smurf just came back from Dong Ha. He got the scoop on where we are going next."

"Spain?" I asked.

Rail wasn't laughing. He took another toke as the rain came down harder. "We're going to Khe Sanh, bro."

Everyone in Vietnam had heard about this small isolated outpost in the corner of South Vietnam and Laos. We had heard stories of divisions of NVA infantry dug in, of flame-throwing tanks overrunning a nearby Special Forces Camp, and where over twelve hundred rounds had screamed down in a twenty-four hour period. The place was a never-ending nightmare where Marines left every day in body bags. We soon learned all the stories were true, including the one about it being our turn to go up there.

Rail frowned, "This is gonna be a gut check, Buddha. Every swinging dick in Fox is gonna have to turn it up a notch. Some of us aren't gonna make it outta there."

We finished the joint and stepped inside the door of the bunker to get out of the rain. I opened a can of peaches and shared it with Rail.

I looked at him, "Anybody who says they aren't scared about going up there is a fucking liar!" I ate the last of the peaches. "It's all in the cards, my man, a roll of the dice while the Devil fades all bets. If the shell has your name on it, there ain't a damn thing you can do about it."

Rail smiled, "It's the one that says 'to whom it may concern' that bothers me."

I laughed at this skinny Marine from Chicago.

"Rail, you should have joined the Navy. Right now, you'd be finishing up a professionally cooked meal eaten with silverware on a real plate and getting ready for a nice hot shower before slipping between some clean sheets for eight hours of peaceful sleep in a nice safe bed."

The night was turning cold and I wrapped a poncho liner around my shoulders.

Rail lit a cigarette. "Hey, I take a shower every time it rains, and around here it rains a lot."

We sat in the door of the bunker and watched the rain fall. We tried not to think about tomorrow and what lay ahead.

The officers and men of Fox Battery sat in the back of duce-and-a-half trucks and waited for the word to move out. We would travel south to Cam Lo and join up with another convoy going west past Camp Carroll and the Rock Pile to a small deserted village called Ca Lu. We would wait there for some tanks that were coming down from Khe Sanh to escort us back to the beleaguered outpost. I was sitting on a stack of C-rations when the distinct aroma of marijuana floated past my well-trained nose. I looked upwind towards the front of the convoy and saw Rail passing a joint to Koontz.

"This truck feels unlucky," I said to the driver as I hopped down and walked over to ride with Rail and Koontz. We were bound for the deadliest piece of real estate in Vietnam. It was the only place where the Marine Corps stopped sending out patrols. They did that after nobody came back from one. When they sent a second patrol to check on the first one, only a few Marines made it back inside the wire. Everyone else was dead. The bodies were not recovered for over six weeks.

"Good morning, Mr. Buddha! It's a beautiful day to die!"

Rail passed me the joint as I settled in. As I took a hit, the convoy started moving.

"What are we hauling?" I asked, as I loaded a magazine into my M-16.

"Don't worry about it. You won't feel a thing."

Koontz smiled at Rail as we picked up speed. I looked around. On my left were cases of 105 shells. On my right were boxes of white phosphorous shells. I was riding on a fucking ammo truck.

We rolled through the village of Cam Lo. The other convoy was waiting for us on the side of Route 9. We joined up and headed west towards Camp Carroll.

A lot of the truck drivers flew their state flag from the cab of their truck. We must have looked like some kind of United Nations convoy as we rolled along creating a cloud of dust that you could see for miles. West of Camp Carroll an NVA machine gun crew and a mortar crew set up on top of a hill and waited. They ate some cold rice and watched the red dust cloud getting closer. The second convoy was glad to turn off and head through the gate at Camp Carroll as we rolled on towards the small Marine base called the Rock Pile.

The rules of the road were the same for Marine convoys in the DMZ in 1968 as they were for wagon trains in 1868 traveling through Geronimo's back yard: No matter what happens, keep moving. Don't stop for stragglers. Don't stop for anything!

As the convoy crested a hill and approached a bridge that crossed a small river the NVA sprang into action. We drove around a truck that was stopped in the middle of the road and on fire. The windshield was full of bullet holes. There was no sign of the driver or anyone else. A large spout of water rose up about fifty feet as the first mortar round landed in the river. The next round hit beside the bridge as we began to cross over. I don't know why the NVA didn't just blow the bridge before we got to it. I am just glad we made it across in one piece. We kept rolling and watching the countryside for something to shoot at. We saw no real targets in the rolling clouds of dust.

We drove into the deserted village of Ca Lu just before dark.

Koontz, Rail, and I picked out a house with a good roof and moved in. First we checked for trip wires and booby traps. We broke out some C-rations and cooked supper. After dark it began to rain hard. Our humble home did not leak a drop.

We turned in early. Sometime in the night, Koontz had to pee. It was still raining and he tried to put it off as long as possible. Finally he got up and stumbled out into the darkness. While he was pissing, Rail got up and pulled the plug on Koontz's air mattress. He got back under his own blanket and waited.

Koontz was getting soaked as he tried to pee faster. Finally, he stumbled back inside and collapsed on his nearly flat air mattress. He knew instantly that he had been fucked.

"Goddammit! Motherfucker! When I figure out who pulled this plug, I'm gonna kick their ass! I know it was you McLane!"

Koontz sat down and started blowing his air mattress back up. Rail and I tried our best to laugh without making a sound. The rain outside helped to hide our chuckles. We spent the next day waiting to hook up with some tanks that were going to escort us the last two miles to Khe Sanh. Koontz was writing a last letter to his girl. He was milking our dire straits for all it was worth. A lot of guys wrote letters while we waited. Late in the day we got the word that we would not leave for Khe Sanh until the next day.

We cooked some more C-rations and spent another night in our waterproof house. The next morning we got the word that the tanks weren't coming. The scuttlebutt was that seven tanks left Khe Sanh yesterday bound for Ca Lu.

NVA soldiers destroyed five of those tanks with rocket propelled grenades and the two surviving tanks aborted the mission and headed back to Khe Sanh.

The next morning our convoy drove over to LZ Stud. Some C-46 helicopters were waiting to take us to Khe Sanh. The countryside surrounding the isolated Marine base had so many craters from B-52 strikes that it looked like a close-up of the moon. Surrounding the perimeter of the base was a winding series of Zig Zag trenches. Each night, the NVA dug the trenches a little closer to the wire. The Zig Zag pattern minimized the damage caused due to a five hundred pound bomb direct strike from a B-52. The landing zone looked like a graveyard of burned out hulks of helicopters and cargo planes. A bulldozer would push the crashed aircraft off of the runway. Sometimes the planes would land intact, but incoming artillery rounds destroyed them while they were unloading their passengers and cargo. Pilots soon learned how to land and slow down just long enough to off-load their supplies and take off again the second the last pallet had bounced on to the runway.

Incoming artillery rounds started screaming in and exploding as we ran down the ramp and raced to the nearest trench. Once the last helicopter had taken off, the shelling stopped long enough for us to grab our gear and head for our new home. Captain Stack glanced over at me.

"Well, McLane, what do you think of this place?"

I was amused that a Captain would be asking the opinion of a lowly private, but I knew better than to let him see a smile. I reached down and picked up a handful of red dirt.

"We are walking on sacred ground. Thirty years from now, a lot of Marines would give their right arm to be able to honestly claim that they ever spent an hour here. Someday our children will study this place in their history books."

The gunny looked around at our new living quarters. He was not pleased.

"This place looks like a goddamn dump!"

It looked like whoever lived here before us never left their bunkers except to take a shit. Whenever they finished a meal, they stepped to the entrance of the bunker and threw the empty C-ration cans as far as they could.

"Buddha! Smurf! I want all of this shit picked up and buried. I don't care how long it takes! Get on it now!"

We crouched down and started picking up empty cans. Seventy-five feet away, an artillery shell screamed in and exploded, sending up a huge cloud of smoke and red dust. I stretched out on the ground and cursed,

"Shit! We're gonna get killed on a fucking trash detail!"

It took a full day to pick up and bury all of the empty cans.

Fox Battery's guns were shooting fire missions constantly. The Fire Direction Control teams worked an eight-hour shift. After a four-hour break, they worked another shift. There were no regular meal times. A large pallet of C-rations sat beside the door of the bunker. You could go over and grab a meal anytime you had a chance to eat. A wide variety of North Vietnamese long-range artillery shells rained down constantly. The worst was recoilless rifle fire. Because we were set up in a valley, they were able to fire these weapons directly down on us from a short distance away. That meant we could not hear the shells coming in. They blew up without any kind of warning.

The corpsman discovered I had a fever. He called it a "fever of unknown origin," fancy words that meant he didn't have a clue what I had. If it reached 104, I would be medevaced to the rear. I was short by two degrees. I knew it wasn't malaria because I had no chills, just cramps and diarrhea. I walked around with a gallon of Kaopectate that I would swig on like some Kentucky moonshiner.

I was on my fifth visit to my favorite plywood shitter when more rounds started screaming in. I could hear the shrapnel whistling through the air as the big shells continued to impact. Fuck it. I kept sitting in my plywood shelter. I just couldn't see myself racing to a trench with my pants down around my knees and shit running down my legs. I went on sitting and staring out of the open door of the small outhouse as more shells blew up around me. If I got hit, at least I would get the hell out of here.

The days at Khe Sanh flew by in an almost never ending rain of hot shrapnel. Each morning, after the fog had cleared, more helicopters and C-130's flew in more fresh Marines and ammo and took out the wounded and dead.

Captain Stack was going home. He was replaced by another asshole named Lieutenant Chase. Chase was fucked up from the get go. For starters, his dad was an Admiral in the Navy. Captain Stack picked up his gear and headed for the LZ.

He stopped and looked at me, "I know what you think about me, McLane and if I ever see you in the States, we'll settle it then."

I laughed, "What is wrong with right now? I smiled and slowly scratched my ass, "You know I have as much respect for you as I do any officer."

Bold words coming from a wise-ass PFC talking to a Marine Corps Officer in a combat zone, but I had this asshole right where I wanted him. In order for him to bring my smart mouth up on charges, he would have to postpone his departure date back home indefinitely. As much as he hated me and all the grief I had given him, he hated the idea of spending even a single extra day in Vietnam even more.

He picked up his gear and started walking toward the Landing Zone.

I was enjoying my morning cup of C-ration coffee when I first noticed him.

This must be some kind of James Bond character. He couldn't arrive in a helicopter like everyone else, he was slowly drifting down in a parachute. Then I saw the ejection seat tumbling down as a large explosion shook the side of a nearby hill.

It was the impact of the Phantom jet he had just bailed out of.

"Shit," I thought, "there went six million taxpayer dollars!" Planes that got hit over North Vietnam tried to make it over us before they crashed.

The pilot drifted down into the minefield. He stood in one place until a passing helicopter dropped him off inside the perimeter. He refused the jeep that was sent to pick him up. He was still pissed off at the idea of losing his plane. He cooled off as he took the long walk over to the regimental command bunker.

The incoming artillery never let up for more than an hour or two during the day. Often they would shell us in the middle of the night. When it was too hot to sleep inside the bunker, I slept on the sandbags on the roof. One night as more shells started to fall, I woke up running. I was instantly knocked on my ass. I thought I had been hit, but I realized I had only run into a wire that was holding up one of the radio antennas. I was glad nobody saw what happened. I went back to sleep.

Everyone knew if General Giap wanted to, he could overrun this place in a couple of hours. If he did, General Westmoreland was prepared to carpet bomb the entire area with massive B-52 strikes. We thought any such attack would start with an air strike by Russian MIGs. The enemy aircraft would punch open a hole in our lines and the waiting NVA would pour in before the smoke and dust settled.

The Communist ground troops would be supported by flame-throwing tanks that would quickly clear out the bunkers of Marines who refused to surrender. We sat at the base of a 50 caliber machine gun and scanned the skies. Some guys carried one bullet in their pocket for themselves, they swore that they wouldn't be taken alive.

Lieutenant Chase yells, "Fire mission!" Does that make four this morning or five? This fever just won't let up. It's not getting any worse, but neither it nor the diarrhea will go away. I'm getting skinny, and I look like hell. I feel like I am awake in a bad dream as I walk over to a card table and pick up a slide rule and wait.....crunch the numbers.....the Fire team leader passes the data on to the gun crews....wait for new adjustments from the Forward Observer.....crunch the numbers again.

Suddenly an artillery shell fired from almost seventeen miles away, screams down into the hard dry clay less than a hundred feet from our bunker. The next minute seems to take forever as dust swirls and dances like red snowflakes, covering the field radios, maps, logbooks, and the faces of the officers and men of Fox Battery. Shells called "bunker busters" carry a delayed fuse and if this one has one, we will know about it when it goes off in the next few seconds. It doesn't.

"Azimuth!" Sergeant Medford shouted.

I looked at my slide rule and called out, "Seven...four......eight."

A voice from the secondary fire team called out, "Negative, Sergeant!"

"Work it again." Sergeant Medford gave the command.

I picked up the slide rule and repeated the procedure.

"Seven...one......"niner!"

The voice from the secondary team yelled, "Affirmative, Sergeant!"

Hal gave the OK to relay the data to the gun crews. Lieutenant Chase gave the command to fire.

Sergeant Medford walked over to me, "Are you alright?"

I smiled, "I'm fine, Sergeant."

A few minutes later the forward observer radioed the end of the fire mission.

I walked outside and leaned against some sandbags. It was almost noon. I took a swig from the Kaopetate jug. Sergeant Medford walked up beside me and touched my forehead. He frowned.

"How's your fever?"

"About a hundred and one today. But I feel fine."

I tore open a box of C-rations and pulled out a can of ham and lima beans. Sergeant Medford spat on the ground and lit a cigarette.

"Look, Buddha, why don't you go to Dong Ha for a couple of days? Get some sleep. Get rid of that fucking fever. You can be back here next week, good as new."

I tore open a heat tab and lit a match.

"We're short-handed enough already. If I'm not here. That means the rest of the guys will have to pick up the slack. We're thin enough as it is."

Sergeant Medford frowned, "Damn it, Buddha. It's not worth the risk of getting our own people killed!"

I stared up at the section chief as I heated my lunch, "Look Hal, the system's working. That's why we have a secondary team. They caught the bogus numbers. I have had this fever for over two weeks and this is the first time I made a mistake. Just let me eat these beans and I'll be as good as new."

Sergeant Medford shook his head and crushed his cigarette. "I want the corpsman taking your temperature twice a day!"

I held up the gallon of kaopectate. "Doc is already on top of this, bro, so relax."

My beans were ready. I found a little shade and sat down to eat.

Smurf walked over.   "I hear we are getting outta this hell hole."

I smiled, "Yeah, we're going to France to help out with the grape harvest."

Since I had no use for them, I gave Smurf the small box of smokes that came with my C-rations. Smurf put them in his breast pocket for later.

"No shit, I heard it from some engineers. They're shutting Khe Sanh down, dude. Everyone's getting the fuck outta here! They are bringing in extra C-4 to blow up all of the bunkers! I'll bet you a hot beer on it."

"Bet." I finished my beans and opened a can of fruit cocktail. This was a bet I would be happy to lose. The rumors were true, but they took their sweet time about it.

We spent the next week shooting fire missions while the engineers walked around blowing up perfectly good bunkers. A few more outfits left each day. Fox was one of the last artillery batteries to leave. A plywood shitter was the only structure standing was we humped our gear out to the landing zone. A single bulldozer was filling in collapsed bunkers as more shells continued to rain down on the deserted base. Koontz's folks had sent him a Monopoly set. He was still waiting for the chance to play his first game with it. I don't think Koontz wrote his folks very often.

I'll never understand how they thought he had the time to sit around playing Monopoly. He should have thrown it away, but he carried it under his arm along with all of his other gear as he ducked and ran up the ramp of the waiting helicopter. As he was running, he dropped the box.

The prop blast scattered all the play money, the small plastic green houses and blue hotels, the board, and every game piece including the little silver Scotty dog, into a huge swirling cloud of red dust as the twin bladed revved up to take off. The landing zone looked like the set of a Fellini movie as gold-colored five hundred dollar bills tumbled end over end through the swirling red clouds.

A lot of good men had died in this place, others had lost arms and legs and everyone carried nightmares that would awaken them years later in the middle of the night as the echo of incoming artillery shells roared through their dreams again.

Even Ray Charles could see that we were losing this war and all of the gallant sacrifices that these brave men had made for country and corps would not change that. I made a promise to myself to someday take a piss on LBJ's grave.

I was proud to be in the company of men who had learned to stare death in the eye on a daily basis. On most days, death blinked first. When all the names of the other battlegrounds of Vietnam have faded into dusty history books, there will still be storytellers and old men who will talk about a place called Khe Sanh.

It was the closest thing to the Alamo since Davy Crocket and Jim Bowie watched Colonel Travis draw a line in the sand with his sword and invite everyone within the sound of his voice to cross over and fight 'til the death for Texas. Someday Khe Sanh would be a valley of ghosts where old men with bald heads and beer guts would stand and remember the days when they were young and think about the brothers who never left this place.

* * *

Fox battery was bivouacked on a small hill in an ocean of elephant grass. Less than a mile away, a mountain river snaked around and over boulders as big as boxcars as the roaring white water raced down to the sea. The gunny organized a swimming party of about twenty happy Marines. Half of them stood guard while the other half swam and played in the rushing water. We were lucky no one got their skull crushed against some rock as we swam over waterfalls and jumped from high boulders into the swirling currents below.

I decided to do a little exploring. I drifted downstream past more big moss covered rocks. Around a curve in the river, I discovered a small cave hidden in the shadows of a huge rubber tree. I wondered if the cave was the entrance to a hidden NVA bunker. I half expected to see some sentry dozing in the afternoon sun.

The water wasn't just going past the cave, thirty feet inside the dark walls was a huge whirlpool that was the beginning of an underground river. My adrenaline started pumping as I started swimming for my life towards the outer edge of the strong current. I managed to catch on to the side of a large rock and pull myself out of the water. A search party would have found the cave, but if I had been sucked into the swirling currents, I would have been listed as missing in action.

Everyone else was still swimming back upstream. I was stupid to be swimming alone. I swam back upstream and rejoined my buddies.

It felt great to be clean, really clean. At Khe Sanh, we only got to bathe whenever it rained. My fever was finally gone. After a couple of days of resting in the tall elephant grass, we flew back to C-2. The guys in FDC moved back into our old bunker. The homecoming was short. In less than a week we left in another convoy for LZ Stud. The big C-46 helicopters were waiting to take us on another operation.

We knew the drill. Silently we carried our gear up the ramp and found somewhere to sit. We took off with Gun Four slowly swinging back and forth underneath us.

Thirty minutes later we landed on the top of a small jungle hill. It was almost dark. Engineers had blown up almost every tree in any direction for about fifty yards. A company of infantry had established a perimeter and was setting in for the night.

It was starting to rain. We snapped the edges of two shelter halves together and tied them to the top of a splintered stump. We quickly dug a drainage ditch in the fading light. I knew we would begin shooting fire missions in the morning. I walked over by some bushes and took a piss.

"Get down!"

A voice about ten feet away called out to me. I could barely make out a grunt lying behind a rock. I looked at him and smiled. Sometimes the grunts like to have a little fun with the arty boys. I walked over and stood beside him.

"What's up?"

He looked at me and pointed down the hill.

"There is somebody down there."

I walked past him about ten feet and stuck out my hand. I looked back over my shoulder.

"Well, where the fuck is he? I want to meet him."

It was fun to turn the tables on these clowns for a change. While I was standing there, my eyes peered into the shadows past the guy behind the rock.

Every grunt as far as I could see was lying flat on the ground. I looked the other direction and saw more grunts crouched down behind rocks and tree stumps.

In less than a second, I was flattened out on the muddy ground.

I crawled back to join the grunt behind the rock. He smiled, "You still want to meet him?" He pointed with his finger, "He's right down there."

They had been listening to someone crawling up the hill for the last ten minutes. As far as they could tell, it was just one or two guys. Since early that morning, helicopters had been flying in and out of the small hill, and the NVA wanted to know why. They sent a couple of scouts to find out. Lying on the ground, I could clearly hear somebody. The guy behind the rock used a field telephone to get permission to throw a grenade. He tossed it down the hill about fifty feet.

The bushes came to life as someone jumped up and ran about ten feet and dove back to the ground. This guy had played this deadly game of tag before. He was off and running as soon as the spoon on the grenade popped.

Now there was nothing but darkness and silence. I waited a few minutes and crawled back to my makeshift tent. The rain fell harder. At sunrise I got up and lit a heat tab under a canteen cup full of water. The C-ration coffee was delicious and warmed me up. I heated up a small can of ham and eggs. The sky went from black to gray as I began another day in the Nam.

They named this place LZ Winchester. It was two miles from the Laotian border. The grunts were searching for any North Vietnamese units operating in this area. We were to provide them with artillery support.

Fire Direction Control was a fairly easy job. We set up a tent that would serve as a command center. Wire men ran two parallel telephone lines to each of the six guns. Radio operators established contact with the forward observers.

We unfolded some card tables and spread out maps. We put colored pins in the maps. The radio came to life.

"Red Dog One, this is Red Dog Two. Over."

I grabbed the handset and answered, "Red Dog Two, over."

"I need one spotter round of Willie Peter."

The forward observer was asking for a round of white phosphorus.

He gave me his coordinates. I wrote them down and handed the paper to Lieutenant Chase. He looked at the paper and called out, "Fire Mission! Gun One, get on the hook."

The crew from Gun One sprang into action. Quickly the white phosphorous shell was loaded and ready to fire. I keyed the handset.

"Roger Red Dog One, your Willie Peter is ready."

This was a locator round used to make sure Fox battery and the forward observer were on the same page. The white phosphorus burned like the tip of a huge match as the shell exploded and a large cloud of white smoke filled the air.

The forward observer spotted the smoke through his field glasses.

"Looking good, Red Dog Two. Let me have another one. Right five hundred, drop one hundred."

He would use the second round as a starting point for any fire missions he would shoot that day.

"Thank you much, Red Dog Two. This is the end of mission right now. Don't wander off."

Lieutenant Chase told Gun One to stand down. I heated up a second cup of coffee. I was glad to be on duty this morning. Other FDC guys who weren't so lucky spent the day filling sandbags or humping boxes of artillery shells from the landing zone to the various gun crews. Marines were using the empty ammo boxes to build small hooch's. The next day I was assigned to a working detail filling sandbags.

Judging by the number of ammo pallets being dropped off, this was going to be a long operation. Smurf passed the word to me to report to the captain. Rail got the same message. The captain told us to report to an infantry captain waiting for us over at the grunt headquarters. He didn't tell us why. We knew better than to ask. Rail and I walked over and reported in. The captain returned our salute.

"I understand you gentlemen know how to play bridge." The statement was put like a question.

I smiled, "Yes, sir, we do." I didn't know if Rail knew how to play bridge or not, but if he didn't, he could fake it until he caught on. This beat filling sandbags. The young grunt Captain handed me an old deck of cards. We sat down on the ground and I shuffled the cards.

I had learned to play bridge in college at the Methodist Student Center when I should have been studying. Rail didn't know how to play, but he caught on fast.

For his benefit, I reviewed the rules out loud. After a couple of warm-up rounds, he played like a veteran. The grunt gunny sergeant walked over to report on the progress of the various working parties under his supervision. He gave me a hard look. I ignored him and called out, "Two spades."

The young captain upped my bid with a call for three hearts. Rail upped the spade bid to three. My hand looked pretty strong, so I raised the bid to four spades.

Rail and I beat the grunt officers like a rented mule. It was a great way to spend an afternoon in the middle of a war. We should have let them win. The next day we were not invited back. We were too busy shooting fire missions anyway.

Our first target was some NVA bunkers that had been discovered. Next, we silenced some snipers. Suddenly Red Dog One was taking incoming mortar rounds.

"Red Dog Two, we need some rounds up here on the double. We're taking mortar fire from a hill on our left."

In less than a minute, Fox battery had rounds on the way.

"Looking good, Red Dog Two. Give me left fifty and fire for effect!"

Twenty rounds later, the mortar tube was knocked out and the fire mission was over. We could rain down hellfire and damnation on anything or anybody within six miles of LZ Winchester. We heard stories of Marines getting killed from friendly fire by accident. It had never happened on any mission I shot with Fox battery.

The regimental commander set a high standard for accuracy. The commanding officers of each battery were expected to meet that standard or find their asses in a sling. The standard was met with excellent forward observers, experienced fire direction control teams, and veteran 105 artillery crews.

Shooting artillery missions was no different in Vietnam than in Korea or World War II. The laws of physics did not change over the years. Fox battery shot as straight and true as similar 105 crews did in the Frozen Chosen or on Iwo Jima. Because of the fire power of artillery batteries like Fox, Marine casualties in Vietnam were kept to a minimum. We shot 13,000 rounds at LZ Winchester in ten days. The next morning we flew back to Camp Carroll.

* * *

It was time for my R & R. Every GI in Vietnam eventually got a week off sometime in their tour of duty for "rest and relaxation. Mine came during July, 1968. I was headed for Japan to meditate at a Buddhist Temple on Mt. Fuji.

I loaded up my gear and walked over to the LZ. I caught a helicopter going to Dong Ha. It felt strange being back in the rear. I walked out to the front gate to get a haircut. The local Vietnamese had a gaggle of little shops set up right outside the gate. They were just plywood shacks with tin roofs. Cheap guitars hung from the rafters and sandals made from rubber tires were piled on crude tables.

At the end of the row of hooch's was a small barbershop. There was an ongoing coincidence that some Marines considered a little odd. It seemed almost every time these guys didn't open up for business was another day that Dong Ha took a bunch of incoming artillery fire. I entered the barbershop and sat down on a stiff wooden chair. I was the only customer.

A large piece of broken mirror hung on a bare wall in front of me. I wondered if this guy was a member of the local Viet Cong. Everyone and everything that rolled in through the front gate went right past him. I hoped he was just a man trying to feed his family. He gave me a pretty good haircut. Just when I thought he was finished, he grabbed my head and snapped it to the right. For a split second, I thought he was trying to break my neck. Next, he snapped my head to the left. I had forgotten that getting your neck popped was a normal part of a Vietnamese haircut. Back in the bush, the gunny cut everyone's hair with a pair of shears that he always had on him. I was glad to pay the local barber a dollar and get the hell out of there.

I decided to visit my old pals in the motor pool. Doyle was slowly putting a new water pump on a truck. He took a break and we smoked a joint. A bunch of soldiers had moved into the area next to the motor pool. Marines like to call soldiers Doggies. This was not meant as an insult, but it was never forgotten that these not Marines. These were new guys. They were all wearing brand new jungle boots and jungle fatigues. They had been in Vietnam for less than a week. After setting up tents, they were busy digging trenches. Every soldier was wearing a helmet.

Most Marines in the rear wore soft covers. Just as we finished the joint, a lone artillery shell screamed in and exploded about two hundred yards away. Doyle and I laughed as we watched our neighbors scrambling into to their new trenches.

The shells would have to get a lot closer before anyone in the motor pool took them seriously. Minutes later, another one exploded about twenty yards from the first one.

Doyle had a cassette tape of the Beatles album, "Sergeant Pepper's Lonely Hearts Club Band." He put it in his tape player and cranked it up. The other mechanics stood around laughing while Doyle and Walsh started dancing in circles.

The Doggies stayed down in their trenches and stared out at the crazy Marines frolicking in the motor pool.

"You assholes better get back to work!" Lieutenant Wheeler yelled as he looked over and saw what was going on.

Another ten minutes passed before the soldiers cautiously climbed out of their trenches and went back to filling sandbags. I lay underneath the truck and watched Doyle checking the brakes. The entire undercarriage of the truck was covered in dried mud. I stared up at the dark mess.

"You know, this mud looks just like one big piece of homemade fudge."

"Maybe it is," Doyle replied as he pulled on a wrench.

"Why don't you bite off a piece and see."

"The only fudge I eat is the kind my grandmother makes. This stuff looks like the crap they sell to the tourists from up north."

I poked at the mud while Doyle finished checking the brakes. I looked over at Doyle.

"Listen Bro, how would you like to partner up with me back in the real world?"

Doyle smiled, "I don't think I would make a very good pimp."

"No, no!" I replied, "I need a good mechanic. I want you to build me a race car and I'll drive it. In no time, we'll both be rich and famous."

Doyle put down the wrench.

"What the fuck do you know about racing cars?"

I smiled. "What's to know? You just keep the gas pedal on the floorboard and hang on!"

I was fourteen the first time I cranked up the family car. One of life's disappointments was discovering that a hundred miles an hour isn't really all that fast.

"What do you say, Doyle? You know you aren't the only good mechanic around. I was thinking about asking Walsh."

"Well, you ain't the only nutcase around either. In the Marine Corps, whack jobs like you are a dime a dozen."

I broke off a piece of mud and threw it at Doyle.

"I got what it takes to be a winner! Just imagine looking in your rearview mirror and seeing me breathing down your scrawny neck on some hairpin curve?"

Doyle laughed, "That would be truly scary, indeed."

"I can make both of us rich, bro. Sleep on it and let me know your answer tomorrow."

I forgot that tomorrow I would be on a plane bound for Tokyo. Doyle stopped for lunch. He cleaned up while I took a knife and broke off a large piece of mud.

I cut it up in small squares and wrapped it in a piece of newspaper. "We'll leave this on the table at the mess hall and see who bites."

Cox came walking by. He was one of the dumbest drivers in the motor pool. Last week he blew up a spare tire. He just kept putting in more air until the damn thing exploded. He tried to explain to Lieutenant Wheeler that he didn't need any air gauge, he could just look at a tire and tell how much air it needed. Lucky for him, he only got a few scrapes and bruises.

"What you got there, McLane?" Cox asked.

"My grandmother sent me some homemade fudge. I'm gonna trade it for a bottle of gin."

Cox stared intently at the squares of mud. "Let me have a piece."

"No way, dude!"

"Come on McLane, you and me are tight."

I frowned, "OK, but you can only have one of the small pieces." I held open the news paper. Cox took a big piece and bit into it. Doyle and I howled and started running as Cox spat out the mud.

"That's what you get for being so greedy. I said to take a small piece!"

We kept running. Cox still had a stiff leg from blowing up the tire, so we got away. I made it up to him later when my grandmother sent me some banana cake.

The next morning I packed a small flight bag and caught a ride to the small airport at Quang Tri. The C-130 dropped off some more replacements and kept rolling while several other Marines and I ran and jumped on board for the flight back to Da Nang. That night I slept between clean sheets for the first time in six months.

The next morning I flew American Airlines to Tokyo, Japan. At the airport, beautiful ladies in bright colored kimonos served cold beers to the arriving Marines. I rode a small shuttle bus with some other guys to a downtown hotel and checked in. I stared at the immaculate bathroom transfixed. I listened to the wonderful gurgling sounds of the spotless commode as I flushed it over and over. The DMZ seemed a million miles away.

I rode a charter bus the next morning to Mt. Fuji. It felt wonderful to meditate with hundreds of fellow Buddhists, high on a mountain, at a temple that was built centuries ago. I found a simple peace in that holy place that I hoped I could carry with me for the rest of my life. Four days later, I caught another bus back to Tokyo. I was riding on one of Tokyo's famous subway trains when I met Tanaka. He was a student at the University of Tokyo. Politicians called people like Tanaka leftists. Back in the States, the same net would have caught me.

In my book, capitalism was rich kids playing tennis at the country club while poor boys like me were ducking shrapnel in leaky sandbagged bunkers. It is a little-known fact that Bob Hope was one of the largest single landowners in California.

No wonder he kept going back to Vietnam. He had a lot invested in stopping Communism. Tanaka and I ate dinner in a small restaurant.

"How are you enjoying Japan?"

"Great! This is a beautiful country filled with wonderful people."

I was elated to find someone who spoke English. This time last year I was attending school at a university in Texas. Our conversation turned to politics. Tanaka sipped at a small glass of sake.

"It is unfortunate that you are involved in such a dangerous war."

I laughed, "In the last few months, I've had a lot of practice ducking and dodging sharp pieces of hot steel."

Tanaka asked me, "Why are you fighting in this war?"

"I would rather be throwing Frisbees in Golden Gate Park in San Francisco. I am in this war because everything I did to avoid going was a disastrous failure. The people in my country don't understand that the war in Vietnam is a civil war. Just like in our own civil war, the South is losing."

I showed him an old SDS membership card I still carried in my wallet.

"I joined the Students for a Democratic Society last year at my university. They were a bunch of longhaired, dope smoking, troublemakers – my kind of people!"

Tanaka stared at the fading card. He had read about SDS.

"You have to understand, Tanaka. The Marine Corps doesn't care about politics. I was just a warm body to them at a time that they needed a lot of warm bodies. If my commanding officer back in Vietnam had his way, I would be on the next plane back to the States. He thinks I am a royal pain in the ass. This war won't last much longer. The American people will not tolerate continuing to bury their finest sons over a bunch of drug dealers and pimps in Saigon."

The next day Tanaka took me over to see the University of Tokyo. We came at a bad time. Rioting students had the place completely shut down. We sneaked in to the campus. A lot of tents were pitched in front of the various buildings. Every door and window was blocked by chairs and desks that were wired together.

At one of the larger buildings someone let us crawl in through a side window.

Political slogans were painted on most of the walls. I saw a peace sign. Tanaka showed me the command center in the occupied office of the President of the University. He introduced me to the leaders in charge of this chaos. I remembered to bow. He handed them my SDS membership card. They passed it around and smiled. They showed me pictures of the President of the University that they had found in his ransacked desk. He was in a geisha house. Up on the roof they had fire hoses hooked up and ready to be turned on in case the police tried to storm the campus. Rocks were piled up in each corner waiting to be thrown down on anyone approaching the building. Because of my very limited Japanese I was forced to communicate with a lot of body language and a huge shit-eating grin.

Tanaka explained that I was a Marine on leave from Vietnam. Someone asked me, "Why are you fighting in that war?"

I looked him in the eye, "Che Guevara writes about how Americans are living in the 'belly of the beast.' Well, I too am in the 'belly of the beast.'"

I felt a genuine bond with these rowdy rebels as I shook hands and looked around at the trashed office. I wished Captain Stack could see me now.

Abbie Hoffman and Jerry Rubin would have really enjoyed this international meeting of angry young men.

The next day I sat at the bar of the Stars and Stripes Club and ordered another Singapore Sling. The alcohol wasn't helping my mood. In a few hours a 707 jet would be taking me back to Vietnam. My vacation from the war was over. I had spent over seven hundred dollars in less than a week and I didn't buy any souvenirs.

I didn't care about the money. Where I was going, I wouldn't need any money. I joined some other glum-faced Marines and soldiers as we boarded a bus for the airport. As much as I hated going back to the war, I was looking forward to rejoining my buddies in Fox battery.

The next day I hitched a ride on a supply helicopter taking a pallet of artillery shells to some isolated outpost. Fox was once again set up on top of a small jungle hill. I found Captain Stack and reported in. He returned my salute and asked, "How was Japan?"

I shook my head, "You wouldn't believe me if I told you. I made friends with some guys you would not have liked. It was all over too soon. It is just as well that I left because I was almost broke."

Captain Stack smiled, "Well I hope you caught up on your sleep. Store your gear and report to the fire direction control tent. Sergeant Medford will work you back into the rotation this afternoon."

I tied my shelter half to the splintered stump of a tree and put my gear under it. After checking in with Sergeant Medford, I spent the rest of the morning humping cases of shells from the LZ to the gun crews.

Rail slapped me on the back.

"Welcome home, dude. Koontz picked up another heart while you were gone. They had to send him to Dong Ha and take some shrapnel out of his leg. He's still in the rear. One more heart and he's outta here for good."

The next day we packed up and flew out to a new fire support base. It was just another pin on a map.

* * *

This place is called the Rockpile. It has been raining almost nonstop for three days and nights. Half of Fox battery's six guns were down because of fogged sights, sights that had to be clear in order to accurately shoot. We wouldn't be doing much shooting today. The same monsoon rains slowed down the North Vietnamese too.

The river at our back was flooding. Yesterday a Marine had drowned when a recon team tried to cross the raging waters.

I woke up around 7AM to the sound of rain and wind slapping at my tent.

I rolled over and went back to sleep. I think everybody except the guys on watch slept in that morning. There wasn't a lot to do with three guns down. Finally, the need to piss made me leave a warm blanket. On days like this one you just stood in the door of the tent and stuck your pecker out. I tore open a heat tablet and picked up a mess cup that was filled with rainwater. I had stuck the cup outside the tent the night before. I opened a can of C-rations for breakfast. There are twelve different meals inside a case of C-rations. Eventually you learn to hate them all.

Yesterday a truck had delivered some fresh eggs to the cooks, still-in-the-shell eggs. The next morning Marines got in the chow line early. They were afraid that the precious eggs would run out. They looked heavenly sitting in neat white rows in the corrugated gray box. When I was at Camp Pendleton I used to eat six eggs every morning. Back at Dong Ha, only officers ate fresh eggs while the enlisted men were served powdered eggs that tasted like carpet pile. Most guys believed the rumor about the powdered eggs being laced with saltpeter to keep anyone from having an erection. A lot of uneaten powdered eggs got thrown out every morning. Any eggs served at the Rock Pile would have to be shared with everyone or else the officers ran the risk of facing incoming eggs with fragmentary edges in the middle of the night. This morning the cooks had determined that each man in Fox Battery would get two eggs. I passed the time in line keeping an eye on the cooks and enjoying the delicious smell. Mine were sunny side up and perfect. I stared transfixed as the cook flipped the eggs on to my metal tray.

"Move it!"

Someone behind me yelled as I stared at my beautiful eggs. I looked back over my shoulder, "Sorry boys, but I just got the last two."

I laughed out loud. I was still laughing as shells screamed in and began exploding less than a hundred feet from my precious eggs. The closest trench was over thirty feet away.

Any North Vietnamese Forward Observer looking at us through high powered binoculars must have had a good laugh watching me slipping and sliding as I ran through the mud and stinging rain and exploding shells while doing my best not to spill my beautiful eggs. I made it! Crouched knee deep in cold muddy trench water, I smiled down at my lovely eggs. Other Marines were running towards my trench. Suddenly a huge clump of wet red mud from someone's boot landed in the middle of my tray. I stared in disbelief at my eggs. The bright yellow yolks were smashed and the white outer edges were now orange as muddy red water ran over them in every direction.

"Fuck it!"

I screamed as I stood up and threw the tray as far away as I could.

The guys sharing my trench howled in sadistic laughter as the rain and more NVA shells continued to fall. I never tasted the eggs. It was 7AM and the war had just said, "Good morning." It was the start of one more day in the Nam and I didn't care if I ever saw another egg for the rest of my life.

Little bubbles started to form in the bottom of my tin mess cup. The water was hot enough to add the small packets of C-ration coffee and the sugar and powdered milk. It was a pretty good way to start the day. I thought about yesterday morning. It could have been worse. I could have lost a lot more than a couple of eggs.

"Hey Buddha!" a voice called from outside my tent.

"The Captain wants to see you."

"What the fuck?" I wondered, as I put on my poncho. What could he possibly think of for me to do on a day like this? I put on my helmet and slogged over to the battery headquarters tent.

"Good morning, Buddha!" Captain Cook smiled as I stood at attention in the door of the tent.

"I heard about your eggs. How would you like to have lunch in Dong Ha? While you are at it, you can pick up the mail. Keep your eyes open. Yesterday a duce-and-a-half was ambushed less than a mile from here. Go get your rifle, Marine. Miller's leaving in ten minutes."

I saluted and headed back to my tent. I couldn't believe it. This was the kind of job they usually handed to some kiss ass. Why me? A trip to the rear meant a chance to eat a real meal in a mess hall, a chance to see my old pals from Headquarters Battery. It would also be an opportunity to pick up some more marijuana. Everyone was out. I didn't have much time as I ran around taking orders. Two guys wanted a bottle of the rotgut whiskey the Vietnamese sold anyone crazy enough to buy the stuff. I climbed in the jeep and we headed out the front gate and turned south.

I would much rather be riding in the rear of a large convoy on a sunny day with a couple of big tanks leading the way. A jeep traveling alone down a muddy road through the heavy monsoon rain is what the NVA sees a soft target, an easy way for some green troops to get their first kill. At this stage of the war I wondered how there could be any green NVA troops left. We did our year and went home.

Goodbye, Vietnam! The guys on the other side were in this war for the duration.

I smiled at Captain Cook's advice to "keep your eyes open."

In dry weather you watched for the subtle signs of an ambush or fresh dug dirt that could conceal a land mine. Today, we just stared at the windshield wipers fighting back the rain and hoped for the best. The jeep driver was a guy named Miller. Because of his buck teeth and squinty eyes, he had been called "Mouse" ever since his first day in boot camp.

"Wake me up when we get to Dong Ha."

I dozed off to the hum of the windshield wipers. It seemed I had barely fallen asleep when Mouse announced the front gate of Dong Ha was just ahead. We drove in and headed straight for the mess hall. We were just in time for a hot lunch. The mail could wait. We looked out of place in our scruffy clothes and muddy boots, standing beside guys who took hot showers at night. I picked up a tray and waited. I didn't recognize anyone from my days in Headquarters Battery. I was amused to hear some guys bitching about the food. It looked good to me. Let the bastards try eating dehydrated food and C-rations for a couple of months. After lunch, we picked up the mail and headed back out the gate. The rain continued to fall. About a minute later we saw a young Vietnamese girl waving at us from under a small piece of tin she was using as a roof. We stopped and she ran over to me.

The going rate for a plastic bag of ten machine rolled joints or a bottle of rot gut whiskey was ten bucks. I wasn't going to haggle in the pouring rain. I quickly purchased ten bags of weed and two bottles of booze.

She counted the MPC bills and smiled. I tucked the weed in a dry pocket and we continued our slow journey down a winding river of mud. It was late in the afternoon by the time we got back to the Rock Pile. I hopped out of the jeep and carried the mail over to the headquarters tent. The Captain wasn't around so I headed back to my tent. I had hardly taken off my wet poncho before guys started coming around to pick up the smoke and the rotgut booze. The boys knew this wasn't bonded bourbon and they didn't care. This stuff would eat the bottom out of a Styrofoam cup before you finished your cocktail. That problem was solved by stacking two cups together. The weed was less messy. It was sealed in small bags.

In less than ten minutes, everyone had picked up their contraband. I walked over to Steadman's tent.

"Yo, Buddha!" He smiled as I came in out of the rain. I found a dry place to sit.

"Break out some refreshments."

Steadman smiled, "Where's my manners?"

He pulled out a joint and lit it up. We heated some water for coffee. I smiled at my buddy, "If this rain doesn't let up soon, the whole DMZ is just gonna float on down the Qua Viet River and into the South China Sea."

Steadman was an easygoing Marine from Foxboro, Massachusetts. He was rotating home in September. I walked back to my tent and went to sleep. I woke up around midnight with a flashlight in my face.

"Outside! In formation! Now! Let's go!"

The flashlight stayed on me as I got dressed and stepped outside. I joined the rest of the guys standing at attention in the rain.

A guy in front of me whispered, "I've got a bag of weed in my pocket."

"Toss it down behind you," I whispered softly. Slowly, I ground the bag into the wet mud.

"Stay at attention, Marines!"

One by one, our names were called, and we were marched into our tents and stood at attention in front of our racks.

"Is this your shaving gear?" One by one, each item was acknowledged and then thoroughly searched.

"McLane!"

The Captain only called me Buddha when he was in a good mood. I dropped out of formation and slowly walked to my tent. I stood at attention at the foot of my cot. My mind was racing wildly. I knew I didn't have anything in my gear. Was there a forgotten butt of a joint somewhere that I had over-looked? Piece by piece the gunny searched my stuff.

"Nothing here, Captain."

"Search it again."

This time I started to relax. I even got cocky.

"Is this your gas mask?"

I stared straight ahead at the darkened back of the tent, lit only by flash-lights.

"Is it green?"

"Get outta here!" The Captain yelled.

I walked out of my tent and went back to standing at attention in the rain. After the shake down was over, we were allowed to go back to our tents. I searched in vain for the bag of weed I had ground into the mud. The next morning I found out that three of the Marines I had sold weed to were facing charges for possession of drugs and possible brig time.

Steadman stood at attention in front of Captain Cook.

"I'm very disappointed in you, Marine. Do you have anything to say for yourself?"

"No, sir."

"Look, Corporal, I know you got that shit from McLane. You idiots were set up yesterday. If you agree to testify against McLane, I can promise you that your cooperation will go a long ways towards helping you out of your legal problems. You can probably put this behind you with just a fine. What about it, Marine?"

"Sir, I am afraid I can't help you."

The Captain stared at him in silence for about a minute and told him he could leave.

Steadman walked back to his tent. Steadman and Koontz each lost a stripe and got a fine. Nobody went to jail. We were unhappy about being set up, but there was no finger pointing. Shit happens, and there was nothing anyone could do about it except be more careful. Shakedowns were a part of the game.

I made it a point to never keep any marijuana on me or anywhere near me. The bill of rights didn't exist in Vietnam. You had to rely on your wits to stay one step ahead of these Keystone Cops. Sandbags were my favorite hiding place. To find any contraband of mine, they would have to look under every sandbag in the DMZ. Even if they found a joint under some sandbag, they could never prove it was mine. The good news was there were nine other Marines who didn't get caught. There was plenty of pot and one bottle of unbounded rotgut whiskey still floating around Fox battery.

Fight hard, party hard. Most Marines were responsible about getting stoned. They left the stuff alone until they were off-duty. It was a way to detach from the absurdity of watching your friends get hurt or killed while trying to win an unwinnable war. Under fire, these guys were the coolest customers around. If you didn't like them, you should have joined the Navy. If you wanted to judge them, you better keep the verdict to yourself. This wasn't the rear. You couldn't fuck with people up here for free, not for long. Paybacks were just too easy, easy to do and easy to get away with. Everyone was a team player, whether or not you liked them didn't mater. If they could carry their own weight and be counted on when the shit hit the fan, you didn't give a damn about their personal hobbies. You didn't fuck with them and you didn't want anyone else fucking with them. These were guys you could count on whenever your ass was in a sling. They would be there. Anytime. Every time. Each one of them had his own personality and style. They didn't take shit off of anyone, including officers, not up here.

The main thing they had in common was their courage and their uncanny ability to know when to zig and when to zag when shells were screaming down. These guys had nothing to prove to anyone. What was at the top of their priority list was staying alive and keeping dry. They were still Marines and if some officer gave them a direct order they would follow it no matter how stupid the order appeared to anyone else with a brain, but God help your ass if your bullshit got somebody killed. The scales of justice stayed balanced in a combat zone.

* * *

We are camped out on a hill about two miles from the Laotian border. Last night six C-46 helicopters dropped off the men and guns of Fox battery. This morning we quickly set up the guns and started firing missions. I have been in Vietnam now for eleven months. In less than sixty days I will be going home. No officers want to play bridge today so my time is spent humping boxes of artillery shells and filling sandbags. In the afternoon, the Captain lets me sleep for a couple of hours. I have duty later that night in the FDC center. The Marine Corps likes their Fire Direction Control people awake and alert when they are crunching numbers and shooting fire missions.

I heard the bad news when I woke up. Earlier that afternoon we were shooting a mission for some grunts about three miles away when the radio went silent. Several attempts to contact them failed. About two hours later, another patrol found what was left of them.

Eight Marines were dead, including the forward observer, Lieutenant Doug Paige and his radioman, Lance Corporal John Stall. We went over the log books looking for any sign of a mistake. I didn't understand it. Some thought that Lieutenant Paige made a mistake about where he was on the map and called the lethal rounds by accident. I didn't buy it. Lieutenant Paige was an experienced FO with almost a year in Vietnam. Two days after he was killed, he was supposed to become the new executive officer for Fox battery.

I had shared a bunker with Stall at C-2. The Marine Corps takes friendly fire seriously and even after a big investigation, they still didn't have a clue what went wrong. Lieutenant Chase flew to Dong Ha to identify the bodies.

In October we flew back to the Rock Pile. The North Vietnamese welcomed us back with a fresh volley of hot steel. Rail and I ran inside the FDC bunker just as a piece of shrapnel hit the sandbags behind us and bounced across the bunker floor. Rail picked up the hot metal and tossed it from one hand to the other.

It was a piece of the copper band that went around the tip of each NVA artillery shell. He tossed it on to the map table. More shells continued to explode as Lieutenant Chase examined the copper band.

Koontz ran over to the door of the bunker. He pointed at a duce-and-a-half behind him. "That truck is loaded with cases of white phosphorus! We've got to unload it now!"

Rail and I followed Koontz as he climbed into the back of the truck. We started throwing the gray metal boxes of willie peter over the side of the truck.

Since the shells were well packed, it was safe to toss them directly to the ground. This was supposed to reduce the chance of one of the highly explosive rounds getting hit by a piece of red-hot shrapnel. In less than two minutes the truck was empty and we ran back inside the shelter of the FDC bunker. If shrapnel had hit one of those cases of white phosphorus, there would not have been much left of three Marines.

I had heard that in cases like that, sandbags were added to give some weight to the empty coffins. Thankfully no such sandbags would be needed this time.

"Good job, Marines!" The gunny smiled as he walked by. In the Army, they would have recommended everyone involved for at least a Bronze Star, maybe even a Silver Star. Not in the Marine Corps. That kind of courage was expected of a Marine. No more, no less. Medals were reserved for something the Marines called, "Above and beyond…"

Rail and I walked over to the mess tent for supper. "I'm getting too short for this shit," I said as I dipped my metal tray into a GI can of boiling water. We ate some dehydrated hamburger and instant potatoes. That evening I had duty in the FDC bunker. The night was quiet and we played cards by the light of a lamp as the hours dragged by.

Suddenly a shell slammed into the mud less than twenty feet from the bunker. The sandbag walls of the bunker shook as the heavy shell exploded.

I heard Lieutenant Chase's voice cry out in the darkness. "I want a crater analysis, McLane!"

"You want to ask for a volunteer, sir?"

"No, I want you."

I had four weeks left in Vietnam. There were guys standing around that had only been in country for a couple of months. One of the tricks the NVA liked to pull was to wait five minutes and shoot another shell with the same coordinates. They try to catch some Marines standing around inspecting the first shell.

"Do you mind if I wait a couple of minutes to make sure they've stopped?"

"No! I want it now!"

I knew if I opened my mouth one more time, the bastard would write me up for cowardice. Slowly, I picked up my helmet and a bayonet and crawled on my knees and elbows about twenty feet through the mud to the still smoking shell crater.

I used the bayonet to dig through the hot shrapnel as I searched for the tip located in the very bottom. I gathered the twisted steel in my helmet. Finally, I found the damn fuse. It was made of brass and in perfect condition. There was even a serial number etched on the side. I pushed the helmet in front of me and crawled back inside the bunker. Lieutenant Chase examined the fuse.

"Good job, McLane. This will make a hell of a souvenir."

I could tell that the bastard planned to keep it. "Lieutenant, I was planning to give it to my grandfather."

"You can get another one." He smiled and put the fuse in his pocket.

"Twenty-eight days," I tell myself. "Twenty-eight days and a wake up."

My clothes were covered in mud from the crawl out to the shell crater. I walked over to my tent and put on my only extra pair of jungle utilities.

I went back to the FDC bunker and finished my watch. I kept my mouth shut. I knew Lieutenant Chase was looking for any excuse to write me up. I would not give him one tonight. When my shift ended, I walked back to my tent and went to sleep.

July 1947. My father is holding me, my mother is holding my little sister. Shortly after this photo, we both came down with polio but recovered fully. My brother is between us.

My sister Kathryn and me in Austin. I am 8, she is 7 and taller.

Mother and me. My sister Kathryn is 8 days old.

Robert (3), Roy Joe (10), and Kathryn (2)

Tyler, Texas. Even at 9, I had a lot of attitude.

Tyler, Texas, 1966. High school graduation.

May 1966. Just released from active duty.

New York City at 28.

AP wire photo of me in Washington at VVAW march in 1971.

Singing at Folk City in Greewich Village, 1976.

A Polaroid of me in New York City at 31.

San Antonio in 1983. Tiffany is 4 months old.

Tiffany at 3.

With activist Cindy Sheehan and Phil Donohue at New York City rally in September 2005.

With Martin Sheen in Crawford, Texas in August 2005.

The rug I wove in the Waco VAMC in 1974 where I was hospitalized for 4 months with PTSD.

Sailing off the coast of Mexico during the winter of 2005. My Yelapa neighbor Kat is sitting behind me.

Tun Tavern
November 1968

S hort is a phrase Marines use to describe the lucky bastards who are getting close to returning to "The World." Today I am one of those lucky bastards. I am so short that I have to wait outside the battery shitter until some tall person comes along to give me a boost up! Yes, sweet Jesus, I'm going back to "The World"—so soon I can't stop thinking about it. I know it could still happen. We all had heard stories of someone buying the farm on their last day in the Nam. But I had a good feeling I was going to make it. I like the name of this new fire support base, LZ Tun Tavern.

This little hill somewhere in the DMZ was named after a Marine shrine.

The Corps was actually born in that Philadelphia tavern one night in 1775.

When the original Jarheads met some stout fellow back then who looked like he could hold his own in a good scrap, they invited him over to Tun's Tavern to have a free mug of ale with some of their pals.

This is just another hill, covered with splintered tree trunks and freshly dug holes. Fox Battery's six guns are set up and blazing away across the morning sky. So far, no one has shot back. One night I got a little drunk while I was on duty. Lieutenant Sterling stumbled into the FDC tent carrying a case of hot beer.

"Have a brew, McLane!"

Foolishly, I accepted the offer from my new drinking buddy.

We were supposed to be on duty. Lucky for everyone's ass, including my own, we finished our watch without shooting another mission.

The Captain found out about it the next day. He couldn't write me up without charging the Lieutenant also and he wasn't going to put a bad mark in an officer's record book over a little beer. Once again, I got a pass on any kind of formal punishment. I was exiled from the FDC. The Captain sent me over to Gun Six.

These guys had no use for me. They knew I was leaving Fox battery for good in a couple of days. I would spend my final days in Vietnam just like I spent my first month at Camp Pendleton, laying low and trying my best to be invisible.

After eight months with an active Marine artillery battery, I was amazed how well I could still hear. Some guys had a John Wayne attitude whenever they worked on a gun crew. They thought it looked unmanly to cover their ears whenever the big guns went off. I never had a problem covering mine. These same guys would be asking me to repeat myself whenever I talked to them. Sometimes I spoke even softer just to fuck with their head.

It may have seemed strange to some of the new Marines watching the way I shot a fire mission with the guys on Gun Six, but I didn't give a shit. I discovered a technique that won't be found in any Marine Corps manual. The other boys would hold their shell with their hands as they waited their turn to shove it into the open breech of the 105. After the gunner pulled the lanyard on the big gun, the next Marine stepped up and followed suit. Once, when I was back at C-2, I almost cut off the tips of my fingers when I forgot to make a fist before I slammed the shell into place. At Tun Tavern, I held my hands over my ears while I hopped along in line with my shell held firmly between my legs. Only when I was next to load the cannon, would I hold the shell with my hands. I didn't care about what the rest of the crew thought, I had more time in country than any of them and if my luck held out, I would be the next guy going home. The guys on Gun Six cut me a little slack. They knew I had been assigned to their gun as punishment. Laying low and staying out of the Captain's way turned out to be a fairly easy job. I even slept late in the mornings.

After my last C-ration breakfast, I walked down to a small winding river that ran past the edge of the perimeter. I took out the small acorn that I had picked up from my grandparents' farm back in Texas. The guns of Fox Battery had been silent that morning. I dug a small hole and planted the acorn where I thought it would get lots of sunlight. It felt strange sowing life in a place that had known so much death. Perhaps someday, it would grow into a mighty oak and children might even build a clubhouse high up in the strong limbs, children who might never have to play the game of War.

Suddenly there was a gulf between me and my buddies in Fox Battery. They were staying. I was leaving. I was no longer one of them. Strangely, I felt like I didn't belong here any more. That night I packed my gear for the last time.

The next morning, I walked down to the LZ, ready to climb on the first helicopter that had a reason to land here.

I heard Captain Cook yell, "Fire Mission."

Gun Six sprang into action. Quickly they were loaded and waiting for the Captain to give the order to fire. I left my gear at the LZ and ran over to Gun Six.

The crew chief knew what I wanted, he nodded at the other guys and stepped aside. I picked up the lanyard and waited. When the crew chief got the order to fire, he nodded at me. I quickly cranked off five rounds, one after the other. When I fired the last shell, I pulled the lanyard so hard I broke the rope.

Suddenly, I heard the distant whine of a helicopter approaching. I looked around at the guys on Gun Six.

"Well Gentlemen, it's been a party."

I shook hands with each of them and ran back to the LZ. After the big C-46 dropped off a pallet of fresh artillery shells and a couple of new guys, I ran up the loading ramp and settled in as the big aircraft began to gain altitude. I took one last look back at Fire Support Base Tun Tavern and the men and officers of Fox Battery. It was a bittersweet farewell. I was looking forward to going back to "The World" — but I also knew that I would miss these guys forever. I climbed out of the helicopter at LZ Stud, and I hopped in the back of a duce-and-a-half truck that was headed for Dong Ha.

I could have flown all the way back to the rear, but in spite of the potential for ambushes, snipers, and land mines, I still preferred to take my chances on the ground. Marines in a helicopter with the tail rotor shot off at three thousand feet in the air had no chance of survival. We drove through the gate at Dong Ha around noon. I headed straight for the mess hall and a hot meal. Most of my Headquarters Battery pals had already rotated home. After lunch, I walked over to the supply tent. The sergeant in charge had the nerve to bring up certain items of gear that I had signed for back in the spring when I joined up with Fox Battery, items that were now missing. What was he going to do? Send me back across the DMZ to look for them? The supply sergeant offered a suggestion.

"Go over behind the motor pool and look around."

Scattered in the grass were many of the same items I was missing. I had a list. I didn't have a clue who left these things behind. It was the Marine Corps way of dealing with a bureaucratic snag. I gathered up the canteen covers and other things on my list and walked back over to the supply tent.

I was waiting for the sergeant to come back, when my eyes wandered over to a row of gray metal boxes at the rear of the tent. There were small white labels on the front of the boxes. This was the personal gear of the officers who were out in the bush. One of the labels read, "Lieutenant Chase." I looked outside the front of the tent. There was no one in sight. I walked over and opened the gray box. Inside were personal items, including a brand new pair of spit shined officer's shoes. I felt like Cinderella as I tried one on. It was a perfect fit.

I picked up a blank form on the supply counter and wrote a short thank you note. I put it in the gray box and stashed the shoes under my shirt. I walked over to the tent where I was spending my last night in the DMZ. I cleaned my rifle and turned it in to the armory.

Just like my first day at Dong Ha, all the people who processed me though the paperwork were total strangers. I didn't care. I felt a kind of high you can't get from drugs as I walked around the place for the last time. The next morning I skipped breakfast and caught a ride in a mail jeep out to the small airport.

My eyes scanned the skies for the prop-driven plane that would take me out of here, the same kind of plane that flew supplies into Khe Sanh. Slowly I watched it circle and land. Ten Marines and two Special Forces guys were headed to Da Nang.

The plane was still moving as we scrambled up the loading ramp. In less than a minute we were approaching take off speed. There wasn't a window near my seat and I didn't care. I had seen enough of the DMZ to last a lifetime.

Danang, Vietnam
November 1968

The enlisted men's club started serving beer at noon. After a couple of brews I headed over to the Red Cross center to see some real live American women. They looked like movie stars to my hungry eyes. I tried not to stare. They were used to it.

I walked over to the paymaster and drew a year's back pay. Mercenaries in the Congo were making $8,000 a month fighting Communism in Africa. I was working in the wrong army. I rode a bus over to China Beach and stared at guys riding surfboards. It felt great to use flushing toilets again.

Delta Airlines brought me here a year ago and Delta Airlines would bring me home.

I watched a fork lift carrying a stack of aluminum coffins into the cargo hold below. God rest their souls. I took a window seat and fastened my seatbelt. It seemed forever before we took off. I kept looking out of the window for any sign of incoming until we were finally in the air. Vietnam got smaller and smaller as the big plane climbed into the big clear sky. Once everyone knew we were out of range of every weapon the NVA had, a loud cheer broke out from all of us on board. I started to relax as we began our journey to Okinawa. At Kadena Air Base, I picked up the sea bag I had left behind a year ago and opened it. Inside at the top was a short note I had written to myself.

"See, I told you that you would make it!"

The next morning I flew back to Travis Air Force Base in California. I didn't go anywhere near San Francisco. I wanted to remember Haight-Ashbury the way I left it in the summer of '67.

I hitched a ride on a military plane going to Oklahoma. An Air Force General was kind enough to let me have a seat on his personal jet. First I watched his valet bring his luggage on board, including two sets of golf clubs.

Finally, the man himself walked aboard and sat down on the solitary bed that was waiting for him. He looked at me with the jaundiced eye of some jaded Caesar while an Air Force Staff Sergeant loosened his shoestrings and took off his shoes and put them under the bed. He then pulled the curtains to give the General privacy.

I remembered the night at the Rockpile when Rail and I tried to make a floor out of boards from some ammo crates while the rain poured down through the leaky ponchos we had snapped together in a vain effort to stay dry.

Camp Lejeune
1968

In Oklahoma City I caught a Greyhound Bus to Shreveport, Louisiana. I rang the doorbell and waited. I wanted my mother to see with her own eyes that her son was in one piece. The next day I bought a red MGA and drove to my grandparents' farm. It would cruise at ninety. I crossed the railroad tracks and followed the dirt road to the small white house that held so many of my childhood memories. My grandparents waved to me from the front porch. No one asked me about Vietnam. I was glad I didn't have to talk about it.

After lunch, I took a walk down to the remains of the old tree house I had sat in a year ago. The old oak was alive and well.

The next day I headed for Camp Lejeune. I still had three months left on active duty. I was assigned to an artillery battery that didn't shoot missions. Their main focus was a long running pinochle game. A lot of the guys were Vietnam veterans like me with less than six months left on their time in the Marine Corps.

The Corps was wasting as little time and money on these soon-to-be civilians as possible. The stateside Marines who had never been to Vietnam just shook their heads and left us alone. I ran into Micarelli and Smurf at the PX. We got stoned and went to see a movie at the base theater. Each movie began with the American flag appearing on the screen followed by a tape recording of the national anthem.

A split second before the music started, Rail yelled, "Mein Führer!"

His voice reverberated throughout the crowded theater. Immediately everyone stood up for the national anthem. Some of the lifers looked around and tried to identify the wise ass while the lights began to fade. Rail got away with his little prank.

"Die, Motherfucker!"

I screamed at Scott Camil as I chased him down the middle of the squad bay. The rubber tipped dart was locked and loaded while I did my best to aim the red plastic gun I held at the center of Scott's shoulders as he ducked and ran between the wall lockers and leaped over bunk beds trying to escape. The dart missed by inches and stuck on a wall locker as he turned the corner and ran back up the length of the squad bay while reloading his own blue plastic gun. A couple of young Marines who had just arrived from Pendleton looked at each other and rolled their eyes. They were smart enough to keep their mouths shut. They had correctly assessed the situation the first time they saw the pistol-packing nut jobs with the glazed eyes running amok through the squad bay. They knew that Vietnam vets were crazy as loons. Every one of us was a ticking time bomb, hard wired to go off anytime and anywhere from the slightest provocation. We were men who had lost all use for decorum or manners.

Scott's last shot had also missed. He raced back for the dart stuck on the wall locker at the opposite end of the squad bay. Just as I fired at the center of his back, he snatched an innocent Private into the path of what would have been a clean kill and kept running. Hitting an angry bystander scored no points. Scott grabbed the dart and tried to reload.

I slammed into him and tried to take away his gun as we rolled on the floor. Gypsy Dave walked in. Like most of the guys sleeping in the three-story barracks, Dave had just finished a thirteen-month hitch along the DMZ. He, too, was just killing time until he became a civilian again. He took advantage of his free time by operating a small marijuana dealership. He had the type of knee-high, fringed buckskin boots that Davy Crocket wore at the Alamo. His boots were different from Davy's. His boots were stuffed with nickel envelopes of pot. They made the perfect hiding place. No spit and polish Military Policeman was going to go poking around in Gypsy Dave's smelly boots. They would never tell him to take 'em off. He would deal out the five dollar bags until they were gone and then hitch a ride into Jacksonville and buy some more.

"Hey Dudes! Put the guns away and let's go to town. Lamar says there's a new band coming in and they are hot!"

Scott looked up at Gypsy Dave. "Now, that's the best offer I've had all day."

I looked at Dave's buckskin boots. "Hot band or not, you know those boys will buy a few bags of your North Carolina Wacky Weed."

Gypsy Dave frowned, "How many times I got to tell you, this shit comes from Kentucky!"

I smiled, "Yeah, that's what the pimp you buy it from tells you, pimp's word of honor!"

Scott smiled, "At least we don't have to hitch into town. Sergeant Medford's driving a brand new Buick. He picked it up this afternoon."

We changed into civilian clothes and put away our plastic guns. We walked over to see the new car. I should have guessed Hal would pick the color green. Green had been good to him. At 21, he was one of the youngest Gunnery Sergeants in the Marine Corps. He still had a month to go before going back to New Jersey for good. The Buick looked beautiful to guys who were used to riding in muddy, banged up duce-and-a-half trucks. We cruised past the guards at the front gate and headed for Jacksonville.

Gypsy Dave reached down into one of his boots and pulled out a joint. He fired it up and passed it around. Hal turned on the radio and cranked it up. Vietnam seemed a million miles away. Scott took a hit and looked at me.

"Hey, Buddha! I hear you are leaving for GITMO?"

I laughed, "Hell no, I ain't going to no GITMO! I nipped that shit in the bud." GITMO was the Marine Base at Guantanamo Bay in Cuba. The regiment I was assigned to at Lejeune was going there in January on a twelve week cruise.

They called it a cruise, 'cause you got there by being crammed down in the smelly hold of some rusty old tin can of a ship left over from World War II. They kept you down in there for the two weeks it took for the damn thing to chug along down the Atlantic coast all the way to fucking Cuba. I had been approved for an early discharge in time to enroll for the spring semester at a small university in East Texas.

If I went on that cruise, the Marines would have to fly me back to Lejeune in time for my discharge date. They weren't going to waste their money on a soon-to-be former Lance Corporal. We parked the new car in a small parking lot behind a bar called the Pink Pussycat. They had a house across the street for the band to sleep in.

In the long run, it was cheaper to rent a house than to put a small rock & roll band in a local motel and hope they stayed outta trouble. The old house made a great place to party. Lamar would clue the band members in that

Gypsy Dave and his associates were cool, in spite of their short haircuts. Their common bond was a love for getting high and listening to rock & roll. The new band was setting up when we walked in. Lamar introduced us.

"These are the guys I told you about. Don't let the baby faces and short haircuts fool you. They may be active duty Marines, but they are absolutely the craziest motherfuckers you will ever meet."

Hal brought our new friends a pitcher of beer. The road manager followed Gypsy Dave into the men's room and purchased several bags of pot.

Nacogdoches, Texas
January 1969

I left the Marines on a Friday and enrolled in college the following Monday. First came a mad dash from North Carolina to Nacogdoches, Texas. Stephen F. Austin University was the perfect place to begin my new life as a civilian.

I was trading a world of insanity and combat boots for the sheltered life of study halls and sorority girls, a world of logic and reason and term papers. I signed up for History, Political Science, Creative Writing, German, and Tennis. I rented a small apartment two blocks from a dormitory that was home to eight hundred freshman coeds. A year of celibacy was quickly coming to an end. I immersed myself into the academic life.

Every night the evening news reminded me the war was still going on. I decided to keep a promise I made to myself back in the DMZ. I went to the Dean and asked permission to hold a small peace vigil in front of the student center. He was reluctant but finally agreed. I asked my Political Science Professor and two other students to join me.

The following Monday afternoon, we all stood silently for an hour, holding small signs that just said "Peace," while a couple of hundred pick-up trucks filled with rednecks slowly circled the student center. They screamed insults and threats as they slowly drove by. Peace demonstrations were something that happened in Berkeley or Boston, never in places like Nacogdoches, Texas.

I wore the Marine jungle fatigue shirt that I brought back from Vietnam. Deputies from the Sheriff's department stood by with campus cops in case any fights broke out. Except for the threats and insults, things remained peaceful.

When the hour was up, we took our sign and went home. I doubt if our little demonstration caused the war to end one minute sooner, but I had kept my word. I had stood up in public and protested this stupid war. No one could ever tell me again that, "I didn't know what the hell I was talking about, 'cause I hadn't been over there." I knew that having this peace vigil would make some folks unhappy, but pissing people off had become a way of life for me.

One day I stood in front of my apartment and wondered why several police cars were parked out front. I thought there had been a robbery or someone had committed suicide. I found out they were looking for me. The manager of my small apartment complex had discovered a small bag of pot in a communal refrigerator and called the cops.

I walked in and was promptly arrested. Someone read me my rights while someone else tightened a pair of handcuffs around my wrists. I was placed in the back of a squad car and driven to jail.

After being fingerprinted and photographed, I was put in a cell that would become my home for the next month. My bail was set at ten thousand dollars.

The Sheriff refused to allow me access to my schoolbooks. He said they were, "Communist books." The days turned into weeks as my family tried to raise my bail. One afternoon, they put a guy in the cell next to me. Earlier in the day he had shot and killed his wife. The next morning he was released on fifteen hundred dollars bail.

One day I scratched a freckle on my arm. The freckle moved. A closer study revealed that the freckle had legs.

"Hot Dog!" I called out to the guy in the cell next to me. Charles, "Hot Dog" Holmes was in jail for burglary. "Check this out, man!"

I reached out between the bars and passed a Styrofoam cup over to him. "What are these things?"

Hot Dog looked down into the bottom of the white cup. "Ha, ha, ha, ha, ha. Man, you got crabs!"

"Oh, really? Those are five of the weirdest bugs I ever saw."

Hot Dog studied the small cup. "Five? Man, there's only three crabs in here."

I quietly laughed. "Three? There were five in there when I handed it to you."

Schoolchildren are visiting the jail today. I can hear their voices getting louder as they slowly get closer to my cell door. The deputy is giving them the grand tour.

"Sorry kids," I thought to myself. "There are no elephants or tigers to see in this zoo, just lots of monkeys in all shapes and colors."

I crouched down in the corner at the far end of my cell and stared at the floor. My guests had arrived. I hear them bunching up to stare and wonder at this strange man squatting in the corner. He isn't moving. Is he asleep?

Suddenly the kids screamed and jumped back as I sprang up and ran across the cell. I climb up high on the bars and thrust my hand out as I yelled at the top of my lungs, "Peanuts! I want some peanuts!"

Quickly the deputy herded the howling children out of the cellblock and down the stairs and back to the normal world where men are not caged like animals.

The deputy yells back at me, "The sheriff will hear about this!"

I yell back, "Go ahead and tell him, you little snitch!"

Visiting time at the zoo is over. I sit down on my bunk and close my eyes. I am amazed how quickly my mind can take me out of this dingy cell and transport me anywhere I want to go. I can be sitting on the banks of a rushing river in a South American rain forest or strolling down a crowded avenue in New York City. The choice is all mine. I could stay there as long as I wanted to, as long as I kept wads of tissue in my ears and kept my eyes closed.

Late that night I heard Hot Dog calling out to me. "Say, man! Are you awake?"

"Yeah bro, what's up?"

"Did you know Clarence made bail? He got out about an hour ago."

"Who got him out?"

"Some lawyer named Longdrop."

"Is he any kin to Judge Backroads?"

"Yeah, that's the guy."

I realized that there had been a jailbreak. The cellblock was a quiet as a cemetery. About an hour later I heard the deputy opening the iron door that led downstairs. He quickly discovered the trustee tied up in bed sheets. He ran back to the big iron door and tried to insert a key from his ring of keys. It didn't work.

His hands were shaking as he tried another key. I watched him with a small piece of broken mirror. I laughed out loud and yelled, "The other one!"

Every time he tried a new key, I yelled, "The other one!"

The poor bastard couldn't find the right key to go down stairs and call the sheriff.

"Shut up! Just shut up, McLane!"

He finally found the right key and disappeared. Clarence had already stolen a car and disappeared into the warm summer night. I never saw Clarence again.

A week later my grandfather put up the deed to his farm for my bail.

I went back to school. I had a lot of catching up to do. I was behind in every subject and facing ten years in prison for possession of marijuana. I somehow managed to finish out the semester without flunking any of my courses. Because of my lack of any criminal record and my service in Vietnam, I was placed on probation for ten years.

In the spring of 1971, I got a letter from the Marine Corps. Because of the pot bust, I was facing a court-martial. Even though I was no longer on active duty, I had signed a six year contract. I was still a Marine as far as they were concerned.

This pending military trial turned out to be a blessing in disguise.

I wanted to get the hell out of Texas and move to New York City. I knew my probation officer would never agree to such a move. I made a phone call to the number at the top of the Marine Corps letterhead. I spoke with a Jag Officer concerning my upcoming trial. He informed me that I was allowed to choose the location of the military base for the court-martial.

My face lit up.

"What is the nearest Marine Corps base to New York City?"

"There is a Marine Corps Reserve Center in Garden City, Long Island."

"That is where I want my court-martial. Would you be so kind as to send me a letter informing me of the trial date as soon as possible? Thank you."

The letter arrived in ten days. I went to see my probation officer. He had a small office in the back of the Nacogdoches police department. He looked at the Marine letter. He seemed puzzled.

"Why would the Marines want to court-martial you in Garden City, Long Island?"

I smiled, "I stopped asking why the Marine Corps does things a long time ago."

He still looked puzzled as he typed me a letter giving me permission to travel to New York City.

"I want you to drop me a postcard every month you are in New York and let me know how you are doing. Remember you are still on probation."

"Sir, I will write you on the first of each month. Hopefully, this won't take too long."

A week later I packed a small bag and started hitchhiking to New York City.

New York City, New York
August 1970

I wandered through the streets of Greenwich Village with my sleeping bag and ruck sack on my back. The trip from Texas had taken three days. I had never seen so many bookstores, head shops, and coffee shops crammed into one neighborhood. I noticed a poster on a telephone pole about a peace rally being held next week by something called the Student Mobilization Group. Anyone wanting further information was advised to go by their office at 1501 Fifth Avenue.

I asked a passing hippie how to get to Fifth Avenue.

"Man, you must have just gotten here. Just head up MacDougal Street until you get to Washington Square Park. Cross through the park and you will find Fifth Avenue waiting for you on the other side."

I grinned, "Thanks, man. Have a nice day."

Washington Square Park was filled with hippies and winos sharing the shade from the hot afternoon sun. I headed up Fifth Avenue. After walking about a dozen blocks, I stood in front of a tall old building with a revolving glass door in front.

The letters at the top of the door said, "1501." I stared at a directory in the lobby. The Student Mobilization Group was located on the 14th floor. I crossed the empty lobby and got on the elevator. Finally, I came upon a door that had a large peace symbol painted on it. I wiped the sweat off of my brow and walked inside.

A gray-haired woman looked up from her typewriter and asked, "May I help you?"

I smiled and set down my bags. "My name is Robert. I just got here from Texas. I came to protest the war. Am I at the right place?"

She smiled back. "I am sure you are. We need all the help we can get. My name is Madeline. My son Scott is a Vietnam Vet. I know he would like to meet you. He is down the hall through the last door on the left. Why don't you say hello to him?"

I picked up my bags and headed down the hall. I passed other rooms where folks were sitting around painting anti-war signs and working on new fliers. The last door on the left was open. I walked inside and stood in front of a slim black man.

Once again, I set down my stuff. He wore an afro and a small goatee. The telephone was ringing. He picked up the phone and said, "Vietnam Veterans Against The War."

He listened for a moment and then said, "Please hold." He then turned his head and yelled, "Mike! Line two!"

He then looked at me and asked, "May I help you?"

I smiled at him. "Yeah, I hope you can. I am here to protest the war. Madeline sent me back here to see Scott."

"Well, Scott is in a meeting right now, my name is Al Hubbard. Perhaps I can help you. Are you a Vet?"

I looked around at various anti-war posters on the wall. "I was a Marine in the DMZ. I got home in November, '68. What can I do to help around here?"

Al smiled, "Well, you definitely have come to the right place." He handed me a small clip board. "Why don't you have a seat and fill this out?"

I picked up the clipboard and sat down in an old stuffed chair. I took a pen and started filling in the blanks. There were the usual questions about name and address. Since I didn't have an address, I just put New York City.

There was a space to put who I was with in Vietnam. Another line asked me what kind of job skills I had. I wrote down, "professional agitator." I finished filing out the form and handed it back to Al. He looked it over. He laughed when he read the job skills part. He held out his hand and I shook it.

"Well, Robert, I definitely think we can find a place for you around here."

"Call me Bob."

He looked up to see two guys coming out of a back office. One was tall, with close cropped blonde hair, the other was short with curly black hair and a beard.

Al looked at the tall one. "Scott, your mom sent this person back here to see you." Al handed Scott the clipboard while the guy with the curly hair studied me.

"Hello, my name is Joe Urgo. Where are you from?"

I smiled at him, "I'm just another Marxist ex-Marine from Texas who can't shoot straight. You can call me Bob. "

All my life I had gone by Robert, until the boys in Fox battery had started calling me Buddha. I wanted a new name to go with this grand adventure I was embarking on. I wasn't ready for any wild child hippie name like Dancing Toad or Iron Prod, so I settled for Bob. Scott smiled as he finished reading the clipboard and handed it to Joe.

"Welcome to New York City, Bob. We need all the professional agitators we can get!"

I smiled at Scott. "It's a gift that has been passed down in my family for generations. I got it from my dad. He was a seventh son."

Joe's eyes narrowed. "Besides your gifted tongue, what other skills did you bring with you from Texas?"

I looked at Joe.

"Well, I can drive anything that comes with a steering wheel. I can type about thirty-thirty-five words a minute, if nobody rushes me. I took a lot of journalism courses in college. I can write articles and lay out a newspaper. I can field strip an M-16 or adjust artillery fire. For fun, I sometimes enjoy making people in positions of authority look like the idiots they so often are."

Scott looked at me. "Why are you against the Vietnam War?"

"For thirteen months I watched my brothers-in-arms fighting and dying trying to win an unwinnable war, all because of the stubborn stupidity and overfed ego of a lying, horse-stealing politician from my own home state of Texas, where the bastard often won elections thanks to the swing votes of folks whose home address was the local cemetery. I just spent a year ducking shrapnel in the DMZ while this lying old fart spent the same year giving pretty speeches defending a bunch of drug dealers and pimps in Saigon. He used to sit around in his bathrobe in the middle of the night in the basement of the White House studying a sand castle replica of a place I called home.

I almost got a court-martial last year for putting up a homemade wanted poster about this international outlaw in my tent. Now we got an even bigger liar and crook called Tricky Dick. Lucky for us, he is also more stupid. I got another court-martial coming up in Long Island for possession of pot."

Joe Urgo smiled at me. "You got a place to stay?"

"Nope."

Joe nodded his head. "I'm staying with some folks out in Queens. He's a lawyer, and she works for a publishing company. They told me I could bring anyone over who needed a place to sleep. You can stay there for a while if you like, 'til something better comes along. There's a demonstration today at Foley Square. Would you like to go?"

"Sure," I smiled. "I am new at this protesting business, I could use some field experience."

Joe looked at Al and laughed. "We can always use some more crazy Marines around here."

Joe was Air Force. Scott was Army. At that time, VVAW's membership was in the hundreds. Soon it would be in the thousands.

Joe looked at me. "Are you hungry? Al and I were about to grab a bite. Scott is gonna stay here and answer the phone. There is a little shish-kabob stand around the corner. We don't have time to be sitting around some restaurant. Most of the time we order take out or grab a sandwich somewhere. You can leave your bags here if you like."

I followed Joe and Al down the hall to the elevator. We stood on the corner of 14th street and watched our shish-kabob's sizzling over hot coals while taxis flew by looking for fresh fares. Al was also Air Force. He had been a crew chief on a KC-135. He paid for our food. He picked up an extra shish-kabob for Scott and we headed back upstairs.

These guys worked a six-day week. They had a lot of irons in the fire. They filled me in on current projects as we rode in the elevator. There was going to be a 60 mile march to Valley Forge on Labor Day weekend, led entirely by Vietnam veterans. There was something called guerrilla theater, a life performance by actors where public streets became the stage. For props, a gross (144) of slightly smaller than life, toy M-16's had been ordered from the Mattel Toy Company. The march was being called OPERATION RAW, (rapid American withdrawal). It was a march intended to bring the world's attention to the fact that Vietnam veterans by the thousands were joining the antiwar movement. From now on, antiwar vets would be the tip of that spear. I spent the afternoon stacking fliers, stuffing envelopes, and getting to know these guys.

Joe motioned for me to join him in a small office at the end of the hall. A couple of other guys were sitting around kicking back. A joint was being passed. They talked about the upcoming march to Valley Forge. Joe Urgo tried to stress how important OPERATION RAW would be.

"We are going to be taking the same route George Washington's army traveled over two hundred years ago. We will have media from everywhere, all the networks, radios, newspapers, you name it. They will cover us from the first step to the last."

Scott added, "If we can make a favorable impression on the American people, we will be taking a vital step towards ending this damn war. On the other hand, if we come across as a buncha dope-crazed, wild-eyed crazy Vietnam veterans, we could cause the war to last even longer than if we had all stayed home. We have to think before we act, especially anytime there is a camera or microphone around. "

I looked around. "How do you expect a crowd of long-haired guys in faded jungle fatigues carrying real-looking automatic rifles to look anyway but scary?"

Scott replied, "It's one thing to yell and carry on when we are performing guerilla theater to demonstrate how we searched a village or interrogated prisoners. That doesn't mean that we have to walk around acting like maniacs all the time, now does it?"

Joe passed the joint to me. I took a hit and tried to talk while holding my breath.

"We will always have an image problem. We got a load of squirrelly looking guys out there with hair down to their asses and, yeah, they use a lot of illegal drugs and they have real problems with anyone who is in a position of authority, including us. On the other hand, they are more than ready to join us in a march down any road or highway in America and get in anybody's face to help end this war and they will travel from one end of this country to the other to join us, but right now most of them don't even know we exist."

Al took the joint from me and nodded his head. "OPERATION RAW will change that. Soon, everyone on the planet will know about us, including the guys in Vietnam and the NVA and the VC."

Joe added, "If we just end this war one day earlier, if one less GI comes home in a body bag, it will be worth it. No one wants to be the last American killed in Vietnam."

I looked at Joe. "Everyone knows this war is over and it's high time to get out. The trouble is that we have a President who is living in denial."

Scott laughed, "Well, we are about to give him a reality check. Speaking out like we are against this war will turn brother against brother, father against son, but what is the alternative? To remain silent will only mean more body bags coming home carrying fathers, brothers, and sons."

Joe finished the joint and put the roach in his pocket. We loaded up some shopping bags with fliers and bullhorns and headed downstairs for the subway stop at Union Station. I was amazed how many people could squeeze into each subway car and how quickly we all would be flying down the tracks. We rode for about ten minutes.

The sign on the wall said Foley Square. We got off and headed up the stairs. The demonstration had already started in a small park across from the Federal courthouse. About forty people were chanting slogans and walking around in a circle. Half of them would yell, "What do you want?" The other half would shout, "Peace!" The first half would answer, "When do you want it?" The second half would roar, "Now!" A long row of cops wearing helmets and carrying shields and nightsticks milled around across the street.

Most of the people scurrying out of the huge courthouse hardly noticed the small, but vocal group demonstrating across the street. They tried to hail a taxi or quickly headed for the subway stop. Dozens of fresh demonstrators got off each arriving train and went upstairs to join their friends in the park. The Student Mobilization Group had a permit to have a sound system. There were speeches and more chanting.

Al looked at me and smiled, "Well, Mr. Professional Agitator, it's time to show your stuff." He handed me the bullhorn. I walked up to the top of a small row of concrete steps and faced the crowd.

"Hello, everybody. It's good to see so many people who do care about ending this war. When I was fourteen, I read a book called Exodus. For the first time in my young life, I learned about something called the holocaust. I learned about the death camps and the millions who were murdered there. I asked my parents if these things I was reading about had really happened. I asked them how such things were possible in a civilized world. I wasn't very satisfied with their answers.

"Now, almost ten years later, I am again asking the same questions about another holocaust and once again, I don't like the answers I am getting. Now I am being told to be quiet, while overseas, thousands of bombs are being dropped from planes from my country's Air Force on hundreds of cities and small towns in both North and South Vietnam. Well, I will not be quiet!

These bombings have got to stop! This war has got to stop! Until it ends, these demonstrations will only get bigger…and louder!"

The crowd cheered and applauded while I walked over to Joe and gave him the bullhorn. He smiled and gave me a big hug.

"Well, I guess you are a professional agitator!"

It felt great standing up and saying how I felt about the war and knowing that I was not alone. Night had fallen by the time the demonstration peacefully broke up and everyone headed home to the five different boroughs that make up New York City.

The cops were glad to be going home, too. Some of them shared our subway train as we headed uptown. We dropped the bullhorn and signs off at the office, and Joe and I caught another train to Queens. It was late when we finally got to where we were going. I was happy but tired. First I took a shower. We then shared a small dinner with our hosts. We told them about how well the demonstration had gone.

I lay in the small bed in the basement and thought about my first day in New York City. I woke up the next morning and headed up the stairs. Joe was reading the New York Times. Our friends had already left for work. We headed for the subway entrance. Joe stopped by a small restaurant that had an open window that faced the sidewalk. He leaned his head in and said, "Give me a coffee regular and a bagel with cream cheese."

I had no idea what he was saying, but I said, "Make it two." I discovered on the subway platform what we had ordered. A coffee regular meant coffee with cream and sugar added. I ate my first bagel. We finished our short breakfast as the train pulled into the station.

The subway cars were already filled with people so we rode into Manhattan standing up. Fifteen minutes later we were back at the entrance to 1501 Fifth Avenue. The Student Mobilization Group paid the rent and let VVAW use two small offices in the back. There were two phone lines that never stopped ringing. Some calls were from people wanting to make a donation. Other calls were from more Vietnam vets wanting to join.

I spent the morning answering the telephone and stuffing envelopes. This was boring work for a professional agitator, but work that had to be done.

I was introduced to a tall fellow with an English accent. His name was Mike Oliver. His Irish parents had raised him in England. When he was a teenager, they moved to Philadelphia. In Vietnam, he had been a grunt in the

Army. Soon he would be my best friend. Mike was the level-headed one in this motley crew. Whenever some of the more free-spirited members proposed some wild idea to take over the Pentagon or invade the White House, Mike would be the first one to say, "Now hold on mates, let's talk this over."

Mike was a functional alcoholic. In the afternoon, he would have his first beer of the day. Several more would follow. Even with a good buzz on, his mind stayed focused and sharp. He never slurred his words. His leadership would prove critical in the coming days. One morning a familiar face walked into the office. It was Scott Camil. He had driven up from Florida. He was no longer a sergeant in the Marine Corps.

Now he had a beard and hair down past his shoulders. He wanted to work full time for VVAW. I introduced Scott to a tall, good looking guy in an expensive brown leather jacket named John Kerry. John was the Boston coordinator of VVAW. In recent weeks, the former Navy Lieutenant with a John Lennon haircut had become a familiar face in the New York office. He shook hands with Scott. I smiled at John.

"Scott was in the Navy, too. Just like me, he was in the men's department, also known as the Marine Corps."

John smiled at my friendly jab at the Navy. I continued, "Say John, have you ever been in a chicken wire hotel?"

"No, Bob, I can't say I have."

"Well, I hadn't either, up until last night. I was in the East Village and I didn't want to take the subway all the way to Queens, so I walked over to the Bowery and checked in. The room wasn't much bigger than a broom closet. The walls don't go all the way to the ceiling, so the top is covered with chicken wire to keep my wino neighbors from crawling over and stealing my stuff. At least the sheets were clean. It was a bargain for ten dollars. These are desperate times. It still beat taking the subway all the way to Queens."

John smiled. "I can see I am looking at a desperate man. Coming from the back woods of Texas, your chicken wire hotel must have looked like the Waldorf. You know, I may have to check in myself, just for the experience."

I smiled back, "Just let me make the reservations. I'll book Abbie Hoffman in the room next to yours."

I invited Scott to join me for a shish-kabob lunch. We took the elevator down to the street and walked down to the corner, where my Greek pal had his stand. After stoking the coals, three new skewers of lamb and green pepper were placed over the flames.

"Say, partner, which one of these bobs is mine?"

He pointed at the one on the end. I reached in a side pocket of my jungle shirt and pulled out a small bag of marijuana. I sprinkled a little pot up and down the row of sizzling meat. Instantly the smell of burning weed drifted down Fifth Avenue. I put the pot back in my pocket and smiled at Scott. "Welcome to New York City."

We took our lunch back to the office. As soon as OPERATION RAW was over, we would be moving up the street to a new building on West 23rd Street. We would occupy the entire fifth floor. The night before OPERATION RAW began, I helped load a hundred and forty-four Mattel toy M-16's and our trusty public address system into the back of a Hertz rental truck.

Mike Oliver drilled some holes from the cab of the truck into the back. He then ran some phone wire through the holes so the driver could communicate with the guys illegally riding in the back.

I saw some guy watching us from the shadows near a pay phone. He must have thought he had stumbled onto some kind of paramilitary operation and he was debating whether or not to call the cops. I gave him a hard look and he turned and walked away. In less than thirty minutes, the fully loaded truck was on its way to Morristown, New Jersey. The majority of vets and supporters taking part in OPERATION RAW had left for Morristown before sunrise on chartered buses. By 8 AM they were fully assembled and ready to begin the march. A press conference was held for the assembled media. Al Hubbard spoke.

"Over two hundred years ago, soldiers from the Continental Army marched along this same path to their winter headquarters in Valley Forge, Pennsylvania. The march was long and hard and the men were tired. They were cold and hungry, but they kept going until they reached their objective. Just like those men who went before us so many years ago, we know this march will be a hard one. Just like those soldiers who served under George Washington, we are going to keep going until we reach our objective, to end the Vietnam War!"

The vets standing around clapped and cheered while the cameras rolled and reporters whispered into their hand-held tape recorders.

Just like George Washington's army, these guys were a rag-tag group. Many had long hair and beards. Some were wearing the same faded jungle shirts that they had on when they fought in Vietnam. They wore them as a badge of honor, and it gave them credibility when they expressed their opposition to the war.

Shortly before 9AM they began their journey down Highway 202 for Valley Forge. A state police helicopter hovered overhead. Most of the men carried toy M-16s. Advance people had notified the local cops that we were coming and no one was looking to start any trouble or burn anything down, we just wanted to march through their little town and keep going until we reached Valley Forge.

Cops on motorcycles slowly followed, and we gradually settled in for a long hike. The weather was sunny and hot. Around noon, we stopped for some sandwiches and cold water. Former medics and corpsmen tended to the blisters and sore feet.

I was introduced to a nice couple who had agreed to help us with our guerilla theater. They were Quakers and opposed to the war. They had volunteered to act as Vietnamese civilians. I smiled and said good morning to a slender, meek looking man named John and his wife, Sarah. I explained to them what was about to happen.

"Just remember we are actors giving a performance. We are going to scare the hell out of you, but I promise you won't really be hurt. It's OK to let fear show, but remember this is all pretend, like playing cowboys and Indians when you were a kid. Any questions?"

Sarah spoke up, "I never played cowboys and Indians."

I laughed, "Well, today you two are going to be Indians. Just remember, no one is going to get hurt."

Scott Moore spoke up, "I want to thank you folks for helping us today. Never before have so many veterans joined together to say that a war was wrong while that same war was still going on. You are helping us to make that statement."

Scott's mother gave John and Sarah a ride down the road so that they would be ready and waiting when the cowboys arrived. I joined some guys under a shade tree for a very short nap. In a few minutes the word was passed to "saddle up and move out! One at a time, we got to our feet and started walking down the shoulder of Highway 202.

The stage for our first act of guerilla theater was a quiet cottage on the edge of the next town. The owners of the place were Quakers who agreed to let us use their home. We called the vets who were selected to take part in the guerilla theater our Recon Team. They walked at the head of the march. The media had already been alerted, and they waited with their cameras ready as we approached the small house and went into action. We quickly surrounded the house and yelled for the people inside to come out. John and Sarah stumbled outside with their hands held high.

"Where VC?"

I yelled at John while someone quickly tied his arms behind him. He was told ahead of time not to say anything. Another Vet tied up Sarah and blindfolded her.

Suddenly I reached over and slapped John across the face.

"Where VC? Where VC?"

I could see the fear in his eyes before he, too, was blindfolded. They were quickly led away. This time they were driven to a railway station in the center of town called White Horse. They left their blindfolds and ropes in the car and sat down on a bench and pretended to be waiting for a train. Across the road, a middle-aged woman waited outside for a beauty shop to open. She was shocked to see a long line of shaggy-haired men in jungle fatigues and carrying rifles slowly coming down the street. She didn't know the black weapons were toys. She watched John and Sarah being tied up and blindfolded. Unanswered questions raced through her head.

"What was going on? Had the revolution begun? Is all of New Jersey now in Rebel hands?"

She stood perfectly still and hoped that these wild-eyed hooligans would ignore her and keep walking. Her hopes were dashed when a large black man with a huge Afro stopped and turned towards her. She opened her mouth to scream. Her mouth froze open as he handed her a green flyer. Without saying a word, he smiled and walked away. She looked down at the flyer in her hand and read the following words.

"A United States infantry company has just passed though here. If you had been Vietnamese, we might have burned down your home. We might have shot your dog. We might have shot you. We might have raped the women. We might have turned you over to your government for arrest and torture. We might have taken souvenirs from your home or person. We might have shot things up a bit. We might have done all of these things to you and your whole town. If it doesn't bother you that American soldiers do these things every day to the Vietnamese people simply because they are "gooks," then picture yourself as one of the silent victims. Help us to end the war before Nixon turns your son into a butcher...or a corpse."

The bottom of the flyer said: "Vietnam Veterans Against The War."

Joe Urgo and Al Hubbard and Mike Oliver held a press conference outside the White Horse train station. Once all of the cameras had been set up, Joe began to speak.

"What you have witnessed here today is an example of the way the Vietnamese people are treated every day in Vietnam during so called "search and destroy" missions. This insanity must be stopped! We will keep on organizing marches like this one until it is stopped! This time the people taking part in this march are all men who have been to Vietnam and have seen these kinds of atrocities with their own eyes. Today is only the beginning. We will continue to march until the last American GI has left Vietnam forever. Are there any questions?"

A reporter from the New York Times spoke up. "How do we know you guys are really Vietnam veterans?"

Several men stepped up and took off their shirts to show the scars from shrapnel and gunshot wounds. Others held up DD-214 discharge papers.

A reporter from CBS News asked, "What message are you sending to the active duty GI's who are fighting in Vietnam as we speak?"

Mike Oliver answered, "The message is this: We know better than anyone where you are! We also know the kind of deadly rigged game you are being asked to play along with. Just months ago many of us were fighting right beside you. We have not forgotten you. We have not forgotten our brothers and sisters who we watched lose their arms and legs, and sometimes their lives, trying to win an unwinnable war. We know that back in Vietnam you cannot say out loud what you are really feeling about this debacle.

"We will say it for you and we will scream it from the rooftops and at press conferences like this one until the madness ends! We pray every day for the safe return of all of you. Pray with us for this war to end."

The rest of us listened and cheered as these men spoke for us and tried to explain what we were trying to do. Soon the press conference was over and we began marching again. Up ahead we met more local Quakers and pacifists and took part in more guerilla theater. This time we rounded up three "Viet Cong suspects" who were leaving a post office. We tied them up and interrogated them as some of the startled town folks watched and wondered what the hell was going on.

This time one of the prisoners was Scott's younger teenage brother, Dwight.

After he had been tied up, Bob Hanson handed me a "K-Bar" and I held it against Dwight's throat and screamed, "Which way VC?"

Dwight did as he had been told to do and didn't make a sound.

I slowly ran the tip of the big knife down the middle of Dwight's bare chest while my eyes were locked on his. Hanson forgot to warn me how sharp the blade was.

I didn't notice the thin red line that followed the path of the blade.

Later on some guys thought that maybe I suffered a flashback and perhaps Dwight was lucky he wasn't more seriously hurt. I laughed at that notion. I never for one moment forgot that this was Scott's younger brother and actually hurting him was the farthest thing from my mind. It was just good acting. Dwight's face beamed as he walked around showing off his new, "Combat wound." Nonetheless, we didn't use the "K-bar" for anymore interrogations.

Late that afternoon we crossed the Delaware River into Solebury, Pennsylvania. I had an idea. I knew footage of the march would be on the national news, and I wanted to see it. I looked at my watch. It was 5:40. I walked up to the next farm house we passed and rang the door bell. A middle-aged man answered the door.

"Good evening, sir. I am a Vietnam veteran taking part in a march today to Valley Forge to protest the war. I am sure myself and some of my friends are going to be on the evening news. Would you mind if I came in and watched it with you?"

"Hell yes, I mind! I fought in World War II! I think all of you protesters are a buncha nuts! Now get the hell off of my property!"

I smiled and tipped my boonie hat. "I am sorry you feel that way, sir. Have a nice day."

I turned around and walked away. I tried the same approach on three more houses with almost the same result. It was getting close to six. At the fifth farmhouse, a man smiled and said, "Sure, come on in."

It felt weird sitting in the living room watching TV with a total stranger. We chatted while we waited for the six o'clock news to come on.

"Would you like a glass of water?"

"Sure," I smiled.

He brought me a tall glass.

"My brother is over there with the Air Cavalry. I pray to God that he makes it back in one piece. I think the whole thing is a crock."

"Most of the guys on this march today made it home in one piece. I hope we can end this war soon and bring everybody back, including your brother."

The evening news started and OPERATION RAW was the lead story. I watched footage of me holding the knife against Dwight's chest.

"Wow!" My host looked at the TV and looked back at me.

"Do you mind if we switch over to NBC? I want to see if they are covering this too."

We switched to NBC. I watched film of the guys marching along. The same thing was happening on ABC. The whole country was watching this march into history. I thanked my host and rejoined my friends outside. I walked over to where Al and Scott were leaning against a car listening to the radio.

"Hey guys! Guess what? OPERATION RAW was the lead story on all three networks!"

Scott's eyebrows went up. "How did you hear about that?"

I laughed, "Hear? I not only heard, but I saw! I watched the whole thing on the TV of a guy in that farmhouse behind me!"

Scott shook his head.

"You mean you just walked up and rang the bell and asked if you could come in and watch his television?"

I shook my head.

"Well, the first four houses I asked all told me to go fuck myself. But the fifth said, 'sure, come on in.' You should have been there. We looked great!"

Scott frowned, "You are lucky you didn't get your head blown off. I am starting to think you really are crazy."

I laughed, "Crazy like a fox! Just remember, I saw us on the evening news and you didn't!"

As the sun sank slowly on the New Jersey countryside, we set up camp under a grove of trees on the farm of another Quaker supporter. Some of the guys went for a swim in the Raritan River. I would never have guessed that there were so many Quakers and pacifists in New Jersey. After marching over thirty miles, these guys were hungry. Someone drove up in a rental truck with a hundred and fifty boxes of Kentucky Fried Chicken. They also unloaded several coolers filled with sodas.

Al and Joe nixed the idea of bringing in any beer. There was too much on the line this weekend to take any unnecessary chances. One thing was certain, no patrol in Vietnam ever ate this good. Blankets appeared from the back of another truck and people gathered wood and built small campfires. Once again, the former medics and corpsmen tended to the various blisters and sprained ankles. For the most part, everyone was in good shape.

I grabbed a box of chicken and a soda and joined a circle of guys sitting around a large campfire. Such a fire in Vietnam would have been unthinkable. Hanson was gnawing on a drumstick and rolling a joint with greasy fingers.

I looked around and asked,   "OK, who's got first watch?"

Everyone laughed. It felt great to know we were safely camped on the large farm of a local Quaker who had welcomed us like lost sons. A small breeze carried the smell of burning pot and our circle soon got bigger. Hanson looked at me.

"Today, for the first time, the American people watched a peace march against a war being led entirely by veterans from the same goddamn war!"

I laughed, "You can bet that Tricky Dick was watching too! He knows, just like every other politician, that the end game has begun. It may take another six months, or even a year, but our guys are coming home, every one of them."

Mike Oliver and Joe Urgo walked over and sat down with us.

Mike spoke up. "I have been dreaming about this day since I left Vietnam."

Hanson added, "I just hope that someday my folks will understand why I am doing this."

Joe Urgo looked at Hanson.

"They may never understand or forgive you, but if you hadn't been here today, you might never forgive yourself."

Mike nodded. "Each of us has his own reasons for being on this march. For a lot of us, the reasons are too personal to even talk about. We have zipped up our brother's still warm bodies into rubber bags, and we haven't stopped asking why they had to die, or what the fuck we were doing there in the first place."

Joe looked around and nodded his head. "One thing is for certain. VVAW is about to take the anti-war movement to a whole other level. In the spring, we are all going down to Washington, DC, and meet face to face with some of the lying politicians who started this war."

Hanson finished his chicken leg and rolled another joint. "This weekend there are less than two hundred of us. In DC, I bet there will be thousands."

Joe smiled, "Where will we all sleep?"

Mike laughed, "Anywhere we want to!"

The first day of OPERATION RAW came to an end. We began the next morning studying a Pennsylvania map while drinking instant coffee in Styrofoam cups. We still had a long way to go. Someone brought over copies of the morning newspapers. There was a photo of me interrogating one of the "prisoners."

At 8:45 AM we moved out and started walking towards Valley Forge. We didn't get there until the next afternoon. We were joined by vets who had seen us the night before on the evening news and left the local Veterans Hospital AMA (against medical advice) to be with us for the final day.

As we walked down a gentle slope into Valley Forge, vets chanted, "Peace!"

Other vets shouted in answer, "Now!"

We formed ranks and stood at attention as we sang a line over and over from a John Lennon song: "All we are saying…is give Peace a chance."

Finally we stood for a moment of silence. On command, we broke the toy M-16's in half. OPERATION RAW was over.

* * *

A week after we got back to New York City we still had the rental truck. Now it was parked in a loading zone in front of 1501 Fifth Avenue. VVAW was moving. From the two small offices in the back of the Student Mobilization Group we were headed to a new location on West 23rd street. It only took half a day to move everything we had.

Scott came up to me and asked me to go with him. I followed him down the hall and into an empty office. Joe Urgo and Al Hubbard were sitting on the only chairs. Joe looked at me.

"Well Bob, how do you like our new digs?"

I smiled and looked around. "This is great. I can't believe we have the whole floor. Do we really need all this space?"

Al smiled. "We're gonna need it alright. Things are happening fast. Now, instead of two phone lines, we're gonna have five and every one of them is going to be ringing off the wall. Every one of us is going to be working our ass off from now on and that includes you. That's why we are having this little meeting."

I looked at Al. "What do you want me to do?"

Scott spoke up. "We have just had a discussion about that very question. We are starting our own newspaper. We want you to be the editor. You will have total control of content and layout. We want you to have the first edition ready for publication in less than a month. There will be stories about VVAW from all over the country, even stories from our members on active duty. You are going to be on the national staff. You will have a salary of fifty dollars a week and an expense account that you will turn in receipts for at the end of each month. Putting out a newspaper is a big job so you will get the biggest office. Danny Friedman also has some journalism experience so he is going to be your assistant. From time to time we may ask you to speak at a fund raiser or a demonstration. You brought a lot of different skills with you from Texas and we intend to use each and every one of them. We'll shut this thing down and go home when the war is over."

Joe looked at me. "This is why you came all the way to New York City, isn't it?"

Al joined in. "Well, Bob, are you going to accept our offer?"

I looked around and smiled. "I don't have a car, so I won't need a parking space. You got things to do and I got a newspaper to put out."

Joe walked me further down the hall, and we turned into a large empty room.

I looked around. The place was huge. There was even a small room in the rear. There was only one small desk in the corner. A guy from the phone company was installing phone lines, at least I hoped he was from the phone company.

Joe smiled. "You are going to need several desks to put out a newspaper. They will be arriving in a day or two. In the meantime, you can use the one desk that is here. Now tell me what you need."

I looked at Joe and laughed. "Well to start with, I need a shit load of office supplies, pens, pencils, legal pads, typing paper, rubber bands, and paper clips. I will need at least two typewriters."

Joe nodded his head. "What else?"

I looked around as I thought long and hard. There was so much to do. I picked up a small pad and started taking some notes. Suddenly my face lit up.

"Articles! I need every one of you guys to write articles and turn them in to me as soon as possible. Write about why you joined VVAW, what it felt like to take part in OPERATION RAW, or a dozen other things. Don't get mad if I don't like them and ask you to do them over. Each month we will take the best stories we got and turn out the most ass-kicking newspaper the anti-war movement has ever seen."

Joe said, "OK. We will all write articles. Now what else do you need?"

I inspected the small office in the back. It was perfect.

"I waste too much time riding back and forth from Queens on the subway every day. I am going to start sleeping in this back room. That way I can be here all the time."

Joe agreed. "That is an excellent idea. Find a chair to go with that desk and get to work. I got things to do. We will have another meeting first thing in the morning."

The following month, twenty-five thousand copies of "The First Casualty" were printed and mailed out to VVAW members all over the world.

* * *

Daylight was fading as I walked down Fifth Avenue and approached 13th Street. Halfway down the block, I saw Abbie Hoffman coming towards me.

I had read in the paper that Abbie was doing research on STEAL THIS BOOK, a working manual for urban guerillas actively plotting to overthrow the government.

I called him on the phone.

"Hey man, I got a great idea for your book, but I can't talk about it over the phone."

He agreed to meet me in front of the deli around the corner from his apartment. As he stopped in front of me, I cupped my hands in front of my mouth.

"How about a CO2 pistol that shoots hits of LSD?"

Abbie's face broke into a big smile. "Wow! That is a great idea! How do you know it will work?"

I kept my hands cupped around my face as I replied. "Of course it will work. You know how small a hit of Orange Sunshine is? That's the perfect size to fit inside the barrel of a CO2 pistol."

Abbie's eyes narrowed. "That would be the perfect weapon to use on some cop who's busting some kid's head at a demonstration."

I nodded my head. "Or a Mayor, or a Senator, or maybe even a President."

Abbie grinned. "Thanks Bob, this is definitely going in the book. When it gets published, be sure and call me for some free copies."

I left Abbie buying Yoo-hoo chocolate drinks and headed back up 5th Avenue.

Washington, D.C.
April 1971

Dewey Canyon III began with a trickle and soon turned into a flood. Ranger Benefield watched the scraggly-looking men getting out of a VW bus, slowly looking around. They began unloading tents, sleeping bags, blankets, and ice chests. The bus drove away. Ranger Benefield approached a short, bearded guy wearing jungle fatigues.

"I hope you fellows aren't planning on camping here. That's not permitted on park grounds."

Joe Urgo looked up at the tall young man in the immaculate gray uniform and the brown Smokey-the-Bear hat.

"Your captain didn't give you the word? We have a special permit that was just granted by the 12th District Federal Court. That's the one that represents the District of Columbia."

The park ranger looked down at Joe Urgo.

"I didn't hear anything about a special permit. You guys are gonna have to pack that stuff up and take it all out of here."

Joe pointed over at a flatbed truck loaded with portable toilets.

"Now who do you suppose all those out houses are for? By dark, there will be hundreds of Vietnam veterans here and they are planning on camping here for the entire week. Let's not get off on the wrong foot. We aren't going to damage any property and we aren't looking to start any trouble. Our only fight is with those politicians up on the hill."

Ranger Benefield was beginning to get nervous. More VW buses and old cars were stopping and dozens of other guys with long hair and beards were getting out and unloading more sleeping bags and tents. He called his captain on his two-way radio.

Joe walked over and said hello to the guy with the truck load of portable toilets.

He looked Joe over. "My boss says to get a five hundred dollar deposit in cash before I start unloading anything."

Joe smiled and reached into his breast pocket and peeled off five brand new hundred dollar bills.

"I hope you have some advice about where to put them, preferably downwind."

The truck driver nodded.

"At most parades and festivals we usually unload them on the southeast corner of the mall."

Joe smiled. "Sounds good to me."

More vets were unloading tents and coolers and moving them into the shade of the trees. The captain told Ranger Benefield that he didn't know anything about any permit. By now, over a hundred vets had made themselves at home.

Over a dozen tents had gone up by the time the park ranger captain had arrived in a golf cart.

"Who's in charge here, Benefield?"

Ranger Benefield pointed at Joe Urgo. He walked over to Joe.

"You know there is a federal injunction against you and your group camping here. I have a copy of it with me. Captain Shepherd was prepared. He handed Joe a copy of the court order that President Nixon's attorney had obtained on Friday. Joe began to look over the lengthy document.

Mike Oliver looked at Captain Shepherd.

"Did you get our letter? We sent one to the park rangers, the Capitol Police, and every police chief in the district letting you know that we were coming. Like we said in the letter, our fight is with those fools on the hill. We're not here to blow anything up or burn anything down. We will be camping here through Sunday. We aren't looking for trouble, but if your men or anyone else comes busting in here looking for trouble, they will find more than they ever dreamed possible."

Suddenly Joe began reading in a loud voice. "It says here that between 4:30 PM and 9:30 AM that we are prohibited from sleeping, lying in or under any bedrolls or blankets, making any fires, or erecting any kind of shelters other than medical tents."

Joe looked at Mike Oliver. "Are all the medical tents up?"

Mike didn't miss a beat. "Not yet. Remember, we have more medical tents on the way. We will put them up as soon as they arrive."

Joe smiled at Captain Shepherd. "I guess we will have to pass out a lot of coffee tonight. We wouldn't want to break the law. A lot of these men are on medication they get from the VA to keep them calm. If they aren't allowed to sleep tonight, they might get a little rowdy. Thank goodness we will have plenty of medical tents available, if they do." Al and Mike walked away. As soon as they were out of ear shot, Mike whispered to Al. "Pass the word that every tent is to be designated as a medical tent. Send someone to buy some red magic markers so we can put red crosses on all of them."

Joe extended his hand to both of the park rangers.

"I want to thank you in advance for your cooperation. Don't worry fellas, most of these men are combat vets, they know all about staying awake through the night."

He left the two park rangers standing at the edge of the mall and walked into what was quickly becoming a VVAW campground. He walked over to where Al and Mike were standing.

"Tell everyone to get some Z's as soon as possible. From 4:30 on, we all have to stay awake."

Mike smiled at Joe.

"Do you really think any of those park rangers are gonna walk in here in the middle of the night and check to see if anyone is sleeping?"

Joe shook his head. "We'll have a perimeter guard awake in case you are wrong."

By nightfall, every tent had a red cross painted on it. The park rangers set up a command post across the street and kept their distance. Music blasted from radios as guys ran into comrades they hadn't seen since they left Vietnam. Small campfires sprang up as the night got colder.

The Air Cavalry, the 101st and the 82nd Airborne settled into one area. The Marines made camp in another. The pungent smell of burning marijuana drifted through the air. By midnight, over a thousand vets had showed up and moved in. The idea of being busted for sleeping was a joke. Most guys were too excited to think about sleeping.

They were keeping a promise they made to themselves back in the Mekong Delta or the DMZ. They were here to protest this war. Tomorrow they would track down some of the politicians who started it. Their message would be up close and personal. I sat down beside Mike Oliver and some other vets who were sharing a small fire. A bottle of wine and a couple of joints were being passed around.

I looked up to see a bald-headed man in a suit and tie walking towards us. I realized he was Ed Koch, the Democratic Congressman from New York City. He was one of the good guys. His opposition to the Vietnam War was well known. He accepted our offer to join us. As he sat down, the vet sitting beside Koch passed him the bottle of wine. He took the bottle and turned it up and took a long swig.

I nudged the guy beside me. "Take a good look. It's not every day you see a United States Congressman drinking wine from a bottle in a paper bag."

Koch looked around and quietly spoke. "The hardest thing we have to do is to get the folks in the heartland to understand that this war is never going to end until we get out. You are the people who have a chance to bring that message home. You were there. No one can tell you that you don't know what you are talking about. You have to tell everyone and anyone who will listen that this war must stop. I will help you in any way that I can. Together, we have a chance to end this war, once and for all. "Anything you need, just come by my office and let me know."

A Marine with hair down to his shoulders spoke up. "Give us a list of the war lovers. We're gonna give these dickheads a visit tomorrow."

Mike Oliver spoke up. "We've already got our list boys, and in the morning, each of you will get a copy. In the next five days we are going to visit every one of them."

Congressman Koch stood up and dusted off the seat of his pants. "Well men, I just wanted to stop by and welcome you to your nation's Capitol and thank you for the valuable part each of you is playing to help end this damn war. I have a committee meeting in the morning so I better go home and get some sleep."

Mike Oliver spoke up. "Tell those park rangers across the street that we are all wide awake. They said that we can't sleep here tonight."

Congressman Koch disappeared into the dark night. One by one, we drifted off to sleep as the campfire slowly turned to coals.

I awoke the next morning to the smell of a pot of coffee boiling on a Coleman stove. It was a big pot and several vets were milling around waiting for a cup. A guy with an Air Cav patch on his arm walked by, passing out a piece of paper. It had been prepared back in New York by Scott Moore. There was a list of "do's and don'ts" to follow if you wanted to stay out of jail. There was the phone number of a local lawyer to call if you screwed up the "do's and don'ts." On the second page was a list of Congressmen and Senators and the location of their offices.

I stood in line to have my face painted into a bone white death's mask, with black eyes. I wanted to look like some guy who had escaped from a freshly dug grave at Arlington Cemetery who was looking for the assholes who sent him off to war in the first place.

I joined some other vets headed up to the hill. The receptionist for Senator Bentsen didn't seem all that shocked when twelve scraggly guys in faded jungle fatigues strolled in and asked to see the Senator. She had seen it all before. Every week some new circus rolled into town beating their drums and blowing their horns for this bill or against that bill. We were just the new flavor of the month. She smiled and called the Senator to let him know he had guests. He walked out and invited us into his spacious office. There were plenty of couches and stuffed chairs.

Senator Bentsen looked sharp in his long sleeved pressed shirt and silk tie. He walked around shaking hands. I stared at his open hand and then looked up at him. My hands remained at my side.

After an awkward moment, he spoke. "Well, I guess it's not your custom to shake hands."

I shot back. "Not with everyone."

Senator Bentsen fumed. "Well, this is a fine thing, when someone won't even shake your hand."

Some of the vets who were hoping to win the Senator over to their point of view were glaring at me. One of them asked, "Are you sure you're from Texas?"

I reached in my breast pocket and showed them my DD-214. It listed my home address as Tyler, Texas.

Senator Bentsen spoke up in a loud voice. "I want each of you fellows to know how much I appreciate your honorable service to your country in Vietnam and I too, look forward to the day when all of the boys can come back home. I want you to know that getting out of Vietnam is one of our highest priorities and your government is moving in that direction as quickly as possible."

John Kniffin's eyes narrowed. "We need to get out of Vietnam now, Senator. No one wants to be the last guy to die in a war that's already lost."

Senator Bentsen looked at John. "The withdrawal has to be orderly. Otherwise, even more Americans will be lost. We also need assurances about all of our POW's."

John replied, "Every week we are still in Vietnam there will be more body bags and more POW's."

Someone brought up our overcrowded veteran's hospitals. The Senator replied that this was a grave concern to him and he would look into it. He politely expressed his interests in every issue we tried to raise. He gave this little speech every week to a new audience of believers. After a few minutes, he looked at his watch.

"If you fellows will excuse me, I have an important committee meeting this morning. I want to thank you for taking the time to see me this morning and again, let me say that I share your concerns about getting the rest of our troops out of Vietnam as soon as possible. Please let me know if there is anything I can do for you while you are visiting your Capitol. If I can be of any help in the future, please drop me a line."

He nodded to an aide who quickly opened a side door. In a couple of minutes we were standing on the grass outside of the building wondering what to do next.

Another Marine from Texas looked at me. "Why did you have to be such a rude asshole? We need guys like him on our side."

I smiled. "Bentsen is a gas and oil man. The people that put him in office have made billions selling Uncle Sam jet fuel and diesel. They are going to keep milking that cash cow 'til the day we leave Saigon. Bentsen may pretend he wants to stop the war and help vets, but don't forget—he's a gas and oil man and his ass is in their pocket."

Another group of vets walked past us. One of them called out, "Were any of you guys Marines?"

Several of us raised our hands.

"The Commandant of the Marine Corps is testifying this morning at a congressional committee meeting. We're gonna go over there and ask him a few questions. Care to join us?"

First, we had to stand in line and go through a metal detector at the entrance.

As I got closer to the front of the line, I noticed the Capitol cops were patting down anyone in jungle fatigues. Suddenly I remembered an ounce of weed I had in one of my side pockets. It was too late to get out of the line. I only had a couple of minutes to figure a way out of a looming arrest. I got an idea. When it was my turn to be frisked, I did my best imitation of Mae West. In a sultry voice I purred,

"You wanna search me, big boy?"

The cop stiffened with a look of revulsion as he waved me past without even touching my arm. I pranced past the cop with my ounce of weed undisturbed and headed to see the Commandant, Leonard Chapman.

The large committee room was packed. About eighty former Marines had gotten there in time to get a seat. Another twenty were standing in the back.

The Commandant looked splendid in his dress uniform as he sat erect and alone at a large table. He patiently explained to the skeptical Congressmen why the Marine Corps needed another general on the payroll. A row of four silver stars sparkled on each shoulder.

Other than some soft grumbling, the former Marines were behaving themselves. The Commandant's testimony came to an end. I knew that once the chairman of the committee adjourned the meeting, all of Roberts Rules of Order went out the window. As soon as he banged his gavel, I was on my feet and walking past the Capitol cops to the large table where the Commandant was rapidly stuffing papers into a briefcase. He was well aware of the former Marines with long hair and dirty fatigues sitting behind him, and he was hoping to quickly slip out through a side door. That hope was dashed when I walked over and stood beside him. He tried to ignore me as he fumbled with the clasp on his briefcase.

I slowly reached out and held the small handful of ribbons I had acquired while on active duty under his nose. He looked at the tiny bits of colored cloths in my hand and froze. In an instant, I slammed the ribbons down hard on the polished table. They bounced off the shiny surface and on to the floor. I yelled in his ear.

"I've had it with all officers, especially generals like you! You're nothing but a punk with stars!"

I was ready to get into a fistfight. I waited for him to swing first. I wasn't expecting what happened next. He straightened up and his hand flew to his throat. He face turned white and when he looked at me, I could see fear in his eyes.

Suddenly, I felt like some street thug mugging an old man for his Social Security check. I felt terrible. I spun around walked away. I left the general standing there fumbling with his briefcase. I walked back and joined my fellow former Marines who had been watching me harassing their former commandant. Bobby Dunn gave me a bear hug. We left the room and headed back out into the hall. It was almost lunchtime.

Someone said there was a cafeteria in the basement. We crammed into an elevator and headed down. I had an idea. "Well, I hope you boys are hungry. Senator Bentsen told me that lunch today was on him. Eat anything you want, boys. The Senator is picking up the tab."

We got in line and loaded up our trays. I smiled at the cashier, "We just left Senator Bentsen's office. He will be joining us for lunch.

He asked me to tell you to keep the checks of all of the Vietnam veterans and as soon as he gets here, he will put them all on his tab. He will be down to join us as soon as he gets off of the telephone."

She stared at me in silence. I kept smiling.

"Remember to hold the checks of all the vets in line here for Senator Bentsen and tell him we are holding a seat for him at our table. Thanks!"

I picked up my tray and walked away. The other guys took my cue and followed me. As they sat down around me, I looked up. The cashier was talking to someone on the telephone.

"Boys, I don't know how long it will be before they wise up. We've got to eat fast and get the hell out of here!"

We quickly stuffed ourselves and headed out of the door. As we stood in the hall, the elevator opened. It was filled with Capitol cops. No one said a word.

They filed out and headed into the cafeteria. We got on the same elevator and took it to the first floor and left the building. I never got the chance to thank Senator Bentsen for our lunch. We headed back down the hill to our campground.

A large meeting was already in progress. John Kerry was standing on a makeshift stage and addressing the crowd. John had joined VVAW several months ago and was a regular at our 23rd street office. In the years ahead, he would become the junior Senator from Massachusetts and a Presidential Candidate. Today, he was just another long-haired vet in a faded fatigue shirt.

"On Friday, President Nixon sent some of his attorneys to see Judge Hart over at the U.S. District Court. They went back to the White House with an injunction that said that we can't sleep here on the mall. Well, we got our own attorney, former Attorney General Ramsey Clark. This morning Ramsey Clark filed a brief with the Washington District Court of Appeals. The judges have voted to lift the injunction."

Kerry waited for the cheering to die down and then he continued speaking. "The Court of Appeals ruled that as veterans, we ought to enjoy the same rights and privileges as the boy scouts who were granted permission last year to camp on these very same grounds. The judges asked that we provide our own sanitary facilities and clean up after ourselves. We aren't supposed to dig any holes or start any fires. We are complying with their demands. President Nixon is still trying to get our asses kicked out of here.

"Yesterday, he sent his lawyers with an emergency petition to Chief Justice Warren Berger asking that the ruling of the Court of Appeals be overturned. Now, Justice Berger has granted the petition. Ramsey Clark requested that the entire Supreme Court be polled regarding Justice Berger's ruling. With the exception of Justice Douglas, they all agreed with Justice Berger. This morning, we have been told, in no uncertain terms, that we will not be allowed to camp here tonight."

The chant began slowly and soon swelled into a roar.

"Hell no, we won't go!"

Next, Ramsey Clark addressed the crowd.

"The Supreme Court has voted that you can't sleep here. The Justice Department has declared that if you do, all of you are subject to arrest. I would ask you to honor the Supreme Court's ruling."

John Kerry spoke again. He agreed with Clark. He urged the crowd to comply. Al Hubbard walked to the stage. He spoke in favor of moving.

"The whole world is watching what we are doing here. Last night Walter Cronkite began the evening news with a story about our little campground. We cannot let ourselves turn into a lawless mob. The Washington National Cathedral has offered to let us use their courtyard for a campground. I propose that we move over there and not defy the Supreme Court."

Mike Oliver got up on the stage and addressed the crowd. He was pissed and it showed.

"Fuck that! We're gonna sleep right here tonight. If we have to go to jail, we'll all go to jail!"

The crowd of veterans roared their approval. John Kerry tried to change their minds.

"That is exactly the kind of confrontational tactics that can destroy everything we are trying to accomplish here this week."

Mike Oliver responded, "I came down here to raise some hell with Nixon and the lying politicians who want to keep this fucking war going on forever, and if I have to go to jail to do that, so be it! Each vet has to make up his own mind. For me, the choice is easy. Jail doesn't scare me. At least I'll have a bed to sleep on, instead of this hard ground."

Sam Schor and his band of California crazies had been going nonstop for three days. When he tried to address the crowd, Joe Urgo tried to stop him.

He glared at Joe. "If you don't allow me to speak, our guys are gonna break away from VVAW for good."

Joe looked at Al Hubbard. Al rolled his eyes. Joe stepped back and Sam moved to the podium and began to speak.

"Listen up, brothers! We all got on the plane and went over and fought in their damn war! We slept in mud and lived on C-rations for months at time! If anybody in America has earned the right to sleep on this ground, it's us! If we have to go to jail for exercising that right, then, goddamn it, we'll go to jail!"

It was decided to vote on staying or leaving. The vets voted by state caucuses. California voted thirty-nine to one to sleep on the mall and damn the Supreme Court. Some states voted to leave peacefully. The final count was going to be close. I voted with the Texas vets to stay and go to jail if we had to.

The official vote was 480 to stay and 410 to go. The crowd roared their approval. A motion to make the decision unanimous quickly passed. Mike Oliver spoke again.

"Listen up, brothers! Many of the cops here in DC are Vietnam veterans just like us. They won't be coming in here tonight to bust our heads. If we do have to go to jail tonight, we will go peacefully. If any undercover federal agent here tries to start a fight, I will personally kick his ass! We had a good day today up on the hill talking to these politicians about ending this fucking war. I suggest we get some sleep and get ready for an even bigger day tomorrow! Now this meeting is adjourned!"

As night fell, a steady rain began falling. Vets without tents broke out ponchos and shelter halves and did their best to stay dry. Around 10PM we got the word that no police would be coming to arrest anyone tonight.

The good news quickly spread across the campground. Joints and bottles of wine were being passed around as vets shared the warmth of small campfires.

Again, a few sympathetic Congressmen slipped in after darkness and showed their support for these tired and dirty veterans. Around eleven, the cast of the musical Hair came in and treated the boys to an impromptu USO show. Shortly after midnight, Senator Ted Kennedy walked in alone and sat down on the wet ground and listened and talked with a small group of vets. Reporters from various newspapers wandered around interviewing vets about why they were opposed to the war and jotting down quotes in their notepads.

John Kerry did not sleep on the mall that night. Earlier, he had gotten a message that Senator William Fullbright wanted him to address the Senate Foreign Relations Committee the following morning. He worked alone in a local hotel until almost dawn, organizing his thoughts into words that could hasten the end of the war. The park rangers sat in their command post across the street and monitored their radios. One by one the campfires went out, and the campground was swallowed up in darkness.

The morning headline of the Washington Post said it all:
VETS OVERRULE SUPREME COURT!

The park rangers made the decision before dark not to enforce the injunction. No one had gone to jail. At the campground, vets toasted the headlines with their morning coffee.

United States District Court Judge George L. Hart was not amused. He sent for Nixon's lawyers to find out why the injunction had not been enforced.

Nixon had breakfast with the Attorney General and the Deputy Attorney General to discuss the situation. In a couple of years, both of these guys would be in a Federal prison because of their involvement with the Watergate break-in and the cover-up.

After breakfast, John Mitchell sent the Chief of the Justice Department's Civil Rights Division, L. Patrick Gray, to explain to Judge Hart that since the Vietnam Veterans Against the War had been peaceful, the Justice Department decided to request that the court dissolve the injunction.

Judge Hart was livid. He was outraged to see his court manipulated in such an outrageous manner. These anti-war vets had made Nixon and the

Supreme Court look like fools on the front page of every major newspaper in America.

L. Patrick Gray put his tail between his legs and headed back over to the Justice Department.

The VVAW leadership decided to hold off on any other major actions until after John Kerry addressed the Senate Foreign Relations Committee. They wanted the national spotlight today to be focused solely on the message of this rising star of the anti-war movement.

Sam Schor and Barry Romo had other ideas. They wanted to rub last night's victory in the faces of the Supreme Court.

They gathered about 150 vets and headed over to the Supreme Court Building to do just that. They were dismayed to find the doors locked. They locked arms and began leading anti-war chants, some of them filled with the kind of words that once got Lenny Bruce arrested. They kicked their legs as they chanted. They looked like a rag-tag male version of the Rockettes as the network cameras captured it all for the evening news.

Finally the Supreme Court police had enough. They told the vets to leave. The vets promptly sat down. The city police were called and began making arrests. They were charged with a federal violation, obstructing the administration of justice. The vets clasped their hands behind their heads like POW's and walked onto buses that were waiting to take them to jail. Police Chief Jerry Wilson called them a "very cooperative group." He ordered his men not to arrest any vets in wheelchairs. That pissed off Bill Wyman and William Henschel, two vets who lost their legs in Vietnam and wanted to join the others on their way to jail.

Bail for a federal charge like this one was five hundred dollars. Each vet was facing a year in jail. VVAW was not prepared to post the $50,000 needed for bail.

Richard Nixon didn't like the idea of more negative headlines and ordered John Mitchell to reduce the bail to ten dollars for each vet. In a couple of hours, all of the arrested vets were back on the street.

Meanwhile, John Kerry was addressing The Senate Foreign Relations Committee. It was time for America to face the ugly truth about the Vietnam War, and John Forbes Kerry would show it to them in living color. He told the assembled Senators that America had created a monster in Vietnam, a monster with an insatiable appetite for death and destruction.

Thousands of America's sons were being killed or horribly wounded every month and millions of tons of bombs were continuing to fall, yet still the end of this madness was nowhere in sight. There was no light at the end of any goddamn tunnel. Kerry spoke of the insanity of America asking her best and bravest young men to die for "the biggest nothing in history."

Somehow he found the words to express the anger and outrage that was in the heart of every Vietnam veteran who had traveled that week to protest in Washington, D.C. He spoke of the irony of Vietnam veterans who had faced going to jail the night before, just for daring to sleep on some open ground that Richard Nixon had declared private property. Finally, he asked the sitting Senators a question that shook them to their core:

"How do you ask a man to be the last man to die in Vietnam? How do you ask a man to be the last man to die for a mistake?"

Kerry ended his speech on an up note. He turned and asked his fellow veterans to "...continue the struggle to pacify our own hearts, to conquer the hate and fear that have driven this country for the last ten years and more."

Kerry spoke of Dewey Canyon III as a turning point, "In thirty years from now, when our brothers go down the street without a leg, without an arm, or a face, and small boys ask why, we will be able to say 'Vietnam' and not mean a desert, not a filthy obscene memory, but mean instead, the place where America finally turned and where soldiers like us helped in the turning."

Senator Stuart Symington asked Kerry when he was finished to move his microphone so he could have a better view of the medals on his fatigue uniform.

"That's a Silver Star?"

"Yes, Senator."

"And a Purple Heart?"

"Yes, Senator."

"With three clusters on it? You have been wounded three times?"

"Yes, Senator."

Senator Symington looked at his fellow members of the Senate Foreign Relations Committee. He looked back at the young man in the faded fatigue uniform.

"I have no further questions."

That night over four hundred officers on active duty risked court-martial by attending, in uniform a "reading of the names of the dead" ceremony at the Washington National Cathedral. One by one, the name of every known American killed so far in Vietnam was slowly read while over three thousand people listened in silence. They heard William Sloane Coffin give a short speech thanking the vets who had gathered in D.C. for proving, "the war is a lie."

That night, VVAW gathered once again on their now-famous campground to discuss final plans for the last day. There was only one action scheduled and it would be the most dramatic event of the week. One by one, each veteran who chose to would step up and throw back the medals that they had earned in Vietnam.

This image would be forever etched in the hearts and minds of the American people. Napoleon once joked to his generals about "what men would do for a few bits of cloth." The men who gathered in front of the nation's capitol that Friday morning had done a lot. Under fire, they had given everything they had, and in turn, a grateful nation had awarded them it's most sacred treasures: Silver Stars, Bronze Stars, Purple Hearts, and dozens of other awards for valor that had been demonstrated in combat, for actions that were always described as above and beyond the call of duty.

The line of over eight hundred Vietnam veterans waiting to return those medals seemed to stretch forever. It ended at a six-foot fence that had recently been erected at the foot of the Capitol steps. This was the most disciplined action that the men of VVAW would take that week. For once, even the crazies were quiet as the line slowly inched forward. Some vets were in tears as they patiently waited their turn to throw back their medals. Other vets reached out to each other as they made up their minds whether or not to participate. Some just couldn't do it, no matter how much they hated that damn war. Jack Smith went first. He offered an apology to the Vietnamese people for acts of "genocide, racism, and atrocity." He declared the medals a "symbol of dishonor, shame, and inhumanity."

After throwing his medals, Smith turned around and checked the credentials of the next man behind him. He would continue verifying each man in line that morning before allowing him to approach the fence.

Some gave short speeches about whatever was in their hearts. Others were crying so hard that they were unable to speak. There was no script. There was no band.

It would take over two hours until the last veteran had thrown back his medals. Finally, a World War II veteran, who had lost a son in Vietnam, stepped forward and played taps. Two of what would later be known as Gold Star Mothers stood nearby. One of them said, "I am here to join these men. In every one of them I see the face of my son."

When it was over, the veterans walked back to their campground in silence.

Some were already packing and getting ready for the trip home. They had done what they came to Washington, D.C. to do. More than any other day, this day marked the beginning of the end of the Vietnam War. Many more petitions, demonstrations, and even riots lay ahead, but the face of the anti-war movement had been changed forever. No longer would protesters be thought of as only wild-eyed hippies and naïve college kids.

After cleaning up all the trash, some veterans participated in the planting of a fifteen-foot elm tree purchased from the National Parks Service. Dewey Canyon III was over.

* * *

Back in New York, I reported to the Marine Base at Garden City, Long Island for my court martial. I wore my jungle shirt with my beard and my long hair.

It was over in less than an hour. The three officers recommended a bad conduct discharge because of the pot conviction.

The final decision was made by a Marine major I never met. He looked over my service record and rejected the recommendation and ordered that I receive an honorable discharge.

I got the word a couple of weeks later in a letter.

* * *

I took the subway uptown to Columbus Circle. I walked into Roosevelt Hospital and asked the lady at the front desk for the room number of Hugh Romney. I took the elevator up to the eighth floor and went in.

There were several people sitting or standing around when I walked over to the foot of his bed. He was in obvious pain as his eyes darted back and forth across the room.

"Hello, Wavy. I read in the paper that you were in here, so I came by to cheer you up."

Wavy Gravy looked up at me. "Do I know you?"

I smiled down at him. "I met you last year in Lewisville, Texas. I was there the night you got your name."

Wavy was the non-leader of a commune called the Hog Farm. They were tending hogs in New México when they got a call to come to Woodstock and help feed some people, or as Wavy put it, "breakfast in bed for 500,000 people."

One of the promoters named Mike Stone chartered a plane to bring them to Woodstock. Before the Hog Farm, Wavy had been one of Ken Kesey's Merry Pranksters.

After Woodstock was over, the bands and the Hog Farm packed up and went to Lewisville and did it all over again. One night at three AM, B.B. King was playing on the free stage while Hugh Romney was rolling around on the stage floor muttering into a microphone when the legendary blues singer looked down at him and said, "Man, you look just like some wavy gravy."

Now, Wavy was lying in a hospital bed in New York City.

Wavy looked up at me and asked, "How are you doing, man?"

"Great! When I met you I was just bumming around Texas. I left Texas for New York City. Now, I am on the national staff of Vietnam Veterans Against The War."

Wavy's face tightened from pain. "Well, I just got back from India. I had surgery on my back and I'm kicking a heroin habit, so I am really hurting."

Wavy introduced me to his wife Bonnie and a fellow named Lou. He referred to Lou as "the Hog Farm's Minister of Money." Sitting on a couch was an attractive woman from Holland named Calico. I reached in my pocket for a small bag and dumped the contents into my hand.

"Well, I thought you might be a little tired of lying in this bed, so I thought I would take you to the races."

Wavy looked a little irritated. "Take me to the races? Man, I can't even get out of this bed."

I smiled as I held out my hand. "That's why I am bringing the races to you." Inside my hand were eight Mexican jumping beans. He looked at the small brown beans as I rolled a bedside table up to Wavy's chest. I placed a blank sheet of paper on the table and drew a circle in the middle of the paper.

"Let me explain the rules. We each pick out a bean and the first bean that makes it outside the circle wins."

Calico asked, "Do you know which bean is the fastest?"

My eyes twinkled. "Yes, I do. I have already raced these beans a couple of times and I marked them."

Wavy's eyes narrowed. "You got marked beans in this race, mister?"

I laughed, "Yes, but only I know if I marked the fastest or the slowest beans, so I will pick my bean last."

Everyone picked out a bean and when Bonnie Jean gave the word, I poured the beans in the middle of the circle and the race was on. It got a little loud and crazy for a few minutes as the Mexican jumping beans slowly began to hop towards the edge of the circle. Everyone cheered their bean on to victory. Calico's bean won.

After the race was over, Lou and Calico, and Bonnie Jean said they were going to leave. I offered to stick around and keep Wavy company.

Wavy frowned, "I don't know if I would be much company right now. I am half-crazy with pain."

I smiled at Wavy. "Well, I am about half-crazy most of the time, so we should get along just fine."

The others left and I pulled a chair up beside Wavy's bed. It was quiet for a few minutes. Finally, Wavy spoke. "It seems like that war is going to go on forever."

"Well, it looks like the end is getting closer. All kinds of people are rethinking how they feel about it. I'll give you an example. Last week I went to see the Mothers of Invention playing at the Fillmore East. For the occasion, I took some mescaline. I was surprised to see John Lennon jamming with Frank Zappa during the second set. Later that night I took the subway. As I was riding along, I noticed that the only other guy in the car with me was a subway cop and he was reading a book. I decided to sneak over and see what kind of book he was reading.

"I got up and slowly edged over beside him. I was still flying high on the mescaline. Imagine my surprise when I saw the cover of the book. Wavy, he was reading a book about Gandhi! He looked up at me for a moment. I looked back at him and smiled. 'You know, officer, if you keep reading and I keep reading, maybe someday, we won't have to kill each other after all.'"

Wavy looked at me.   "Are you a killer, Bob?"

"Wavy, I was a Marine in Vietnam. I was assigned to an artillery battery. I know that we killed a lot of people. Now I am working full time to stop any more killing."

We sat in silence for a while. I wondered if someday my antiwar activities would cause me to become a fugitive. If they did, I would need a place to go, someplace safe to hide.

"Wavy, I want to ask you something. If you were ever on the lam, where would you go?"

Wavy smiled, "That's easy. I'd go to Yelapa."

"Yelapa? Where the heck is Yelapa?"

Wavy gave me directions while I wrote them down on the back of a business card.

"Take a bus to Nogales, Arizona. Walk across the border and catch a train to Tepic. In Tepic, take a taxi to the bus station. Take the bus to Puerto Vallarta. When you get there, find a cargo boat called the Lucinda. Take it to Yelapa. When you get there, say hello to Benny and Mickey Shapiro. Tell em Wavy said 'hi.'"

I put the card back in my wallet. "Well, I hope I never need this, but if I ever do, thanks."

I sat with Wavy until he drifted off to sleep. I slipped quietly out of the room and caught the subway back downtown to VVAW headquarters.

Gainesville, Florida
May 1972

Welcome, Brother!" Scott Camil smiled and gave me a big hug as I walked in and set down my backpack. I had been in San Diego, doing advance work for the Republican Convention when Nixon decided to move the thing to Miami. I packed my stuff and hitchhiked to Gainesville. Scott was the Southern coordinator for VVAW.

He had organized chapters in Florida, Georgia, and Alabama. On December 22, 1971, the Jacksonville Office of the FBI had received a memo from J. Edgar Hoover. Former Marine Infantry Sergeant Scott Camil was the subject of the memo. Hoover described Scott as "an extremely dangerous and unstable individual whose activities must be neutralized at the earliest possible time."

Watching him frying glass marbles on his kitchen stove as he smoked a joint, he looked perfectly normal to me. Scott explained how frying the marbles would make the glass shatter more easily when fired from a slingshot.

Scott had a case of slingshots to go with the fried marbles. Next, he demonstrated what happened when you mix potassium magnate and glycerin in a test tube. He shook the test tube up and then put it in the corner of an empty fireplace. It sat there for about a minute and then burst into flames. Scott was a fun guy. We shared the same barracks in Camp Lejeune, North Carolina, while we were waiting to be discharged. A friend of Scott's named Bruce stopped by. Bruce was a Vietnam vet and a member of VVAW. Bruce was really proud of his new Trek bicycle. He spent seven hundred dollars to buy it. I decided to hang around Gainesville for the next month. The first thing I had to do was get a shot of penicillin for the gonorrhea I had picked up while hitchhiking through Arkansas.

Free love wasn't always free. I thumbed a ride over to the Gainesville public health center. My penis was in hell. I quit drinking water, because every time I had to pee, I felt like ripping the urinal off the wall. The old biddy behind the desk looked down at the form I had filled out and looked up at me. "I am afraid we can't help you, young man. You are not a resident of this county."

I looked down at her and smiled. "If I don't get my shot, there will be five or six young ladies in here next week wanting shots and they will all be residents of this county."

I got the shot.

Back at Scott's house, they had just heard the news that Nixon had mined Haiphong Harbor. Scott and I decided to walk over to the University of Florida and see what was going on.

A large group of kids had gathered outside the student center. On the way across the campus, we noticed someone wearing jungle fatigues sitting in an unmarked police car. The brown Crown Victoria really stood out in the parking lot. I walked by for a closer look. We then walked on over to the student center.

About three hundred students were having a heated discussion about how to respond to Nixon's obvious escalation of the war. I couldn't believe my eyes.

Standing at the back of the crowd was the same guy I had seen in the jungle fatigues sitting in the front seat of the unmarked police car. I walked up to the top of the stairs where a public address system had been set up. I told the person speaking that I had an important announcement to make. He handed the microphone to me.

"Brothers and sisters, before we go any farther, I want everyone here to meet a pig. I'm talking about the asshole standing over there in the jungle fatigues wearing the dark shades. Five minutes ago, he was sitting in an unmarked police car. Now if I made a mistake, come up here and tell us all who you really are, you pig motherfucker!"

The guy in the jungle fatigues turned around and walked away. By now, the crowd of angry students had quickly grown to over five hundred people. They decided to walk over to the middle of Highway 441, which ran along the edge of the campus, and sit down. In less than five minutes the road was completely blocked off.

In a few minutes a large group of cops wearing helmets and a contingent of deputies from the Sheriff's department arrived. A fire truck pulled up. The police chief picked up a bull horn and told the sitting students that they had five minutes to clear the road. Nobody moved. The cops formed a line at the edge of the crowd.

I tied a bandanna across my face. A couple of minutes later, the firemen turned on a hose and pointed it at the crowd. They turned their backs to the stream of water and locked arms. I walked into the path of the fire hose and held my arm up like I was taking a bath. The blast of water knocked me over like a bowling pin. I was unhurt and soaked. I got up and waved to the firemen. Someone threw a bottle toward the fire truck. A pair of ecology students ran over and started picking up the broken bottle. A couple of Gainesville cops walked up and started clubbing the kids picking up the glass.

A sheriff's deputy fired a tear gas canister into the sitting crowd. Someone threw it back. Thanks to the fire department, most of the students now had some kind of wet cloth to hold up to their faces. Gandhi would have been proud of this feisty crowd. They ignored the fire hose and the tear gas and kept sitting together in the middle of the road. Finally the cops moved in and started arresting people.

Scott and I decided we weren't ready to go to jail and we slipped away and headed back to his house. It was starting to get dark. We talked about what to do next. Some wanted to burn down the R.O.T.C. building. We knew it would be guarded. Earlier we had passed a half a dozen mail trucks parked on campus.

They were federal property. We decided they would make easy targets. Scott prepared six test tubes of potassium magnate and gave them to me. I put them in the side pocket of my fatigue jacket. We waited for dark. Bruce and I headed back to the campus. Scott stayed behind. He had plans of his own. Over seven hundred students who were blocking Highway 441 had been arrested and hauled off to jail. Clouds of tear gas hung in the air. The scariest part was crossing 441 again.

There were cops with helmets and clubs standing on every corner approaching the campus. We ducked our heads and bolted across the street. We kept running until we were sure no one was following us. We headed for the mail trucks. They were gone. A roving band of students ran by us. We decided to join them. Their numbers kept getting larger as more students joined in. It was a hot night and I took off my fatigue shirt and hid it in some bushes. Since the mail trucks were gone, we abandoned the idea of using the potassium magnate to burn down a major target. I tossed them in a trash dumpster. In a few minutes, it was blazing away. I pointed out a guy in bib overalls to Bruce.

"Watch out for that guy. I think he's a cop. He's too old to be a student and he looks out of place."

Bruce was skeptical. "Awwwwww. You're just being paranoid. "

I replied, "Wait and see."

A few minutes later the same guy started chasing Bruce. I couldn't help but yell, "I told you so!" as he ran past me. Bruce was younger and faster and very scared and he got away. I noticed a small crowd of guys who didn't look like students. Their short haircuts gave them away. Slowly we formed a circle around them and started closing in. Someone yelled, "Look at all the little piggies!" Suddenly, one of them threw a tear gas grenade at us and we showered them with rocks and bottles.

We scattered into the night. Bruce and I ran back over to the edge of the campus.

A lone cop car was driving down Highway 441. We picked up rocks and hurled them through the air. Both of them slammed into the side of the car. It kept going.

Around two o'clock in the morning, we headed back to Scott's house. Tear gas hung heavy in the night air. We decided it was just a matter of time until the cops raided the house and took everyone in it to jail. Bruce had a girlfriend who lived a few blocks away. We walked over there and called it a night. We saw no point in going to jail. I went back on campus the next morning to get my shirt. It was gone. I had worn that shirt in the DMZ. I never saw it again.

A month later, Scott answered his doorbell and discovered an FBI agent standing there holding a piece of white paper. It was a subpoena for Scott to appear before a federal grand jury in Tallahassee, Florida the following week.

Twenty-two other members of VVAW from around the country received similar subpoenas. I was disappointed not to get one. The following week, all twenty-two people had testified before the Tallahassee grand jury. They were questioned under oath about their lifestyle, their sources of money, their drug habits, their girlfriends, and any traveling they had done in the recent past. A couple of days later, six members of VVAW were indicted for: "Conspiring to promote, incite, and participate in a riot at the upcoming Republican Convention in Miami."

Three months later, two more people would be indicted, including the guy who sold Scott the case of sling-shots.

Miami Beach
August 1972

In August, a convoy of cars carrying Ron Kovic and other California members of VVAW left Los Angeles for the Republican Convention in Miami Beach. They called themselves The Last Patrol. As they drove along, they picked up more vets along the way. A week later they rolled into Miami Beach and slowly drove through the city. The Miami City Council decided to let all of the protesters use a city park known as Flamingo Park for their campground and sanctuary during the week that the Republican delegates would be having their convention. The park looked like a mini-Woodstock as thousands of hippies and various anti-war groups set up tents, a stage, and a public address system. Many began rolling joints and throwing Frisbees as more protesters continued to arrive.

I felt someone pulling on my shirt. I turned around and was delighted to discover it was Abbie Hoffman standing behind me. I walked him over and introduced him to Scott Camil. Scott had been advised to stay out of Miami this week, since he was under a federal indictment.

Wild horses could not have stopped Scott from being here, much less some silly piece of paper. I looked at Abbie, then Scott.

"I would like the convictee of 68 to meet the indictee of 72." Scott laughed and hugged Abbie. They disappeared into a nearby tent.

Earlier in the year, Presidential candidate George Wallace was shot by a lone gunman. Here, wild and crazy guerilla theater was the order of the day. A mob of crazies who called themselves the Godzilla Brigade, wore cut-out face masks of would-be assassin Arthur Bremmer while they chased another member of the brigade pushing a fellow wacko in a wheelchair who was wearing a George Wallace face mask. As they ran down the street, they chanted, "Free Arthur Bremmer! Give him another chance!"

The Youth International Party (Yippies) used an entire field to make a huge face of Richard Millhouse Nixon out of fresh cut watermelons. They got his nose and eyebrows just right. After the media had finished taking photographs, everyone was invited to eat free watermelon.

I wandered into one of the fancy beach hotels to check out a reception that was open to the public for some rich nobody who wanted to be the next Republican Vice-President. I was amazed at how easy it was to crash these events. I recognized a couple of Yippee women standing in the crowd listening to this asshole give a speech. Nearby, coffee was being served and in the middle of the table was a small bowl for donations to help defer the costs of the refreshments. I was determined to get the small pile of coins and get away with it. There had to be a way. My mind was racing as I stood in line for a cup of coffee.

Suddenly it came to me. I deliberately only filled my cup half way. I added a little cream and sugar. In the next motion, I added my bowl of coins. It slurped right into my cup without making a sound. My cup of coffee felt like it weighed a pound.

Quickly one of the rich Republican women, who was supposed to be keeping an eye on things, discovered the empty donation bowl. She looked around in vain for the thief. I pretended to drink my coffee as I strolled towards one of the Yippee women.

"I want you to hold this cup of coffee for a moment and be careful not to drop it."

She laughed when she realized what I had done. Next, I wandered into the men's room, and when the coast was clear, I washed the coffee away from my pile of booty.

I dried the coins off with a paper towel and left the hotel. I went into a nearby deli and ordered a roast beef sandwich. Back on the street, things began to turn ugly. The Godzilla Brigade got bored chasing the George Wallace impersonator, and decided to attack several charter buses filled with terrified Republican delegates. As they circled the trapped buses, many of them were chanting,

"Burn them! Burn them!"

Poor middle-aged ladies from Kansas wearing plastic boater Nixon hats stared down from their bus windows at the grinning masses of the great unwashed, blocking traffic and dancing around while waving lit cigarette lighters.

Members of VVAW, wearing marshal armbands, arrived just in the nick of time to save the delegates from the mob of crazies. This was the same organization that had been indicted for coming to Miami to cause riots. Later that day, twelve hundred members of VVAW silently marched down Collins Avenue to the Fontainebleau Hotel. This was the hotel where President Nixon would be staying. Several hundred state troopers in riot gear were waiting. Hunter Thompson stood on the sidewalk taking notes. After a short meeting, the state troopers agreed to let three disabled vets enter the lobby and wait for Nixon's arrival. Bill Wyman, Bobby Muller, and Ron Kovic were chosen. Outside, the rest of the vets decided that wasn't good enough and moved towards the solid line of state troopers. Hunter put away his notepad and braced himself for a riot.

Suddenly, Barry Romo grabbed a bullhorn and gave orders for everyone to return to Flamingo Park. A lot of vets were upset with Romo. Later we would learn that he had been working for a Stalinist group out of Chicago called Revolutionary Union. RU was eating away at the core of the leadership of VVAW like a cancer. First Joe Urgo, then Ed D'Amato, and now, Barry Romo had quietly joined their ranks. Members of RU got their marching orders from a guy named Bob Avakian. The litmus test to determine that a member of VVAW was a secret member of RU was to ask him how he felt about Joe Stalin. Avakian worshiped this Marxist psychopath. I would look at my suspect veteran and comment,

"Say, that Joe Stalin was a real nut job! You know what I'm saying?"

If I saw his body stiffen and his eyes tense up, I knew without even having to ask, that the dude had crossed over. There were guys like Mike Oliver and Scott Camil and Scott Moore who would never fall for the RU party line, no matter how many women Avakian sent after them to try to win their soul.

On the last night of the Republican convention, the gloves came off. Helicopters swooped down on Flamingo Park dropping canisters of tear gas. People in the park fled into the night. Earlier that afternoon, thousands of protesters had marched down Collins Avenue right into a wall of waiting state troopers. Over fifteen hundred people would be arrested and hauled off to jail.

I came upon some members of the Godzilla Brigade stacking trash cans in the center of a side street. "Screw blocking this side street. Take this stuff out in the middle of the intersection and set fire to it!"

They looked at me and smiled as if to say,   "Duh, why didn't we think of that?"

Later that night I found myself trapped on another side street. Both ends were blocked off by cops wearing helmets. Slowly each end moved towards the middle of the block. The party was over. I clasped my hands behind my head and was arrested along with several dozen of my associates. I stood in line with my hands bound behind me with a pair of plastic handcuffs. I waited to have my photo taken with a Polaroid camera and then I was stuffed into the back of a paddy wagon and hauled off to jail.

Two days later I was released with no fine. I didn't even go before a judge.

"Just get out of here," The jailer growled as he led me to an exit. I walked out into the bright light of a hot August morning. I bought a newspaper and started looking though the classified ads. I was looking for a job. I slept that night on a clean bed at the Salvation Army. I figured that whatever I did next would require some money.

I walked into the office of a small security company and applied for a job. The guy behind the desk handed me an application.

"You need a shave."

"Yeah, I been fishing. Now I need a job."

He looked over my application and told me that I was hired. My two year hitch in the Marine Corps was good enough for him. He handed me a razor. Next he issued me some dark blue pants and a short-sleeved guard's shirt. I put them on.

Then, he handed me a gun belt and a loaded .38 caliber pistol. He gave me bus fare to the address of a construction site. I was amused how quickly I went from being a wild-eyed revolutionary to a uniformed, armed security guard.

The guy who was supposed to relieve me never showed up and I ended up staying there for twenty-four hours. I had nothing to eat. With my first pay check, I paid the rent in a cheap hotel and bought some better clothes. Besides my night gig as a rent-a-cop, I got a day job as a salesman in Burdine's Department Store, in Miami Beach. One day Police Chief Rocky Pomerance came in and I helped him find a belt. I didn't mention my recent stay in his jail.

* * *

In November, I hitchhiked to Shreveport, Louisiana. I wanted to spend Thanksgiving with my mother. I hadn't seen her in over a year. She picked me up at a truck stop on the outskirts of town and drove me back to her house. I was dirty and tired. My mother made me a tuna sandwich.

"You'll never guess who stopped by to see you!"

From the look in her eyes, I could tell it wasn't an old friend.

"Who?"

"The FBI. They want to talk to you. They asked me some really strange questions."

"Like what?"

"Well, for one thing, they asked me if I thought you were capable of committing murder."

I snorted, "That's a dumb question."

I put down the sandwich and started looking through my wallet for the card with the directions that Wavy Gravy had given me back in New York. I found it tucked away behind some rolling papers. It was wrinkled but still readable. My mom continued talking to me.

"They wanted me to go to the library and check out some books on Communism."

I laughed. "They wanted you to do what? Look, Mom, I haven't killed anybody. I haven't done anything that would cause you to be ashamed of me. The FBI is just following Nixon's orders to harass anyone involved in anyway with the anti-war movement. I don't have time to explain anything more right now. I have to get out of here."

I decided to take a shower before hitting the road again. In the middle of getting undressed, it hit me: I could be spending the next six months in some stinking federal cell because I stopped to take a shower. I quickly got dressed and grabbed my backpack. My mother dropped me off on the interstate at the other edge of town. Late that night, an eighteen-wheeler let me off on the outskirts of Amarillo.

It was raining. I found shelter underneath a railroad bridge and crawled inside my sleeping bag. In a few minutes, I was sound asleep. A fast freight rumbling under the bridge woke me up early the next morning. I peeped out of my warm sleeping bag at six inches of snow. It would have been closer to head south in Texas to Laredo. But, I figured that was where the FBI would be watching. So I was following the directions Wavy gave me, right down to the letter.

My shoes were soaked by the melting snow. I shivered and stuck my thumb out. I was miserable.

That's all right, I told myself. In a couple more days, I'll be on the beach in México. Finally another trucker picked me up. The next morning, I was in Nogales, Arizona. I called Scott Camil in Gainesville, Florida.

Yelapa, México
November 1972

"Tell the guys not to worry about me. I am ten feet from the Mexican border. Tonight, I'll be deep in México. Good luck with your trial. Tell everyone that I'll see them in the spring. I better not stay too long on this phone, so I got to go. I love you, brother!"

I hung up and quickly walked across the border. Just like Wavy told me to, I bought a train ticket to Tepic. I settled in on a second-class seat and watched the mountains in the distance start to fade as the sun went down. We pulled into Tepic early the next morning. I caught a taxi across town to the bus station and bought a ticket to Puerto Vallarta. I missed the express bus, so I had to settle for the local.

It made all the stops. It was a typical Mexican bus with plastic statues of the Virgin Mary and Jesus on the dash and rosary beads hanging down from the rear view mirror. After riding a couple of miles I was ready to borrow the beads. This guy drove like a bat outta hell. I stuck my head out of the open side window and looked down several hundred feet as he drove around a mountain curve. Late that afternoon we rolled into Puerto Vallarta. I bought some tacos from a street vendor and found a cheap hotel. In 1972, Puerto Vallarta was a sleepy little bump along the road on the coast of the state of Jalisco. It had one working red light.

The next morning I found the boat called the Lucinda and bought a three dollar, one-way ticket to Yelapa. There was a guy about my age, from New Zealand, going to Yelapa, too. His name was Lance. We decided to split the rent on a cheap house. The boat followed the coastline south for about forty-five minutes. Finally, we went around some large boulders sticking up out of the ocean and turned into a small beautiful bay. Yelapa was everything Wavy said it would be. A small canoe rowed out to the Lucinda and we threw down our gear and jumped in. The ride to the beach cost another five pesos. We stood on the beach and looked around. We picked up our back packs and followed a winding trail into town. We passed pigs roaming free. A small kid who spoke a little English asked us if we were looking for a place to stay. We nodded and followed him as he led us to his grandfather's house. We shook hands with a small white-haired man named Juan Carlos. We followed him down a trail that ran parallel to the shoreline. After about a quarter of a mile, he stopped in front of a little cinder block house with a thatched roof. It had running water in the bathroom and a wood burning stove. Juan Carlos spoke no English. We spoke no Spanish. He wrote the number three hundred on a piece of paper. I looked at it and wrote the number two hundred on the back. The old man nodded his head and we shook hands. Lance and I each gave him a hundred pesos. We were renting the house for the equivalent of sixteen dollars a month.

There were two swinging beds supported by ropes. We left our gear and walked back into town. There are no roads leading to Yelapa. There is no airport. The only way to get here is by boat. No one has a car. There are no sidewalks.

There is no electricity. Just like Wavy told me, there were no cops and no sheriff. It was just a quiet little fishing village. A couple of boatloads of tourists from Puerto Vallarta come into the bay every day. The tourists ride a donkey to see the waterfall and eat lunch on the beach. Later in the afternoon, the same boats take them back to Puerto Vallarta. Huge Iguana lizards sun themselves on rocks and high in the trees, while overhead in the sky, large Macaw parrots fly back and forth across the bay, singing a song of freedom. Dolphins play offshore. There are even passing whales. I enjoyed a hot lunch of fresh fish and rice. I washed it down with a cold beer. I remembered the cold morning I spent shivering with my thumb in the air on the side of the interstate on the outskirts of Amarillo. Being a fugitive wasn't so bad if you played your cards right. There were less than a hundred gringos living in Yelapa. They were mostly artists, writers, hippies, and beach bums, living together in peace and harmony as they shared the sand and the sun together.

Around sunset, I took a walk down to a small café on the beach called the Yacht Club. As I walked in, I was surprised to see a poker game in progress. There were four gringos sitting around a small table playing seven card stud. Every hand involved international transactions of Canadian, American, and Mexican money. The currency exchanges went quickly as these guys were old hands at calculating the exchange rates in their head. I put on my best smile and asked if I could sit in.

A guy with pale blue eyes in his thirties wearing a straw boater looked me up and down and said, "Sure. Pull up a chair."

His name was Mel. The other guys were called Steve, Byron, and Pipeline Jim. Pipeline Jim wanted to marry one of the local girls. Her family told him he was much too old to marry their daughter, Antonia. He told them he would pipe running water into every home in Yelapa in exchange for the hand of the fair Antonia. They agreed. He married her and built for her the biggest house in Yelapa, high on a hill overlooking the bay. From that day on, he was known as Pipeline Jim.

Steve was a gray beard who owned the Yacht Club. Byron was a jeweler who lived here with his wife. Mel was a degenerate gambler, a poet, and an artist. He carried a cane and walked with a limp. In San Francisco, he had managed to get run over by a cable car. The money from the settlement, a small Social Security check, and regular poker games enabled Mel to enjoy a quiet life in México.

After a couple of hands, I noticed that Mel had a tendency to try to buy the pot. After the second or third hand was dealt, Mel would quietly toss out a fifty-peso note. The other players often then folded and Mel scooped up the pot. I waited until I was sitting on a good pair. When Mel tossed in his fifty-peso note, I matched it and bumped it with another fifty-peso note of my own. Mel looked at the pot, looked at me and then looked around and asked,

"Who let this guy in the game?"

Pipeline Jim replied, "You did."

I won the pot. It was the beginning of a long night. The poker gods were smiling. Around midnight, the game broke up. I won about five hundred pesos.

Mel invited me up to his house. He had a beach home at the top of a small hill. He broke the seal on a fresh deck of cards and we started playing poker again, one on one. The cards must not have been marked, because by sunrise, I had won another five hundred pesos. Mel suggested that we go back down to the Yacht Club for breakfast.

He explained, "In Yelapa, we have a tradition where the winner always buys the loser breakfast."

I laughed, "My friend, I wouldn't want to break tradition. Order anything on the menu."

Mel had venison with eggs. I paid for it with his money. I asked him where I could buy some marijuana.

"How much do you want?"

"A kilo."

"Talk to an old man named Clemente. He rents horses on the beach."

I finished my coffee and left Mel eating his breakfast. I walked towards the beach. I found Clemente. He spoke a little English. I told him I was a friend of Mel's. I told him what I wanted. He looked at me and smiled.

"I have a little house on the south end of town. Come by and see me after dark."

"How much for the kilo?" I asked.

"Seven hundred pesos."

We shook hands and I told him I would see him after dark. Seven hundred pesos was roughly fifty seven dollars in greenbacks. I stopped at a little store and bought a beer and a box of small plastic bags. I walked back to my house and played gin with Lance until dark. I quietly walked out to the south end of Yelapa and found Clemente's house. I looked around and slipped inside.

The only light came from a kerosene lamp and a small fire in a fireplace, tended to by an old woman. Clemente handed me a large shopping bag. It was filled with fresh picked marijuana, well over a kilo. I held the bag up to my nose and inhaled deeply. It smelled heavenly. I handed him seven hundred-peso notes and slapped his shoulder.

"Gracias, Señor Clemente!"

I slipped back out the door. I was now in the pot business. I looked around at the shadows and a sliver of a moon. I was halfway expecting a bunch of Federales to appear out of nowhere yelling, "Policia!" I had seen too many movies.

There was no one there but me and some barking dogs. Lance couldn't believe his eyes when he looked inside my shopping bag. I spread a Mexican newspaper out on the bed and dumped the weed on the paper. I started filling plastic bags. I didn't have a scale and I didn't need one. I wanted a reputation for selling fat ounces.

Of course, Lance and I had to try some to make sure this shit was any good. I rolled a joint as fat as the paper would hold. I fired it up and took a toke.

This shit was powerful. We sat in the front yard and smoked and watched the moon slowly rise over the bay.

Yelapa was everything Wavy told me it would be and more. I settled into a nice lifestyle. I played poker three nights a week. I sold grass every day. I usually carried a pound around with me wrapped up in a beach towel.

There were plenty of customers. I would sell to any gringo. I would also sell to Mexicans if I knew them. A month later, Lance and I parted company. He wanted to see more of México. I was happy to go on living in Yelapa. I moved into a nice split level house high on a hill overlooking the bay. I hired a mojo named One-Eyed Louis to do my heavy work, like carrying a fresh tank of propane up to my house.

The story goes that one night Louis was drunk and stumbling down the trail when he fell and gouged his eye out on a rock. Legend has it that while Louis was lying there on the ground with his eye hanging on his cheek, a pig came along and ate it. Louis was very muscular and ugly as a wart hog.

I was having lunch at the Yacht club one day when a small boy handed me a note. It was an invitation to come see Joe Treglio. I wondered what he wanted.

Joe was one of the long term gringo warlords who lived up the river about a mile from the beach. I called them warlords because most of them had been in Yelapa for years, and each one had their turf staked out. You had to be aware that making friends with one of them could make you an automatic enemy of their enemies as well. So far, the only warlords I had made friends with were Mickey and Benny Shapiro. Wavy had told me to say hello to them and that was good enough for me.

Every time I saw Mickey in town, I bought her a beer. Often, she returned the favor. Making friends with the Shaprios made me an instant enemy of their next door neighbor, Peggy. They had been feuding for years.

Around sunset, I walked up river to Joe Treglio's house. His dogs started barking as soon as I entered the first gate. I still had three gates to go. Fences surrounded his house in concentric circles.

His home was in the center of the last one. He shook my hand and offered me a joint. I smiled.

"Perhaps, you would like some of mine?" I showed him the pound I had wrapped up in my beach towel. He accepted my offer and we sat down on large leather chairs in his living room. He took a pinch from the beach towel and rolled a joint. He was a small Italian in his forties.

"I been watching you, kid. I like your style. I got to hand it to you for balls. You carry this stuff around like it was legal."

I smiled. "The jail cell ain't gonna be any bigger if I go down for an ounce or a pound."

Joe laughed. "Sometime, we might do a little business. You might meet someone who wants more than a kilo. I been here a long time, kid. I can handle any kind of weight you want. You give me a deposit and a date and on that day, I can bring hundreds of kilos down out of these mountains on the backs of mules. My guys will load them at night on any boat you bring into the bay."

I looked around. "I guess you have got your act together pretty good to be living in Yelapa as long as you have."

Joe smiled at me. "Let me show you something."

He pointed to a framed document on the wall. It looked like some kind of diploma. Except for his name, the whole thing was in Spanish.

"Do you know what that is?"

"Your GED?" I asked.

Joe roared in laughter. "I like you, kid. Besides balls, you got a sense of humor. That document is a Mexican permit authorizing me to have firearms in my home. Do you have any idea how hard that was to get?"

I shook my head. "Well, I hope you don't have a reason to use them very often."

Joe rolled another joint.

"You will find that Yelapa is a very peaceful village. The perfect place to live and do a little business."

Late that night, I said goodnight to Joe and told him that if I met anyone who was looking for any kind of weight, I would be in touch.

✳ ✳ ✳

His name was Lupe. He lived in Michoacan, but he had family in Yelapa. I met him at a cockfight when I bet against his bird. I had discovered a simple, yet effective method of predicting the winner of these nasty battles. I just bet against the more nervous bird. After more than twenty cockfights, I had only been wrong once. Rooster fighting is a bloody business and I would have rather been lying in my hammock, sipping a Margarita, but I needed the extra money. Every Sunday afternoon, there were cockfights in Yelapa under a huge mango tree.

The first time I went to one, I got a little too close to the action. I was standing there wearing nothing but shorts and sandals, with my back to a wall. The birds began fighting right in front of me. If I kicked one of the birds away from me and that bird lost, I would have a mob of very pissed off Mexicans chasing me up river as fast as I could run. Suddenly, a thin red line appeared across my shin. My leg had been slashed by one of the metal spurs lashed to the legs of each bird, before every bout. The birds were fighting so fast, I couldn't even tell which one had cut me. It didn't hurt, but the blood poured down my leg. I smiled and poured some tequila on it. My fellow bettors admired my display of machismo.

After my bird won, Lupe walked over and shook my hand and handed me a wad of pesos. He congratulated me on my wager. Then he asked me if I smoked pot. I told him I did and he offered to bring me a kilo the next time he came to Yelapa.

The price would be one hundred American dollars. I told him we had a deal. We shook hands. I was ready to try some different weed and it gave him a chance to make back some of the money he had lost to me.

The next week he walked up to my house with a kilo of pot inside a large tin can. I opened the can and inhaled deeply. I dug down into the middle of the can and pinched a small bud to sample. I rolled a joint and took a couple of tokes. This was killer bud. I was happy to pay him his hundred dollars. My customers were also happy. Ten days later he brought me another kilo.

Meeting Lupe changed the way I sold pot. The days of walking around with a pound wrapped up in a beach towel were over. Now, anyone who wanted to buy pot from me was going to have to walk up to my house. When the word got out about this new stuff, they would be happy to make the trip. I started to have a daily happy hour for the pot heads of Yelapa. Every day I put a handful of weed on a plate and a pack of rolling papers. I laid out several one-ounce bags of Marijuana beside the plate. Customers were free to sit down and roll and smoke a joint or two. Then, they could pick out one of the bags and leave fifty pesos on the table. I seldom got out of my hammock.

Between playing poker and selling pot I had settled into a nice comfortable lifestyle in México. Things started to go bad when I got a note from Cynthia. She was one of the longtime warlords of Yelapa. She was Mel's girlfriend and she had a modest pot business of her own. After the word got out about my killer weed, a lot of her regular customers were coming to me. The message was short and to the point.

Cynthia said that she and some of the other pillars of the community were fed up with my presence in Yelapa. If I didn't leave town tomorrow on the morning boat, there would be a midnight boat just for me. She said that the Federales would be waiting for me in Puerto Vallarta.

I told the muscle-bound bozo who brought me her note to tell Cynthia that I wasn't going anywhere anytime soon. That night, I laid four sticks of margarine by the front door. I put four pots of water on a low boil. I waited quietly in the shadows of my kitchen. Shit, I thought as I listened for the sound of footsteps coming up the trail. I came down here for some peace and quiet. Now look at me, sitting here in the dark standing watch in a one-man Alamo. Midnight came and went. Cynthia's vigilantes weren't coming.

The Mexicans who pulled tourists around the bay in a para-sail with their boat had problems of their own. Yesterday, a tourist coming in for a landing got caught in some palm trees and ended up going back to Puerto Vallarta with a couple of broken ribs. They needed a gringo today to demonstrate to everyone that the para-sail ride was really a safe and fun thing to do. I made a deal with them. First, I was riding for free. Next, I wanted them to take me across the bay and turn around in front of Cynthia's house.

They hooked me up and off we went. When they made the turn, I was directly over her home, about a hundred feet in the air. I could see her sunbathing below. I cupped my hands.

"Oh, Cynthia, you bitch! What happened to your midnight boat? Fuck you!"

I sailed back across the bay.

I decided to spend a couple of days in Puerto Vallarta anyway, while Cynthia calmed down. That night I was back in Carlos O'Brien's nursing a pitcher of banana daiquiris. I met a guy from Chicago named Dave. I offered to share my pitcher. The small talk soon turned to drugs.

It seemed like half of the gringos in Puerto Vallarta had come to México to score weed. Dave wasn't just looking for a small bag of marijuana, he wanted two hundred kilos. He had a boat ready when it was needed. I told him that I knew someone who might be able to help. It would take a few days to put a deal together. An ex-con I knew named Chico walked over. The guy would do anything other than work. He had introduced me to all the wrong people. He could tell by the way I looked at him that some kind of deal was going on and he wanted in on it.

"Chico, this is Dave. He is a tourist enjoying a couple of days in the beautiful city of Puerto Vallarta. He was just leaving."

Dave took the hint and got up and left. Chico looked back at him and looked at me. "What's up with him, man? He looks loaded."

"He's a school teacher from Iowa. He brought down a big box of bibles in Spanish to teach assholes like you about the baby Jesus. I gotta run."

The next day, I caught a boat back to Yelapa and went to see Joe Treglio. Over coffee, I told him about Dave.

Joe smiled, "Sure, two hundred kilos is no problem. It's gonna cost him eighteen thousand dollars. I can start loading my mules when he brings me half. He can pay me the other half when my crew loads his boat. Let me know what night he wants to do this deal. I'll take care of you when he leaves."

I said goodbye to Joe and caught a boat back to Puerto Vallarta. I was going to make money on both ends. I decided to add ten bucks a kilo to the deal and make a quick two grand from Dave. I met him in the lobby of the hotel. We went up to his room and talked about his two hundred kilos. I told him he would have to put nine thousand dollars up front. He began to get nervous.

"Look, my guy has been living on the coast of México for over ten years. He has a hundred acre ranch. He isn't going to throw all of that away over nine thousand dollars."

Finally the truth came out. Dave didn't have that kind of money. All of his talk about wanting to buy two hundred kilos of marijuana was just talk. He had a big mouth and a bad habit of pretending to be someone he wasn't.

Things turned ugly in a hurry. He called me a motherfucker. I knocked him down. He looked up at me and snarled. "I'm gonna have you killed."

I laughed, "No, you're not. You're gonna get on a plane tomorrow and take your lying ass home." I walked out.

The next day I was eating lunch at Carlos O'Brien's when Chico walked over.

"I ran into your Bible buddy this morning. Funny thing, amigo...he wants to have you killed."

He showed me a hundred dollar traveler's check made out to him and signed by Dave. "This is a deposit. He is going to give me four hundred more when you are dead."

I stared at the check. "That's the most you could get out of him to kill me?" Chico smiled at me. "I tried to get a thousand, but he told me you weren't worth it."

This dude was dumber than I thought. I took out my wallet. I removed the money and the cash in my pocket. I handed what was left to Chico. I gave him my Ray Ban sunshades.

"Show this stuff to him and tell him you dumped me in the ocean. Get the other four hundred from him and meet me on the beach in front of Daiquiri Dick's in the morning. Bring me half of the money.

"I'll go to Guadalajara for a few days until he leaves town. How does that sound?"

Chico smiled and shook my hand. "My friend, consider yourself murdered!"

I decided to lay low until tomorrow. I bought some magazines and checked into a small hotel on the other side of town. The next morning I was sitting in front of Daiquiri Dick's drinking a cup of coffee and waiting for Chico to show up with my share of the money Dave was paying him to kill me.

I knew one of three things would happen: 1. Chico would show up as planned and give me my share of Dave's blood money. 2. Chico would show up and kill me and keep all of the money. 3. The cops would show up and take us both to jail.

I knew the second possibility was not very likely. Puerto Vallarta would quickly lose thousands of dollars in vanished tourist money, if a gringo was murdered on their beautiful beach. The person who killed that gringo would die a slow and painful death. I ordered more coffee and read the morning paper. Finally, two Puerto Vallarta cops walked by. They went about twenty feet and turned around. They came back just as a large Mexican in a flowered shirt walked up to me and asked, "Sir, are you Robert McLane?"

I took a sip of my coffee and smiled, "Yes, señor. I am."

"My name is Detective Ramón. Mr. McLane, you are under arrest. There are two ways we can do this, the easy way or the hard way. Which way would you prefer?" Ramón was the kind of cop who didn't need any handcuffs. If he told someone that they were under arrest, they were under arrest, and going with him.

I smiled up at the big guy. "I always liked easy."

We took a taxi to the jail. I paid the fare. Ramón noticed a large Turquoise ring on my hand.

"Señor, you know they will take that ring away from you, once you are inside the jail. Why don't you give it to me and I'll give it back to you when you are released?"

I took the ring off and handed it to him. I might have a chance of getting it back from Ramón. I knew if I lost it inside the jail, I would never see it again.

We climbed out of the taxi and walked into the jail. I saw Dave for a moment. I guess Chico hadn't convinced him that I was dead. He waited while the cops searched my backpack. The only thing they found was a cheap bottle of Tequila. I winked at Dave and kept my mouth shut. Ramón took me in another room and started questioning me.

"The guy outside says that you are a Mafia drug dealer."

I laughed. "I am a Mafia drug dealer? Where is my Cadillac? I am just a humble traveler, enjoying the beautiful beaches and the warm sun and the wonderful hospitality of the good people of México. I have a small home in Yelapa where I live quietly. The man outside is loco. Everything he says is a lie."

After talking to me for a few more minutes, Ramón led me into the main jail. An iron door led directly into a large open courtyard. The prisoners inside were watching. A short, fat guard closed the iron door and motioned for me to light his cigar. I struck a match and held it low in front of his face. As he leaned forward towards the flame, I took the cigar out of his mouth and locked eyes with him as I put it in my mouth and lit it with the still burning match. I handed him a twenty-peso note and smiled. The inmates laughed as I looked around and blew a smoke ring. The top of the outer wall was covered with broken pieces of bottles that had been cemented in. One deputy with a rifle peered down from a guard tower in the corner. There were about thirty-five prisoners milling around. One guy was sweeping the ground with a broom. I was the only gringo.

I wondered if I was about to refight the Alamo. A small guy wearing sunshades and a clean shirt walked over and introduced himself as Danny. He spoke excellent English. He told me he was awaiting trial for bank robbery. He explained that the prisoners were organized into a sort of community. He was the unofficial mayor. Danny wasn't very big and he didn't look too tough, but he had plenty of friends who were. Once I had determined that this guy was for real, I decided that being his friend was my best shot at getting out of this place in one piece. I took a twenty dollar bill that I had hidden in one of my sandals and handed it to him.

"Perhaps, there is a coffee fund I could contribute to?"

Since Dave claimed all of my money was stolen from him, the police took everything else but the twenty peso note for evidence. They didn't search my sandals. Danny took the twenty dollar bill and put it in his pocket. He smiled and offered me his hand.

"My friend, do not worry about your time here. You do not sweep. When we have food, you will eat too. Welcome to Puerto Vallarta jail."

I began to relax. Things were looking up. About an hour later, they brought Chico in. He was drunk. He saw me and lunged at me. A couple of Danny's associates grabbed him. Danny looked at me.

"Do you want him beaten up?"

I shook my head. "No. When he sobers up, I will have a talk with him."

They dragged Chico over to a corner and threw him on the ground. He sat there glaring at me. Finally, he rolled over and went to sleep. In a lot of ways, this Mexican jail was nicer than jails I had been in back in the States.

For one thing, I was looking up at a beautiful blue sky. There were no foul smells.

Murderers, thieves, and drunks were all thrown in together. When Chico woke up I walked over beside him. He looked up at me.

"Hello, you rat!"

I frowned at him. "Listen asshole, I didn't rat you out. The same guy who got me locked up told the cops all about you. I bet he left out the part about where he hired you to kill me. Why don't you ask them? Do you think he was going to let you get away with beating him out of his money when he figured out that I was still alive?"

Chico sighed. "You are right, amigo. I was drunk and acting like a punde-ho. I hate being in jail over this stupid shit."

That night, most of the prisoners slept on the ground in one long line. The guards let me have my sleeping bag. As I was lying there trying to relax, I fart-ed, a loud one. The two Mexicans lying on either side of me jumped up and ran about ten feet and started cursing in Spanish. I couldn't help but laugh. A few minutes later after they lay back down, I farted again. This time they moved faster and cursed longer. I finally fell asleep.

The next morning I got up and washed my face with the one faucet we all shared. I drank a cup of coffee. The handle on the cup was broken, but the coffee was fresh and tasted great. I didn't believe my eyes. I was staring at a pile of assorted pastries on a plate beside the coffee pot. I picked up a cinnamon roll. I found out that the food that wasn't sold by some of the bakeries each morning was delivered to the jail. I had another roll.

I was eating a better breakfast than I ever had in an American jail. The next day they let Chico go. For some reason they were holding on to me. Since Dave had left for the States, they didn't have much of a case. Maybe they were waiting to see if I was going to start crying, "Won't someone please call my rich Daddy for me?" The subject of a phone call never came up.

On day three, I started getting restless. I walked over to where Danny was relaxing on a bench and getting some sun. "Say Danny, you got a guy in here about my size who can box? Tell him that I want to go three rounds with him. We'll have some fun."

Danny looked over his shades at me like I was asking if I could dig a tunnel. He studied my face for a moment. "Let me see what I can do."

A few minutes later, he introduced me to Paco. This guy used to box in the ring in Guadalajara. He was a couple of years younger than I was, but definitely in my weight class. He had scars on his knuckles and his face. I might get my dumb ass kicked, but I was also going to have some fun. If I was afraid of a little fistfight I never would have joined the Marines. All of the other prisoners and some of the guards got into a large circle.

Paco and I walked out into the middle and faced each other. I looked around and raised my fists. "Remember the Alamo!"

A guard yelled, "You no Davy Crockett!"

The guys in the circle howled with laughter. Danny explained the rules. We would box bare-handed. We could throw punches with closed fists as hard as we wanted to. We were supposed to hit above the belt and no head shots. There would be no referee. The rules sounded good to me. I wanted to leave here with the same pretty face that I walked in with.

Danny looked at us. "Any questions?"

We shook our heads. I snarled at Paco. "Let's get it on!"

One of the guards hit an iron pot with a nightstick, and we started boxing. Paco was a good boxer, much better than me. I winced as he drove a left hook into my ribs. I blocked a lot of his punches with my elbows and shoulders while I managed to land a few punches of my own. When he started to smother me with combinations of shots, I pulled him close to me in a clinch and waited for the pain to pass. Three minutes seemed like ten.

Finally, the guard hit the iron pot ending round one. I sat on a stool and listened to the crowd cheering for Paco. After a short minute, we began round two.

I survived another round without getting too roughed up. I sat on the stool and tried to catch my breath. During the third round, Paco suddenly caught me with a fist in my gut as I was moving towards him. Lucky for me, he pulled his punch a little or he would really have doubled me over. Still, when he hit me, my eyes bugged out and my fists opened up as the force of the blow took me by surprise. The crowd roared with laughter as Paco reached out and shook my open hand and then went back into a boxer's stance. The matador was playing with the tired bull. I never went down and I answered every bell.

After the third round ended, Danny looked around and raised Paco's hand as the crowd roared their approval. Bets were paid off and I shook hands with Paco to congratulate him on his victory. My boxing career began and ended in that Mexican jail.

The next afternoon, I passed a note to a guard to give to the head of immigration. The note said that I was sure we could find some kind of solution to bring an end to this unfortunate misunderstanding. About an hour later, the same guard escorted me into his office. Juan Penja was a short, thin man, wearing glasses and sitting behind a large desk. I noticed my backpack in the corner. He offered me a cigarette. I don't smoke tobacco, but I accepted his offer anyway.

"So how do you like living in México?"

I smiled. "It is a beautiful country filled with very nice people." I took a drag on the cigarette and tried not to gag. "You know, back in Yelapa I am sure they must have heard about my being arrested on the beach. I bet there are some very nervous gringos hiding up river right now. They think that you are probably beating me with a rubber hose and making me write a list of the names of every pot smoker in Yelapa."

Juan Pena smiled. "We know everyone in Yelapa smokes marijuana except the alcoholics."

I looked at him as I finished my cigarette. "Señor Penja, I want to apologize for the unfortunate misunderstanding that I had with that gringo."

I explained in my best broken Spanish, how this person had insulted my mother with his vile tongue and I had punched him one time to defend the honor of my mother. I told him that he swore to me that he would get revenge and then he went to the police with this crazy story about me being some kind of a Mafia drug dealer.

Señor Penja looked at me. "Well, this person has left our country and since he was the one who made the complaint, all charges against you have been dropped. My friend, you are free to go."

We stood up and shook hands. I picked up my backpack. As I was walking out of his office, I stopped and asked him a question. "By the way Señor, the next time I visit México, is there something I could bring you from the United States as a token of my thanks for your fine hospitality? Perhaps a small TV?"

Señor Pena looked at me for a moment. "Perhaps, there is something you could bring me. I would be very grateful. Have you seen the movie Serpico?"

I smiled. "Sí, Señor Penja, Al Pacino is one of my favorite actors."

Juan Penja nodded his head. "Well in the movie, he has this Browning nine millimeter pistol that could be fired fifteen times without reloading. I would be most grateful if possibly you could bring me two of those pistols."

"Señor Penja, how am I going to bring a pistol into México? For a gringo like me to be caught with even a bullet in your country would mean spending several years in a Mexican prison far worse than the jail I just got out of."

Señor Penja proceeded to explain to me how easy it would be to bring him two guns. "You must catch a direct flight from Houston to Puerto Vallarta. You put the guns in a bag to be stored in the cargo hold with my name on the outside. When the bag is unloaded at the airport, it will come straight to me."

I nodded my head. "I suppose I should throw in several boxes of shells while I am at it?"

Señor Penja smiled. "That would be a nice thing for you to do."

I raised my eyebrows. "I suppose after delivering those pistols, I could do a little business uninterrupted here in old Vallarta?"

Señor Penja laughed, "Bring me those guns and you can dance naked on the tables at Carlos O'Brien's if you want to. Have a good day, Señor McLane."

As I was walking out of the jail, I saw Detective Ramón. He smiled. "Well, I see our little bird has flown from his cage. I hope your stay wasn't too unpleasant? I heard about your boxing exhibition."

I smiled at Ramón. "You may take pride in knowing that my stay here was more pleasant than any American jail I have had the misfortune to be in."

He took my ring off of his hand and gave it back to me. I smiled and thanked him.

"You know going to jail in Puerto Vallarta has been a good thing for me. I got to know the Police Chief, the Mayor, the head of immigration, even the undercover cops like you. So long, my friend."

I started walking. There were still a couple of hours of daylight left and I wanted to get as far north as I could go before dark. I didn't have a peso to my name, but I was free. I caught a ride in the back of a pickup to the outskirts of town.

Thirty minutes later, I was riding in the cab of a large eighteen-wheeler headed to Guadalajara. The driver had a gallon of tequila on the seat beside him. He wasn't drinking but he invited me to have all I wanted.

I took a couple of shots as I watched the sun beginning to set over the ocean. On the edge of Guadalajara, I walked into a small restaurant. I looked at the man behind the counter and showed him a shirt.

"Señor, I have this nice shirt that was made in the United States. Perhaps, I could trade this fine shirt for a small bowl of something to eat?"

He frowned. "Please have a seat, Señor, and put away your shirt. María! Bring this man some food!"

A couple of days later, I crossed the border into Texas. I made the journey safely, thanks to the charity and grace of the Mexican people.

San Francisco
1973

M ike Oliver had moved to California. I decided to go visit him. I rode my thumb west. He was living in a co-op in the Tenderloin district of San Francisco. They occupied the entire five story building. We went up on the roof and smoked a joint. He filled me in on some of the things I had missed while I was in México.

"Scott Camil and the rest of the boys who were tried had been acquitted. VVAW had been taken over by the Revolutionary Union. Mike described it like a scene out of Invasion of the Body Snatchers. One day Joe Urgo looked like just another ordinary anti-war vet from Queens. The next day he walks in with the same hollow-eyed stare as the rest of the Avakian Zombie Corps, the same assholes we saw down in Miami who went around screaming at little old ladies. You remember the ones who kept yelling, 'Free Attica! Smash Imperialism now!'"

Mike shook his head. "First it was Joe Urgo. Next, Ed Damato walked in wearing one of those blue Mao caps. That was a dead giveaway. Anytime anyone showed up in one of those caps, we knew he had crossed over. The national headquarters moved to Chicago. It was obvious what had happened.
"

Mike rolled another joint and continued. "I think they just wanted to cut back on their phone bill. One thing was certain. From then on, VVAW became just another front for the Revolutionary Union. All of the vets who were worth a damn had already been kicked out or quit. Scott Camil and I were among the first to go. John Kerry and Ron Kovic quit. Bob Hanson and Jack McCloskey and I are now working for a group called Swords To Plowshares. What are you planning to do next?"

I looked at Mike. "I don't have a clue. A week ago, I was answering the bell for round three of an exhibition fight in a Mexican jail. I made a lot of new friends down there. I think I might go into the import business with a couple of partners."

Mike smiled. "Well, you're gonna have to find a place to crash, if you want to hang around here. I don't have room for you in the small space me and my old lady are sharing. This place is crawling with good looking women, though. I'm sure one of them will be willing to take you in."

I decided it was time to call the Feds. I took a bus across town and found a pay phone. The man's voice on the other end answered with one word.

"FBI."

I spoke slowly. "My name is Robert McLane. M-C-L-A-N-E. I heard you want to talk to me."

The voice replied. "Well, I don't know. I will have to check. Please hold."

I smiled, "No, I will call you back tomorrow. Let me know what you find out. Goodbye."

The next day I called again. "My name is Robert McLane. I understand you want to talk to me."

There was a pause and then the voice answered. "No, we aren't interested in talking to you."

I hung up and released a deep breath of relief. My life on the lam was over. My days in VVAW were over, too. I caught a trolley back downtown.

I decided to go back to New York City. I started hitchhiking east. A couple of days later, an eighteen-wheeler dropped me off in Nebraska. I was standing on the shoulder of the highway when a state trooper pulled up beside me.

After checking my name for warrants, he informed me that hitchhiking was illegal anywhere in Nebraska. As I was talking to him, I heard a train whistle. I noticed a freight yard off in the distance. I looked at him with my best smile.

"Why don't you drop me off by that freight yard? I'll hop in a boxcar and you won't see me again."

It was a funny feeling riding in the back of the big Crown Victoria. This time it wasn't taking me to jail. A long fright train was slowly rolling by as I climbed out of the trooper's car and grabbed my backpack. I looked at the trooper who had given me a lift.

"You wanna go with me?"

He laughed and shook his head. "Get outta here before you get me in trouble!"

In less than a minute, I was rolling east in an empty boxcar. I felt like Huckleberry Finn floating down the Mississippi on a raft as I watched the Nebraska plains rolling by. I wailed on my Horner harmonica as the sun went down.

I rode that freight all the way to Kansas City. Then I started hitchhiking again. In two days, I rolled through the Holland Tunnel into Manhattan.

Veterans Hospital, Waco, Texas
July 1974

"Mr. McLane! Mr. McLane! You have blood work this morning. You need to get ready."

Once again, I had curled up in a large stuffed chair and gone to sleep. I sat up and looked around. Jimmy and the usual suspects were waiting by the front door. "The Price Is Right" was on the TV in the dayroom. People in the audience screamed, "Higher! Higher!" A leggy model strutted around a washing machine.

I stood up and shuffled over to join the line of lucky winners giving blood that day. Jimmy unlocked the door and we walked down to the sidewalk to wait for the rickety old school bus that would carry us over to the lab building. Of course, the bus was late, but no one was in a hurry to roll up their sleeves for those vampires anyway. I felt a gentle breeze on my face and wondered if I would ever be free again. The old school bus pulls up, and we climb in.

At the lab, we follow Jimmy inside and take a number. There are no magazines to read, just some guys in pajamas clutching small bits of white paper waiting for someone to call out their number. I watch the nurse tighten a piece of amber rubber around my arm and start searching for a vein.

After ten straight days of drawing blood, it was getting harder to find a spot that wasn't covered in scar tissue. She finally found a spot. Quickly she pushed the needle in and drew several vials of blood. She looked up and smiled. "That's it for today!"

I walked over and joined my companions. In a few minutes, we went outside and waited for the bus to take us back to Building 17. We bounced along in silence. Back on the locked ward, I headed for my favorite stuffed chair and sweet oblivion. I curled up and closed my eyes.

"Mr. Robert!" It was Jimmy. I had slept for almost two hours. "You have an appointment with Dr. Hoerster."

I followed Jimmy over to the door that led downstairs and waited while he unlocked it. Halfway down the hall, we turned right and entered the office of Dr. Edward Hoerster, MD. I sat down and read an old Time magazine while Jimmy signed a logbook. In a few minutes, Dr. Hoerster opened his door and told me to come in. He sat down behind his desk and pointed at a chair for me to sit in.

"How are you doing today, Mr. McLane?" He asked me in a tone that I had long ago deemed condescending.

"Fine, Dr. Hoerster. I do wish you would give some consideration to reducing my medication."

He smiled. "Well, how are you and the staff getting along?"

I smiled back. "We have all been getting along just fine. They are very nice people. When do you think I will be able to leave this place?"

He looked down at his notes. "Well, Mr. McLane, that may take some time. You do seem to be making some progress. Do you mind if I ask you a couple of questions? Is that all right with you?"

I looked him in the eye. "Sure, Dr. Hoerster. What would you like to know?"

He looked at me for a moment. "Do you ever hear voices?"

I replied, "Do you mean voices that are not coming from real people? Do you mean those kinds of voices, Doctor?"

He smiled. "Yes, Mr. McLane. I mean exactly those kinds of voices."

I smiled back. "Yes, I do. In fact, I hear those kinds of voices most of the day and they are driving me crazy."

Dr. Hoerster made some notes and looked up. "Do you hear these voices every day?"

I nodded my head. "Yes, sir. They start up the first thing in the morning and sometimes, they go on all day."

Dr. Hoerster made some more notes and then he looked at me again. "Do you mean as soon as you wake up? Is that when you start to hear these voices, Mr. McLane?"

I looked at him. "No, sir, I don't hear them as soon as I wake up."

"Well, when do you start to hear them?"

"They start up exactly at seven AM every morning."

Dr. Hoerster looked intrigued. "And why do you suppose that is, Mr. McLane?"

Strange voices seemed to be some kind of tripwire for Dr. Hoerster. I was determined not to set it off.

He leaned forward and looked me in the eye. "Why do you suppose that is, Mr. McLane. Why at seven AM?

This man had my life in the palm of his hand. He held all the strings and I was his unwilling puppet. The keys to my freedom lay somewhere behind those black rimmed thick glasses. My own eyes betrayed my contempt as I looked at him and smiled.

"Because that's the exact time when Nurse Atkins turns on that idiot box every morning and it doesn't stop chattering until fifteen minutes before bedtime."

Dr. Hoerster put down his pen and stared at his notepad. "Other than the television, do you hear any other voices, Mr. McLane?"

"I hear yours."

He continued to look at me. "Let me ask you this, do you think anyone from the government is out to get you?"

I raised my eyebrows. "Well, two suits did show up at my Mother's house in the fall of 1972 looking for me. They had green plastic identification cards that said Federal Bureau of Investigation. They wanted to know when was the last time that she had seen her middle child. I called them about six months later and they said they were no longer interested in talking to me."

I stared at the awards and diplomas on the wall. Several were from Baylor University. My grandmother went to Baylor. My brother graduated from Baylor. My brother the Eagle Scout. The president of the student body, who wanted to become an ordained minister in the Southern Baptist Church. The same brother who went before a judge and arranged for the sheriff to deliver me to this house of horrors. I bet the judge went to Baylor, too.

My brother and I were as opposite as Cain and Abel. I thought I was pretty smart, but his IQ was at the genius level. While he was winning chess tournaments and Boy Scout awards, I was trying to get out of my latest scrape with the law.

Dr. Hoerster had another question. "Other than a visit from the FBI to your mother, do you have any reason to believe that anyone else from the government is out to get you?"

I looked up at the ceiling. "Well, who can really say? We both know what a rogue outfit the CIA has turned into, don't we? And Nixon? Now, there's a guy who knows how to push the envelope on paranoia, Doc."

He frowned. "I would appreciate you not calling me Doc."

"I called some of the most respected men I knew in Vietnam, Doc. They were our corpsmen and some of the bravest guys I ever knew. Doc was a respected title in the DMZ."

Dr. Hoerster put down his pen. "Well, you seem to be responding well to the lithium and in spite of some of your ideas about our government, I have decided to give you grounds privileges, Mr. McLane. You will be allowed to wear your regular clothes. You will be assigned a bed in a dormitory. I am also cutting back your blood work to three times a week.

"You will also be going to group therapy. That will be all for today. Thank you, Mr. McLane."

He was looking down at his notepad while I got up and left. Jimmy saw me smiling. He figured out why. We headed back to Building 17. The next morning he handed me the bag I had put my clothes in. I was given a bed on the second floor. The good news was that I wasn't on a locked ward anymore. The bad news was that I was still living in Building 17.

After an interview with the head nurse, she decided that I would be a good candidate for the music program. I had played guitar and sung in small clubs and coffeehouses in Greenwich Village when I lived in New York City. The hospital had all kinds of programs for their patients. She told me about the arts and crafts department in the basement. She wrote down directions to the music building. I thanked her and went down to check out the basement. There was something there for everybody, everything from plastic airplane kits to ceramic ashtrays.

I looked at a medium sized loom and the partially woven rug. I decided I wanted to make my own rug, my own personal memento of my crazy days. I picked out the yarn I wanted and started weaving. An hour later, I had hardly gone an inch, but it was a start. I decided to check out the music department.

I took out my directions and started walking. I couldn't believe I was going out the front door without an escort. I followed a group of people going into a small building across the street. I had observed through the mesh screen on the porch that this building was some kind of commissary.

People were always leaving carrying white paper bags and drinks. I walked over to the serve-yourself-soft drink machine and poured myself a large Coke. I slipped onto a stool beside a pretty redhead in some kind of uniform.

She was eating a sandwich and looking at some notes. I put on my best smile.

"I am Dr. McLane. How are you doing today?"

She looked up at me. "My name's Holly. I am fine." She studied me with a critical eye. "If you don't mind my saying so, you look a little young to be a doctor."

"Well, I was only twelve when I entered medical school."

She arched her eyebrows and looked me in the eye.

"Perhaps you can help me with a course I am taking in behavior disorders. It seems quite complicated."

I frowned, "All right, I'll tell you the truth. Call me Robert. I am a patient here, a part-time maniac and a full-time lunatic, a certified psycho with paranoid delusions. Have you ever ridden in a spaceship?"

Holly laughed. "No, Robert, I have never ridden in a spaceship. Now tell me the truth. Are you visiting somebody here at the hospital? I can see you aren't nuts. I guess I shouldn't use that word around here. This is my first week. Every student nurse in this area must take a six week course here on psychosomatic illnesses."

She took a bite of her sandwich. I tried another approach.

"Yes, I am a patient here, but I am not crazy. That's going to be our little secret, right? I've got everyone from the doctors and nurses, even the aides, thinking I'm totally bananas. I've got free room and board and I'm in the middle of making a great rug. If you are going to rat me out, at least wait until I've finished the rug. OK?"

Holly laughed again. "Are you ever going to tell me the truth?"

I took a sip of my coke and glanced up at the clock. "I have to leave now. I am giving a lecture over at the music department on the differences between sharps and flats. Since you are new here, perhaps you could meet me tomorrow and I could show you around. What time do you go to lunch?"

Holly studied me for a moment. "Twelve thirty is fine. Do you really know your way around here?"

I smiled, "Show up tomorrow and find out for yourself. I'll meet you out front. I better get to that lecture. Bye!"

I finished my Coke and headed out the door. I took the directions out of my pocket and headed for the music building.

It was just a small, plain, square, yellow-brick building. I went inside and followed the sound of singing to a room where half-dozen patients were listening to someone doing their version of, "Tie A Yellow Ribbon Round The Old Oak Tree." A bald guy in a white coat sat at a desk filled with sheet music.

I walked over and introduced myself. I explained that the ward nurse from my building thought I might be a good candidate for the music program. He invited me to sit down.

"I'm Dr. Gould. The music program is fairly new here, but we have plenty of instruments and you are welcome to use them. Do you play any instruments?"

I glanced around past a couple of trombones and a tuba and several guitars quietly gathering dust along one wall. I could tell, even from my chair, that they were vintage Gibson guitars, made in the late forties or early fifties.

"Yes, Dr. Gould, as a matter of fact, I play guitar and sing. I have had many paying gigs at nightclubs in New York City."

Dr. Gould smiled. "I am sure you will fit right in, Mr. McLane. Perhaps you would be kind enough to play us a song?"

I walked over and picked up one of the Gibsons. Other than a flat E string, it was in tune. I hit a C chord and started singing, "Lost Highway." I used to do this song standing on a corner in Greenwich Village while passing tourists tossed quarters into my guitar case and winos fought over empty bottles.

Dr. Gould encouraged the small group to show their appreciation with some halfhearted applause while I put the guitar back against the wall. I later learned that there was only one other patient who could play an instrument.

Dr. Gould shook my hand. "Next week we are having a talent show. You are just in time to take part."

I smiled. "It would be my pleasure, Doc."

I soon learned that the "music program" consisted of these guys sitting around taking turns singing their favorite songs a cappella while Dr. Gould took notes and told them when it was time for lunch. After listening to a couple of patients sing, I had heard enough. I walked over and whispered in Dr. Gould's ear.

"I do have a small problem, Doctor. I get very nervous whenever I sit still for very long. When that happens, I usually go for long walks until I settle down. I hope you don't mind."

Dr. Gould nodded his head. "Of course, Mr. McLane. I understand completely. Stay as long as you can and come back when you are ready."

I smiled. "Well, thanks for being so understanding. As a matter of fact, I am feeling a little nervous right now, so, if you don't mind, I'll take a little walk right now."

I eased out of my chair and went outside. It was a beautiful day. I walked around for hours. I was still getting used to not seeing the sky through a mesh screen.

I was sipping another Coke the next day when Holly walked up.

"Hello, Robert."

"Aren't you the lady who wants to take a grand tour of the funny farm?" I took her arm and we started walking across a large field of grass.

"Well, I hope you can keep up. This place is huge and there is a lot to see. Now that building to your right is the Vampire club. Some call it a laboratory. That large building off in the distance is the administration building. The people who work in there never met a nut they didn't like."

I slipped my hand into hers and whispered. "Now Holly, do you want the normal, boring kind of tour that we give all the regular visitors and bird watchers, or would you rather have the 'hidden hollow where no one goes' tour that is only shown to a chosen few?"

Holly smiled. "Well, I've already seen the library and the cafeteria and I don't think there is anything normal about you."

I laughed, "I put my pants on two legs at a time, just like everyone else."

We walked along a small path that ended at a fence behind a storage building. I helped her climb through the strands of barbed wire. We followed an old trail across a lush meadow into a grove of maple and oak trees.

Holly looked at me. "I bet we both could get in trouble for crossing that fence. I know you are a patient. If we get caught, they will probably kick me out of school and put you back on a locked ward."

I smiled, "The key word here, Holly, is 'if', but you are right. Crossing that fence makes us a couple of outlaws, just like Bonnie and Clyde."

On the other side of the grove of trees was a long row of cement stalls that used to hold pigs. I looked at Holly.

"Now here is where we used to keep our most dangerous patients. The newspapers found out about it and made us close the place down. They said it looked too much like a pig farm. Now, I admit it was no Holiday Inn, but we never had an escape."

Holly laughed. "I bet this was a pig farm, silly."

I nodded my head. "Your insightful observations tell me you must have grown up in the country, Holly."

She looked around and smiled. "I was raised on a small farm west of Temple, long enough to know a pig farm when I see one, Dr. McLane." She added a little extra sarcasm to her voice when she called me "Doctor."

"You got a problem with country folks, mister?"

I looked at the ground. "No ma'am, I don't. As a matter of fact, I am a country boy myself. I grew up drinking water from a dipper. I didn't get my first pair of shoes until it was time to start school. I'm just one more country boy who went to the big city and crashed and burned underneath all those neon lights."

Holly looked at me. "Were you in Vietnam?"

I smiled and stood at attention and saluted. "Part of '67 and most of '68. Lance Corporal McLane, United States Marine Corps, at your service, madam."

Holly nodded her head. "I figured you were probably a Marine." She took my hand. "Did you see much of the war?"

I looked at Building 17 off in the distance. "Enough to end up in the VA funny farm. But, we can find a much more pleasant subject to talk about on a beautiful day like this."

We followed the path as it continued down to a small creek. I skipped a stone across the water. Holly looked at me again.

"So, did you have some sort of a breakdown?"

I smiled at her. "Last question. No, I didn't have any breakdown. All I did was try to give some blood at a bloodmobile on Cape Cod. This little trip to Waco was my brother's idea. He went to a judge and signed some papers and the rest is loonytoon history. I bet some of these bluebonnets would look nice in that pretty red hair of yours."

I handed her a small bouquet.

"It's against the law to pick wildflowers in the State of Texas, Mr. Barrow." Holly smiled as she took the flowers in her hand.

"You can call me Clyde." I took her in my arms.

She whispered as she looked up at me. "I guess you can call me Bonnie."

"I bet patients kissing student nurses is against the law, too."

I softly brushed her hair back from her face and moved closer to her. She turned her face to mine and kissed me, long and slow. I stroked her hair as my lips explored her neck. I had forgotten how sweet a woman could taste. My healing took a big step forward that afternoon behind the old pig farm.

Later, we followed the same winding path back to the barbed wire fence. After looking to make sure the coast was clear, we quickly crossed it and walked back towards the brick building in the distance. I took my hand out of hers as we walked along.

"We had better not meet in front of the commissary any more. How about seeing me at the same time tomorrow in front of the library?"

She hesitated. "I really don't want to get kicked out of school."

"I don't want to be put back on a locked ward either. How about next time, we stay inside the wire and pretend we are just friends? You can bring some sandwiches and I'll bring something to drink. We can sit on the grass and have a picnic."

Holly smiled at me. "Now that sounds like a plan, Mr. Barrow."

"I said you can call me Clyde."

We both realized any kissing or holding hands ended at the fence. Holly headed for her next class and I walked back over to the music building.

It felt great to be off of the locked ward. I thought about running, but I wondered how far I would get with no ID and little money? Dr. Hoerster held all the cards.

With just a note from him on a piece of paper, I could be set free or put back on the locked ward and scheduled for shock treatments.

The next afternoon I walked across the grounds to a small, two-story building. I was going for my first session of group therapy. I joined about twelve other Vietnam vets who were sitting on folding chairs in a circle. A man in his forties, wearing a shirt and tie walked in and pulled up a chair.

"Good afternoon men, my name is Dr. Talbert. Welcome to group therapy. The value that you will get out of coming here is entirely up to you. If you intend to use this valuable time to joke around or tell tall tales, I would rather you leave now, out of respect for the men who have come here seeking some real healing."

"If I think you are not taking these sessions seriously, I will ask you to leave and you will not be invited back. Each of you has his own reasons for being here. Each one of you carries his own rucksack filled with pain and sorrow and anger over your experiences from being in the Vietnam War."

Dr. Talbert continued, "Hopefully, some of you will find a way to leave here with your rucksack a little lighter. It isn't easy talking about bad things that have happened in our lives. I want each of you to know that you are not alone in how you feel. Maybe some of the answers each of you is seeking will come from something the man sitting beside you says. Maybe from something I say. That is why they call this group therapy. Does anyone have any questions?"

No one raised their hand. After a long minute, Dr. Talbert spoke again. "Each one of you has had to deal with a certain level of grief in your life and now you have to learn to live with the grief and to move on. As the Buddha says, 'Life is suffering.' Some of you are stuck somewhere in the past over some incident that happened where you saw one of your buddies get hurt or killed. There is nothing you can do to change what happened that day. Unless you plan to spend the rest of your life in some miserable place like this, each of you will have to find a way to let go of what happened back then and get on with what is left of your life. Would anyone like to talk about such a day and how it affected them?"

Again, no one raised his hand.

"Perhaps, I can give you an example of what I am talking about. I am not a vet and I have never been in a war, but I have had days where my whole world was turned upside down. It was entirely up to me to see that my problems did not become a permanent rock around my neck. Recently my wife of twenty years informed me that she wanted a divorce. Nothing I could say to her will make her change her mind. She has moved out of our home and now I have to come to terms with her decision and move on with my life. It is not easy. In fact, it is the hardest thing I have ever done. But the only alternative to not moving on is to be a prisoner of the past forever.

"There are hundreds of patients like you here in the hospital who have chosen to be such prisoners. The world will not wait for you while you waste your days thinking about shit that happened in the past. Life is going to go on, with or without you. Right now, most of you are incapable of loving yourselves, much less anyone else.

"Most of you have problems trusting anyone, so you don't have many friends either. A lot of your former friends and your family are afraid of you.

They look in your eyes and search for that special person they used to know and love. Nobody's home. A lot of you have turned to drugs or alcohol. You have learned that isn't much comfort either.

"You can spend the rest of your life replaying those days and nights in Vietnam in your mind over and over again. Most of you are young men and unless you find a way to move on, you will have a lot of wasted years.

"Now, would anyone else like to say something or am I going to spend this whole hour talking to myself?"

The guy beside me spoke up. "What you are asking us to do just ain't that simple, Doc. I watched my best friend get blown to pieces right in front of me. I was covered in his blood and all I could do was watch him die. Now, you want me to pretend like that never even happened. Well, fuck you!"

A small murmur of agreement rippled across the room as other vets looked around and nodded their heads.

Dr. Talbert continued. "First, I want to thank you for having the courage to speak up and tell the others here what you are feeling. There will always be more questions than answers. All of you, to some measure, feel used and betrayed. Many of those feelings are legitimate. Because of those feelings, you have little or no respect for anyone in a position of authority, including me. Sometimes, it feels like there are parts inside of you that are broken or missing. You all have painful memories that refuse to go away. I am telling you today that those same memories will destroy what is left of your life unless you find some way of letting them go."

Another vet from the Air Cavalry spoke up. "Let me ask you something, Doc. You say we don't trust anyone in a position of authority. Let's just say, for the sake of argument, that you and General Custer are the sole survivors of the Little Bighorn massacre."

The doggie continued. "I wonder, Doc, just how quickly you would be willing to saddle up and follow the fearless General back into Indian country?"

Several of the vets laughed out loud at that one. Dr. Talbert smiled and then slowly the smile faded. "Let me tell you my definition of hell. Hell is a place where no one trusts anyone. Learning again to trust is something that some of you may never be able to do.

"Each of you will have to find your own way to get there. Some of you will remain trapped in a world of drugs and alcohol and places like this one. I hope that each of you does find the answers to the questions that brought you here today. The VA hopes that coming to groups like this one may help you. Gentlemen, our time is up. I hope to see each one of you again on Thursday. Have a good day."

I wandered into the small medical library that was tucked away in the back of one of the numerous red brick buildings that made up the Waco Veterans Administration Medical Center. Patients are not supposed to be in there, but there was no one around to stop me. I was looking for the answers to how I was going to get Dr. Hoerster to release me. It had been almost four months since Sheriff Black had delivered me to this place. I browsed the shelves of books and medical journals looking for anything that might give me clues to the right combination of answers Dr. Hoerster was waiting to hear.

I came upon a book called Man's Search for Meaning by Dr. Victor Frankel. I took it and a small medical dictionary and slipped them underneath my shirt and left the building. I followed the same path I had taken with Holly past the old pig farm and sat down beneath the shade of a large sycamore tree. I picked up my stolen books and started reading. I began with the medical dictionary.

Dr. Hoerster kept using the words schizophrenia. I looked it up. The news was not good. For starters, the dictionary said it was incurable. I read that people who have this condition are in and out of institutions all of their lives and often commit suicide. Was I really schizophrenic? I didn't think so. Either Dr. Hoerster was wrong or I was in deep trouble. I put down the medical dictionary and picked up the other book.

I wondered if the hand of God led me to the book by Frankel, or was that the schizophrenia talking? I scanned the pages looking for answers. I found plenty. Dr. Frankel told me that the only real control any of us have over our lives is not in controlling the circumstances of our being, but rather the attitude in which we view those circumstances. According to this Jewish Holocaust survivor, we discover the meaning of our lives by doing deeds, experiencing values, and by suffering.

Well, I certainly had the suffering part covered. Dr. Hoerster had my ass, but according to Dr. Frankel, my mind still belonged to me. He went on to say that a man who becomes conscious of the responsibility he bears towards another human being, or to an unfinished work, will never be able to throw his life away.

Evidently, thousands of Vietnam veterans had never heard of Dr. Victor Frankel. They were committing suicide every year. More vets have now died by their own hand than were killed in action in Vietnam. I wondered where my own responsibility lay. Was I to be a living witness to the Vietnam War, to tell my fellow Americans about the things I had seen? Should I keep protesting and demonstrating until we left Vietnam for good? Doing that would turn many of my fellow vets against me. They would call me a traitor and worse. How could I continue to speak out? The bigger question was, how could I remain silent?

Dr. Frankel was a prisoner in a Nazi death camp called Dachau. I was a prisoner in a mental hospital. He had known what it was like to have his world permanently turned upside down and yet, he somehow found a way to make sense out of that experience and to go on with his life. I quickly realized that there were answers in this book that I could carry with me for the rest of my life. I knew that I had to start over and this time read the book slowly from cover to cover. When I finished, I knew I would be ready to get out of Waco and go on with my life. The sun was going down as I put my books back under my shirt and walked to Building 17.

The next morning I went for my regular appointment with Dr. Hoerster. I had already reached the conclusion that telling this man exactly how I felt about the world, was a sure way to make my stay in his hospital a long one. He didn't like my answers or my attitude. I didn't want him to realize that I was reading books by anyone like Dr. Frankel. I organized my thoughts as I waited outside his office.

Finally, he opened his door and motioned for me to come in. I smiled as I sat down in a chair and folded my hands in my lap. Dr. Hoerster returned my smile.

"And how are you doing today, Mr. McLane?"

I smiled back. "I am doing really well, Dr. Hoerster. I honestly feel that I am ready to leave this place, and I am hoping that you agree with me."

He lowered his head and looked at me from over the top of his glasses.

"Well, what do you want to do when you get out?"

This was his favorite trick question. This was where my plan must work, had to work if I had any hope for freedom. I'd finally realized that telling this asshole the truth about what I really wanted to do when I got out of here was the one thing that was guaranteed to keep me right where I was. I wanted to go back to New York City. That was the wrong answer to give to Dr. Hoerster. He saw the Big Apple as a bottomless pit of illegal drugs and immoral people, hustlers, junkies, and whores who were all waiting for me right back in the same alleys and cheap hotels that I had wandered away from six months ago. The gutters of New York City were home to thousands of dysfunctional lost souls just like me.

I smiled at Dr. Hoerster. "You know, Doctor, I have decided that I want to go back to my hometown of Tyler, Texas. I never should have left that place. I want to get back in school and get a good job. If my old girlfriend is still single, I'd like to start dating her again and maybe get married. If she is not available, then I'll just have to find a new one. I'm not getting any younger and I want to start a family." I knew that keeping a straight face was critical to selling this pack of lies.

Finally, Dr. Hoerster looked up from his notepad and smiled. "You do realize that when you are released, you will have to continue taking your medication. You will be taking lithium regularly for the rest of your life. The good news is that it won't cost you anything. You can pick it up at the VA hospital in Tyler for free."

I remembered not to overplay my hand. "That's great news, Dr. Hoerster! Thank God there are drugs that can help me live a normal life. How soon can I head for Tyler?"

Dr. Hoerster made some notes and then looked up at me. "Well, if you continue to show the progress you definitely seem to be making, I don't see any reason why I can't release you next week."

I stood up and held out my hand. "Thank you Dr. Hoerster! I will never forget what a great help you have been to me!"

He shook my hand and I turned around and left. I quickly walked back to Building 17. I felt like running. If I didn't screw this up, I would be out of this place in less than a week. The next morning I was waiting when Holly got out of her behavioral disorders class. I suggested that she join me for lunch at the commissary. I told her it didn't matter if anyone noticed us. I was waiting in an empty booth when she walked in. I tried to think of the right way to tell her what I had to say while we waited for our food.

"There's good news and bad news, Holly, and I'm afraid it's the same news. I'm getting out of here next week and I'm leaving right away for New York City. I wish there was an easier way to say goodbye. I know I will never forget you."

Holly looked at me with a mixture of anger and disbelief. "Just like that, huh? You're just gonna waltz in and out of my life, Dr. McLane? No chance of any kind of discussion about a future with me in the picture, is there? You've already decided there's no possibility of that, haven't you?"

I reached over and gently touched her hand. She quickly drew it back.

"Holly, you can do a lot better than hooking up with some whacked-out weirdo with no job and a long history of drug abuse and mental instability. I don't have a clue what I am going to do with my life. How could I ask someone like you to tag along while I wander down some highway that may never end? In another time and another place, we might have had a chance to make a life together, but not with the cards we are holding today. There is no easy way to say goodbye, Holly. So I'm just going to get up now and walk outta here. Think of me every now and then. I know I will never forget you."

I got up and paid the check and left. I called my brother and told him that Dr. Hoerster was going to release me. I spent the next week being extra careful not to blow up at anybody or piss off any of the nurses or aides. I was playing out the clock. I put in a half a day finishing my rug. I decided to send it to my grandmother for safe keeping.

Finally, the day came. I bought a small bag at the commissary and stuffed it with the few clothes I owned. I signed some papers and had one last visit with Dr. Hoerster. I resisted any impulse to tell this control freak what I really thought about his theories on schizophrenia and bipolar disorders. The next morning I stopped by the pharmacy and picked up a paper bag filled with bottles of pills of different sizes and colors. Each bottle had my name on it.

I walked out to the front gate and waited for my brother. I watched a guy driving a big John Deere tractor as he mowed the grass in front of the administration building. I watched him get off and walk over and talk to someone. I wondered what Dr. Hoerster would do if I stripped off all of my clothes and hopped on the idling tractor and headed out the front gate for Baylor University. I knew what he would do.

After the cold pack sessions and shock treatments finally ended, I would become a permanent resident on the locked ward of Building 17, a living example of what happened to anyone crazy enough to try to make the powerful Dr. Edward Hoerster look like a fool. I saw my brother drive up in his white Caddy. I tossed my bag in the back seat and we drove away. I declined his offer to buy me breakfast. I wanted to get on the road.

"Dr. Hoerster told me that you want to go back to Tyler. Shall I drop you off on Highway 31?"

I looked at my brother. "You've known me long enough to know I ain't ever going back to Tyler. Lying to that old fart was the only way I was ever going to get out of that place, big brother. I'm headed north to visit a lady friend of mine out on Cape Cod. After I spend some time with her, I'm going back to New York City. I would appreciate you dropping me off on a northbound ramp of Interstate 35."

My brother smiled and shook his head. "Well, I gave up a long time ago on arguing about anything with you, baby brother. Just be careful and remember, you can call me any time you need to."

I shook his hand. "Thanks, Roy Joe. Tell Peggy I said goodbye and I appreciate what both of you have done for me these last four months."

He let me out at a truck stop on the north side of Waco and drove away. I carried the paper bag of pills in one hand and my traveling bag in the other. I passed a large orange dumpster as I approached the ramp headed north.

About fifteen feet away, I turned and deposited the bag of pills squarely in the middle of the dumpster with a perfect hook shot. I stuck out my thumb and waited for my first ride.

New York City
August 1974

I climbed in the cab of an eighteen-wheeler filled with watermelons and settled in. I was going to the small New England village of Chatham, snuggled away somewhere on the coast of Cape Cod. My friends celebrated my return over a lobster dinner in Provincetown. It felt great to be back on the East Coast. After a month of daily walks exploring the empty beaches of the Cape, I was ready for New York City. I packed my bag and told my friends goodbye. I took the train to Grand Central Station. I got a room in a cheap hotel. I went up to West 48th street and started looking at acoustic guitars.

48th Street is Guitar Row in the Big Apple. The folks at the Sam Ash Music Store made me a good deal on a nice Horner. The Japanese got wise that it was better to give their guitars a German sounding name if they wanted to sell a lot of them in the United States. I caught a subway down to the village. I wanted to recoup some of the money I had spent on my guitar so I picked out a spot on Bleecker Street and started playing and singing for quarters. I was in the middle of "Me And Bobby McGee" when Phil Ochs walked up. He was one of the most famous folk singers in America. He stood there for a few minutes listening to me and then he leaned over and dropped a fifty dollar bill in my guitar case. I kept on singing. After another minute had passed, he leaned over and picked it up.

I kept on singing. Another minute passed and he put a hundred dollar bill in my guitar case and walked away. I finished the song and picked up the C note and the other three dollars and change that I had made and I closed up shop. I walked over to Washington Square Park and bought a couple of bags of weed. The Vietnam War was over! Everyone in the anti-war movement was having a big celebration and concert this weekend in Central Park. It was going to be a big party.

I walked over to Omar's Café and ordered a falafel. I lined up a gig that night in Mill's Tavern. On Bleecker Street, some called Mill's Tavern a nightclub. It looked like a run-down beer joint to me. I stopped in the middle of a song to ask a drunk to shut the fuck up at least long enough to let me finish my set. When it was over, I picked up my fifteen dollars and went next door to The Other End. Tim Hardin was playing there. I ran into Phil at the bar. He told me he was broke and asked me if he could borrow twenty bucks. How could I say no? I was lending him his own money. He took the twenty dollar bill and ordered another rum and orange juice. Phil asked me to meet him at O'John's café at 10AM the next morning. It happened to be one of my favorite places to eat breakfast. He walked through the door at ten on the nose. Phil wanted to show me a club on Broome Street in the SoHo district of lower Manhattan. He was thinking about buying an interest in the place. We took a taxi over there and looked around.

It was a huge loft bar with three levels. Phil was going to be partners with a retired math teacher named Bob Bonic. He called his brother and told him to send the cash he needed to close the deal. Phil decided to name the bar after the Cuban revolutionary hero, Ernesto "Che" Guevara. He passed out fliers that described the bar as a "place for revolutionaries and geniuses." Phil and I sat down in a back room and talked about his plans. He studied my eyes for a moment.

"I want you to work for me, Bobby. I need someone I can trust."

It took me a couple of days to realize that Phil Ochs at that moment in time was a very functional and sometimes psychotic alcoholic. My unofficial duties included keeping anyone from hurting Phil and keeping Phil from hurting anyone.

This would be a challenge at times because Phil also had a habit of pissing off some very dangerous people. My first job was clearing up some problems at the hotel where he lived. Phil was staying at the Plaza Hotel on Central Park South.

Each night, around midnight, Phil would hop on his ten speed bike and head uptown to the Plaza. One day the maid cleaned his room and accidentally threw away the lyrics to some songs that Phil was working on. Phil went ballistic. I tried to calm him down. He demanded to have a meeting with the hotel security. I went along.

It turned out that one of the security guys at the meeting had been a

Marine in the DMZ. He had even spent some time at Khe Sanh. Things got a lot less tense after we chatted for a few minutes. The hotel apologized for the lost lyrics and promised that it would not happen again. Outside, the doorman hailed a cab and we headed back downtown. A big part of Phil's personal problems was his insecurity about relationships. He was insecure because the people he tried to bond with kept running down the street in terror.

I am sitting on a milk crate in the back of a white van that is going the wrong way down a one-way street, with my favorite crazy folk singer at the wheel, singing to himself and holding a rum and orange juice in one hand.

"Uh, Phil, you better hang a right at the next corner. OK?" Off we went into the dark New York City night. Phil Ochs played the next night at Gerdes Folk City in the Village. Legend has it that Bob Dylan was discovered there. The ad in the Village Voice said, "Phil Ochs & Friends." That meant that anybody in the world of folk music might show up and play. The first set went fairly smoothly. Phil was in a good mood and the place was packed. There was a thirty-minute break before the second set.

I decided to take a walk and get some air. I found Phil, lying in the gutter, sleeping like a baby. Two blocks away, people were standing in line to get in and hear this guy play and sing his songs. I gently slapped him on the cheek.

"Phil! Phil! You gotta wake up."

He opened his eyes and looked up at me.

"Phil, you got another set to do. You got to get up."

"Is that you, Bobby? Please go over to the Greek coffee shop and bring me two large cups of coffee, regular with extra sugar."

He closed his eyes and went back to sleep. I walked across Sixth Avenue to the small cafe and brought back the two cups of coffee. I woke Phil up. He sat up and started drinking the coffee. By the time he finished the second cup, he was on his feet and back in front of Folk City. The people in line let out a cheer. The second set went fairly smoothly. There was one unhappy customer. I pointed at a now very drunk Phil Ochs and said,

"The ad said 'Phil Ochs Live!' Well, there's Phil Ochs and he's very much alive. If you don't like who you're looking at, the next time, don't come!"

We spent the next day riding around Manhattan in a stretch limousine. We had nowhere to go in particular, but at least we were going in style. After circling Central Park a few times and cruising down Fifth Avenue, we were parked in front of a sidewalk café in the West Village. Phil decided he wanted to sit on the roof. He sat there and stared out at the traffic coming up the avenue. Phil was not a flashy dresser and he looked like some wino meditating on the roof of the limo. I stayed in the back seat. I felt like I was losing a battle not to look ridiculous. A squad car with two of New York City's finest pulled up beside us.

They glanced up at Phil and looked over at me. They asked me if I wanted the bum on the roof arrested. I replied, "That 'bum' is paying for this limo and if he wants to sit on the roof, it is perfectly alright with me."

Finally, Phil climbed down and went looking for another drink. After night fell, Phil discovered that he didn't have the money to pay the limo driver for his services.

He called the former Attorney General Ramsey Clark and arranged a short loan.

Phil handed the phone to the driver to confirm that he could go to Clark's office and collect his money. Phil dropped me off at Washington Square Park. That night, Phil wrecked his own bar. It started when he insisted on playing the jukebox at maximum volume. The people sitting at the bar rolled tissue paper into small balls and stuck them in their ears. Phil got even louder than the jukebox and very belligerent.

Finally, his own bouncer kicked him out the door and turned down the jukebox. Phil beat on the locked door for about five minutes. Then things got quiet. We thought he was gone. In a few minutes he was back. He went looking for a board and he found a large one. Now, he was using it as a battering ram on the locked front door. The bartender and I raced upstairs to the balcony.

The bouncer called the cops. We peered down at the rapidly disintegrating front door. I looked at the bartender. "That's alright. He can break down the door. He's still got to come up these stairs."

Just as the last pieces of the door gave in, the cops arrived. We waited for a couple of minutes and slowly walked back down the stairs. I asked the bartender to pour me a double shot of Wild Turkey. I tossed it down and went outside to check on Phil.

He was explaining to the cops how he had been kicked out of his own damn bar! The police told him perhaps it would be better if he explained it downtown. Phil Ochs was a fairly big guy. He was nervous about going anywhere with any cops. I told them Phil would go peacefully with them if I went along and if they didn't put him in handcuffs.

I looked at Phil. "Don't worry. They wouldn't dare try to hurt you with me watching. Let's go down to the station house and straighten this mess out."

We climbed in the back of the squad car and rode over to the station house. Inside, everyone was talking at once, trying to explain to the desk sergeant what happened. He was a veteran at getting the big picture in a hurry. Clearing this up wouldn't take long. He looked at me.

"Is this the owner of the club that was broken into?"

I nodded my head. "He is one of them."

The desk Sergeant smiled. "Well, it's no crime to break in your own place. We are going to let this man go."

My jaw dropped. "You're going to do what?"

The desk Sergeant glared at me. "I said we are going to let him go."

I replied, "Well, give me a five minute head start before you do!"

Phil laughed, "It's OK, Bobby. I have calmed down. I feel fine. Let's go over to Folk City and have a drink."

We walked out of the station house and hailed a taxi uptown. We walked into Folk City. The band was between sets. Phil sat down at the piano and began playing. The crowd got quiet. I looked out at them and announced.

"Ladies and Gentlemen, Mr. Phil Ochs."

He sang the song "Changes." Phil had written dozens of songs and this one was one of his best. When he had finished, we parted company. We agreed to meet at O'John's the next morning. At ten o'clock Phil pulled up outside O'John's in another limo. He wouldn't get out. I paid my tab and walked over to see what was going on. Phil rolled down the window.

"Get in."

I climbed in the back and closed the door. Phil looked at me and frowned. "We've got to get out of town. The Mafia is after me. I pissed some people off last night. We got to scram. I'm going to LA. Where do you want to go?"

I thought for a moment. "Well, México has been pretty good to me. But first I have to stop in Texas to pick up a couple of pistols."

Phil nodded at the driver and we sped away. I stopped at my hotel and grabbed my guitar and my clothes. In less than thirty minutes we were at Kennedy airport. Phil paid for the tickets and gave one to me. I asked him to book my flight to Puerto Vallarta through Houston. I told Phil that I was going to spend the winter in a little place that Wavy Gravy had told me about.

I asked him to join me. "Come with me, Phil. We'll drink tequila and chase wild women."

He looked at me and shrugged his shoulders. "Maybe I can make it after New Year's Eve. I already promised to play at Max's Kansas City that night."

He gave me a hug and walked away to catch his plane. I picked up a boarding pass and went to catch my flight to Houston. I never saw him again. In the spring, he hanged himself with his belt in his sister's apartment in Queens.

Washington, D.C. November 1992

A soft rain was falling as twilight turned this Veteran's Day into night. Other vets quickly walked past the slow-moving man with the cane and the faded corpsman's shirt. With a little more light they might have noticed the Navy Cross among the ribbons on the faded shirt. Many vets were on their way to reunions that were going on all over town. Thousands of modern day warriors had gathered here to celebrate the ten year anniversary of the Vietnam Wall. Many were seeing the wall for the first time. The man in the corpsman's shirt stopped and gripped the cane tightly.

"Are you alright, Doc?"

I recognized him from a party the night before at the Sheraton where hundreds of Marines and former Marines had gathered to celebrate their 217th birthday. The old corpsman had helped cut the cake with an officer's sword. Any corpsman who had ever served with a Marine combat outfit in a War was considered an honorary Marine by most leathernecks. Jim Mayton was a dues-paid member of that special brotherhood. He had saved hundreds of Marines in Korea and Vietnam. The man with the cane trembled as he looked at me.

"I'm out of gas. I'm only running on two cylinders."

He paused while he fought for another breath. Advanced emphysema and his refusal to quit smoking made even the shortest walk seem like a forced march up hill with a full pack. I nodded at a park bench that was a few feet away.

"Have a seat, Doc. We'll figure something out."

A Green Beret walking by saw what was happening and offered to help. We thought about carrying him to a taxi, but his bad hip killed that idea. A park ranger came by driving an electric cart. I explained the situation.

She asked me, "Do you know how to drive one of these things?"

I smiled, "I'm a golfer!"

She gave me the cart. I drove Jim back up to the street and hailed a cab. He waited in the back while I returned the cart. We took the cab over to the Sheraton. Settled in on a couch in the lobby, Jim ordered a gin and tonic and lit a cigarette. His eyes followed a pretty woman walking by. Other Marines entering the hotel saw Jim and stopped to say hello. Everyone from generals to privates treated the old corpsman with respect and affection. Jim still wanted to see the wall. After a BLT sandwich and one more gin and tonic we hailed another taxi. This time three Marines went with him. We borrowed a wheelchair from the hotel. There are over fifty-eight thousand names etched in gray letters on the black granite wall. That night, Jim went to see just one – Edward Gaffney Creed.

After picking up some wounded Marines, the young corpsman's helicopter went down, killing everyone on board. Among the wreaths of fresh cut flowers, they find the name. Jim's eyes filled with tears as he rubbed his fingers across the gray letters.

"He was a ski bum. Once, he kicked my butt."

Quietly Jim said the goodbye he never had the chance to say in Vietnam. At times like these, some say the wall weeps as raindrops slowly slide down the smooth black granite. James Mayton passed away in the summer of 1993. He was buried with full military honors. At his request, a small piece of black granite was added to his headstone.

Vietnam Veterans Memorials

The Vietnam Veterans Memorial Wall

Groundbreaking: March 26, 1982

Dedication: November 13, 1982

Designer: Maya Ying Lin

Architect: Cooper-Lecky Partnership

Material: Black granite from Bangalore, India

Length: Each wall is 246 feet 9 inches (75.21 meters) long; the total length of the Wall is 493 feet 6 inches (150.42 meters)

Height: 10 feet 3 inches (3.12 meters) at the center of the memorial

Angle: 125° 12"

Density of granite: 210 lbs/cubic foot (3364 kilograms/cubic meter)

Number of panels: for each wall, 70 separate inscribed panels, plus 4 at each end without names

Panel dimensions: 40 inches (101.6 centimeters) wide, 3 inches (7.62 centimeters) thick, between 8 inches (20.32 centimeters) to 10 feet 3 inches (3.12 meters) tall

Number of lines per panel: 1 to 137

Number of names per line: 5 to 6

Height of letters: 0.53 inches (1.35 centimeters)

Depth of letters: 0.015 inches (0.038 centimeters)

Foundation: The granite panels are supported by 140 concrete pilings driven approximately 35 feet to bedrock

Total cost: Construction costs of the Wall totaled approximately $4,284,000 The VVMF raised nearly $9 million in private contributions in its quest to win support and build the memorial.

2003 President George W. Bush signs act that approves planning and building of an underground education center at the Vietnam Veterans Memorial.

The Three Servicemen Statue

Designer: Frederick Hart

Dedication: November 11, 1984

Material: Bronze

Height: 7 feet (2.13 meters)

The Vietnam Women's Memorial
Designer: Glenna Goodacre
Dedicated: November 11, 1993
Material: Bronze
Paving stones: Carnelian red granite
Approx. size: 8 feet by 15 feet (2.44 meters by 4.57 meters)
Approx. weight: 1 ton (907 kilograms)
Trees: Eight yellowwood trees representing the eight women killed in
   Vietnam
Cost: Approx. $4 million
Number of entries in design contest: 317 (Goodacre was originally runner-up)

The Flagpole
Material for base: Bronze
Installed: Mid-1983
Emblems: Around the base of the flagpole are the emblems of the Army,
   Navy, Air Force, Marines, and Coast Guard.
Height: 60 feet (18.29 meters)